FOUR SEASONS
REFLECTIONS, MEMORIES, FLASHBACKS

By
Robert M. Franchino

FOUR SEASONS

REFLECTIONS,

MEMORIES,

FLASHBACKS

Copyright © 2023 by **Robert M. Franchino**

DEDICATION

    I especially dedicate this assortment of writings to my dear wife, Nancy Lee, who has been with me and at my side to share the happiest moments and challenging events of my days on this earth. Fortunately, our vast delightful adventures together have been blessed with an abundance of success, joy, contentment, satisfaction and excellent health

    LIFE is not measured by the number of breaths we take, but by the memories that take our breath away!

    It doesn't matter where you go in life… It is who you have beside you.

CONTENTS

The Table of Contents is organized in a chronological progression to capture tales accumulated over my existence. The four seasons approach records recollections during each of those four periods during my lifetime.

AUTHOR'S NOTE	1
INTRODUCTION	2

SPRING   3
From Birth to age: 20

HALLOWEEN BALLERINA BABY GROWS INTO A LINCOLN CENTER DANCER	4
UNCLE SAM	6
POLIO	8
KIDDIE KIDNAPPER	10
BLACK AND WHITE TELEVISION	12
KINDERGARTEN BANKING SCANDAL	13
LUCK AT THE LIQUOR SHELF	15
CHILDHOOD CAREER CHANGES FROM SINGING COWBOY TO CLUB DATER	16
NAMED MACK	17
MEMORIAL DAY-A DIFFERENTPERSPECTIVE	18
WHAT A MISTAKE	24
CITY CHILD TO FARM BOY	25
TAKE THIS BOY TO A DOCTOR	29
HOT ROD	30
THE BIG ONE THAT SHOULD HAVE GOTTEN AWAY	31
HAVE LUNCH ON DAD	33
MY MUSICAL HISTORY	34

ONLY RATS EAT CHEESE	40
MY LAST COWBOY	41
PASSION FOR ROSES	42
MISS PEEK-A-BOO	44
TELEPHONE CALL FROM THE PRINCIPAL	45
FIRST FIELD GOAL	46
RAILROAD REALITY	47
WHAT SIDE OF THE TRACKS?	50
GLORIA	52
BICYCLE BUSINESS BOY	54
BULLY BEATEN BADLY BY BALLERINA BOY	56
DAD HAS A BOY AND BUILDS A MAN	58
HOLE GANG	63
MY FIRST BAND JOB	65
HITCHHIKER	67
ADVICE AT A PRICE	69
ON THE WRONG SIDE OF A GUN	70
JELL-O JOKE	71
TRAGEDY ON TRACKS AVOIDED	72
WISE GUY	73
PARKING PRANKSTER	74
KIT KAT CLUB CATASTROPHE	76
BAND JOB OFFER FOR MY COLLEGE MUSIC PROFESSOR	78
CLASSIC DATE	79

The First Girl I Dated; I Married

SECOND ENCOUNTER	83

The First Girl I Dated; I Married

THREE ENGAGEMENT RINGS	85
THE BIG ONE THAT SHOULD HAVE GOTTEN AWAY	88
MUSIC ASPHYXIATION CLASS	90
A SHOOTING MACHINE TEAM	91
ENTREPRENEUR EVOLVES TO EDUCATOR	92
I GOT THE JOB	93
INITIATION INTO THE TEACHING PROFESSION	95

SUMMER 96
From age: 21 to 40

YACHT OWNER FOR ONE RIDE	97
CUTTING EDGE SISTER-IN LAW	99
"GOTTA" PEE MIDNIGHT MOONER	100
MANY FIRST AID SAVES	101
BOB CHINO BAND SIGN	104
PAPER SHIRT UNCOVERED	105
DREAM HOME NIGHTMARE	107
HONEYMOON NIGHT	109
MARRIAGE FIRST MEMORABLE MEALS	111
BEN GAY	113
MISSING MOTHER MYSTERY	114
LIFT THE LONG LADDER	116
AMATEUR OUTPERFORMS CONCERT PIANIST	117
HANGING A DECORATIVE CHRISTMAS BALL	118
SCIENTIFIC APPLICATION FOR SARAN WRAP	119
FIRST ANNIVERSARY PRESENT	120
ASTRONOMY	121
MONEY DOES GROW ON TREES	122
MY THREE SONS	125

HAY! LET ME SHOW YOU	126
SEVEN MAPLE TREES	128
RAILROAD TIES	129
IS THAT THE DOCTOR?	131
GREENHOUSE THESIS	132
PREGNANCY AND WHAT SIZE DRESS?	134
MICHELANGELO MYSTERY	136
BUNNY FUN FUR COAT	137
FIRST EAST RUTHERFORD HIGH SCHOOL REUNION DRESS	139
NEGOTIATIONS UNDER THE GUN	141
GOTCHA	143
NEWBORN NBA PREDICTION	144
SWIMMING POOL CONSTRUCTION	145
SILHOUETTES ON THE WINDSHIELD	148
BICYCLE BOARDWALK BATHING BABY	150
"MEASLE" PAINTING	152
SIMPY	153
UNIQUE CHAMPIONSHIP PET	154
MAGIC KEY	155
A FAMILY FANTASY ABOUT SANTA	156
WHY DO ALL MOMS HAVE THE SAME NAME?	157
TINY TOMATO TRADERS	158
A FOOL'S JOKE	160
A NEW TWIST ON TAXES	161
LITTLE LAD BUYS LINGERIE FOR A LOVELY LADY	162
HIP SURGERY MADE SIMPLE	163
LIQUID ORGANIC CLEANER	164

CRUISE FROM HELL	165
SEW GET A JOB	171
FROM GO CART TO SERVICE MANAGER AT LEXUS	172
WORRISOME WEEPING WILLOW TREE	174
MASS. MOUNTAIN MEN ON ELECTION DAY RALLY	176
WHEN I GROW UP, I AM GOING TO BE A DENTIST	178
BEECH STREET ADDITION	179
ROMANTIC BOB WHO	182
ROMANTIC SATIN SHEETS	183
CAMPING AT FORT WILDERNESS	185
FARCE IN THE FOREST	187
THE IMPACT OF A SINGLE PHOTO	188
FADING FAST FEET TO FLASHING PHOTOS	189
STAY AND STAB	190
SNIPE HUNT	192
SPECIAL SALES SPEECH	194
SEE THROUGH BATHING SUIT	196
THURSDAY NIGHT RITUAL	197
A MACHO MAN'S ATHLETIC MASSACRE	198
WHERE ARE THE CHILDREN?	200
KEY CAPERS	202
RENE IS FINANCIALLY INDEPENDENT	203
YOUR CAR IS FOR SALE AND MAKE THE SIGN	204
I CAN START THE CAR	206
WHY IS A TEN-YEAR-OLD DRIVING THE CAR?	207
YELLOW JACKETS	208

AUTUMN 209
From Ages: 41 to 60

THINGS TO CONSIDER: *Splitting the Restaurant Check*	210
COMPUTER AND ME	212
DAD I CAN FIX THE DISHWASHER	214
HOW-TO PICK-UP CHICKS WITH A *"FRANMOBILE"*	215
VETERANS OF FOREIGN WARS	216
A PROTECTIVE PARENT'S PERIL	218
WESTWOOD HIGH SCHOOL MARCHING BAND	219
FIRST MEMORABLE DRIVING LESSON ON THE GARDEN STATE PARKWAY	221
DAD, I CAN FIX THE CAR	222
SENIOR CITIZEN SEASHORE STOLEN SUPPER	223
SENIOR CITIZEN FORCED TO PLAY IN A TEENAGE ROCK AND ROLL BAND	224
CAMERA CONQUERS COLLEGE ENTRANCE CHALLENGE	226
HARD TIMES	228
PAID VACATION	229
JACKSON JONES	230
JACKSON JONES STRIKES AGAIN	232
JACKSON JONES RETIREMENT	233
I DO NOT WANT TO ATTEND COLLEGE	235
INSTALLING A SPRINKLER SYSTEM	236
RENE'S COLLEGE LAVISH LINCOLN	237
SANIBEL SEASHELLS	238
NOTEWORTHY TIPS	240
A DEFINITION OF TIPS	243
HER-O	245
THE ST. LOUIS MAGIC STORY	247

I HAVE A WARRANT FOR YOUR ARREST	249
THE LAST STOLEN SANDWICH	250
UNDER SURVEILLANCE	252
THE GREATEST GIFT A SON CAN GIVE HIS FATHER	254
BLASTER BOYS	255
A PARENT'S WISH	257
FINAL SHOPPING FLING	258
MRI	259
ELIGIBLE WIDOWER	260
THE LAST PAINTING CONTRACTORS JOB	261
SHE WILL NEVER REMEMBER AND GRAMP WILL NEVER FORGET *(CPR Story)*	262
THE HAIR STYLIST	264
THE GREATEST GIFT A DAUGHTER CAN GIVE HER FATHER	265
PARENT'S INCOME TAX SHOEBOX	266
ONLY TWO MORE WEEKS	268
FALLING OFF THE ROOF	269
SNOW SHOVELING	270

WINTER 273
From Ages: 61 to ….???

WHERE DOES THE TIME GO?	274
THE GREATEST GIFT FROM GRAMP	275
RETIREMENT	276
MOVE TO FOUR SEASONS	277
LIFETIME OF LESSONS YEAR `ROUND TAN	279
THE MISSING PROFESSIONAL SILVER COFFEE URN	280
ASTHMA	283

MOTHER HUBBARD MISSING WEDDING DRESS MISSES THE RECEPTION	286
ST. PATRICK'S DAY	288
SURPRISING SENIOR WEDDING	289
SARAH THE HORSE	290
NINE- ELEVEN THROUGH THE EYES OF A THREE-YEAR-OLD	291
I AM NOT GOING TO MARRY GRAMP	293
CRYING DOESN'T WORK	294
HANDYMAN IN MINNESOTA	295
POP	296
MUTUAL RESPECT	298
UNTIMELY HEADACHE	299
CLOTHING CAPERS THROUGH THE YEARS	300
ROB'S DOCTORATE	302
RENE'S MASTER'S DEGREE	304
CHAD'S FIRST DAY OF SCHOOL	306
THE OLD MAN WHO SWIMS WITH A HAT AND GLOVES	307
BOWLING BITS AND BANQUETS	309
BETTER ACCORDION PLAYER LAST YEAR	311
DO I SMELL?	312
THANKSGIVING AT THE FARM	314
MESSAGES	320
IN TIME, THE CHILD BECOMES THE TEACHER	322
TWO BIRTHDAYS PER YEAR	324
GRAMP, HELP ME WITH MY ITALIAN PROJECT	326
NEW YEAR REFLECTIONS, AN AMERICAN DREAM	327
BROKE WITH A POCKET FULL OF CREDIT CARDS AND CASH	329

DO A GOOD JOB GRAMP	330
HAIRCUTS	331
FLORIDA FLAT TIRE	335
HAIR STYLE GELS PERMANENT FRIENDSHIP	337
ACCORDION; A SECOND VISIT	339
UNTIMELY WALK ON WATER	342
TIMELINE	344
KNOW WHAT TIME IT IS	345

EPILOGUE AND PERSPECTIVE — 347

LIFETIME OF LESSONS LEARNED	348
POINTS TO PONDER *Making the Right Choices*	357
NOT A GOOD SIGN	359
QUIPS AND QUOTES	363
WHAT DO I APPRECIATE?	365
WHERE ARE THEY NOW? *(Acknowledgements)*	368
CHRONOLOGICAL CROSSROADS *(Acknowledgements)*	371
NOTE	379
RELUCTANT READERS	380

AUTHOR'S NOTE

Many individuals have come before our time, some are currently with us, and most are in the future. We have had and will continue to experience opportunities to learn from all of them (past, present and future). In essence, a civilization can only advance when the current age group is surpassed by future generations.

INTRODUCTION

This collection of events is devoted to those who have influenced me and provided wonderful opportunities to travel down a road of reminiscence to enjoy reflections, memories and flashbacks.

This selection of stories, during the four seasons of my existence, is the result of being surrounded by magnificent people who have contributed a compilation of events which were harvested to produce an abundance of treasured thoughts, delightful deeds and exciting experiences.

Over many years, as a professional educator and enthusiastic participant in pupils' development, "You should have written a book", has been frequently expressed when a lifetime, significant event or humorous activity associated with my experiences has taken place.

I have been very fortunate to actively accumulate an abundance of these unforgettable encounters which have never been recorded on paper but are only preserved in the depths of my crowded mind. Before they slipped away, an attempt was made to safeguard some of these unwritten encounters, incidents or episodes.

Time was taken: to reflect on the past, revitalize fantastic flashbacks, record the present-day, foresee the future and mull over these magnificent, memorable, treasures. Recalling these pleasant thoughts have brought smiles to my lips, tears to both eyes, happiness to my happy heart and the enjoyable excitement of developing and creating this interesting valued journal, *FOUR SEASONS, REFLECTIONS, MEMORIES, FLASHBACKS.*

SPRING
From Birth to age: 20

HALLOWEEN BALLERINA BABY GROWS INTO A LINCOLN CENTER DANCER

Life as a child involved remarkably close family ties with relatives who lived within the proximity of two square miles. Evenings and weekends were consumed with an abundance of activities that crossed all age and interest levels. Holidays and festivities revolved around merriment and meals that were all day feasts. Throughout the years, these occasions moved from house to house and each individual family took a turn hosting the traditional observances. The lesser events enjoyed similar ceremonial celebrations as did the major ones.

My first Halloween was marked by a special favorite cousin, Marilyn, who was ten years older than me, and she took exceptional care in dressing her little beloved relative as a female ballerina. An expenditure of extraordinary effort and care was devoted in selecting a retired tutu, leotards and tiara for the lovely distinctive outfit. After taking a few steps into the cold night time air, the tyke realized that he was now in an embarrassing situation and quickly returned to the safety of the house.

Years later this latent talent was revitalized when the baby ballerina grew up and became a school principal who made arrangements for his staff to participate in a Lincoln Center Summer Institute. During the next few years, summer vacation periods were dedicated to studying dance with internationally prominent, professional, performers. As a result, many opportunities were presented to be on the same legendary world-renowned stage with these famous artists.

Later, the well-worn pink commemorative rehearsal dance attire was worn at a few costume parties and then returned to the closet. However, the decorative special shirt remains a substantial smidgen of the assorted memories which are a part of my personal dancing profile.

UNCLE SAM

While growing up as a toddler, I lived in a large silk producing center of an industrial section in Paterson, NJ. Homes were built three feet apart and had very long, huge backyards. Our property consisted of a triple sized plot that was approximately ½ acre in area.

During World War II period, families utilized the land to cultivate and grow crops. The sequence began in the spring by hand turning the soil with a garden fork. Once prepared, the seeds were carefully sewn in well tilled loam.

Summer tasks involved: watering, cultivating weeding, pruning and removing bugs with gentle fingers. Fall activities included an extension of all these chores plus the addition of harvesting and preserving the produce. Standard Ball Jars were used during the canning process. Enough fruit and vegetables were processed to supply the relatives for the next year. In most instances, a surplus was created to share with others.

Cabbage was the staple yield and, therefore, became a major component in the weekly diet. No matter how Mom cooked it or attempted to disguise the dinner with beans, potatoes, sausage, and spices; I definitely did not like what was set before me and, therefore, experienced extreme difficulty in passing this food beyond my mouth!

An older couple, with a person in military service, was our next-door neighbor. "Uncle Sam", who seemed to fill the role of my grandfather, took great delight in entertaining me as he went about his yard duties. He patiently taught me about city farming and caring for chickens. One of my jobs was to protect and feed the little peepers so they matured and became food producers. In addition, this little mini farmer collected fresh eggs from the fenced in the chicken coop area. Older hens and roosters were nasty and aggressive when it was their eating time. The fully developed poultry violently pecked at anything near their grain bucket! However, these precious birds provided an excellent source of eggs and meat for many meals.

I quickly learned to pay attention to what was being served for dinner in each of the two homes. When given the choice of eating cabbage at my house or enjoying spaghetti, homemade, rich, red, gravy and beautiful plump meatballs at "Uncle Sam's"; I selected my friend's kitchen, and stated, through the poultry wire fence, that my senior pal invited me to eat in his home. While they complied with this childish prank and considered this ploy to be humorous, I was very serious about avoiding eating the powerful, gassy indigestive supper. Although there were vast differences in our ages, we were very good buddies until his dying day. These episodes resulted in a fond series of wonderful memories!! As the years flew by, I became his assistant in making over a hundred gallons of homemade wine per year.

POLIO

Memory vividly recalls the many nightmares our nation encountered during an era in which we passed through during early childhood. At the time, President Franklin D. Roosevelt managed the struggles associated with World War II and his own personal battle against the dreaded disease of infantile paralysis.

Parents panicked when their youngsters complained of pain, cramps or muscular discomfort. Common reminders of this monstrous affliction left clear mental images of patients requiring cumbersome heavy steel braces to assist them in movement. Restrictions to a wheelchair for mobility issues or confinement, using an iron lung to assist in their very strenuous respiratory process were additional anxiety, producing concerns.

At that time, adult conversations loomed around the facts and myths associated with this frightening horror. Summer activities were limited and constrained attendance at movie theaters, amusement parks, swimming pools, sitting on curbs or lounging in wet bathing suits. At the age of three, the impact of this nasty curse was dramatically illustrated in the neighborhood when a young playmate prematurely died as a result of that affliction. Interestingly, he and I were born on the same day!

Fortunately, and several years later, a scientist named Jonas Salk, who graduated from the same Eastside High School that I attended, made a long-awaited, significant, landmark discovery. He developed a miracle vaccine to eliminate that scourge on society. Years later and as a school administrator, I was charged with the responsibility of ensuring that every child attending the Reynolds building was properly immunized and able to document proof by showing the appropriate health and inoculation records.

Decades later and at one of the national conventions for elementary school principals, Dr. Jonas Salk was the keynote speaker. His message was that medical science had successfully developed techniques to teach the human body how to protect itself against sickness through biochemical intervention and inoculations. He further suggested that, ultimately, knowledge will be able to be transferred from person to person in a similar approach by injecting educational elixirs or learning liquids into individuals. Imagine being enlightened through the services of a new instructional consultant at the local pharmacy.

KIDDIE KIDNAPPER

During my formative tiny toddler years, Dad would frequently take me to work with him. On occasion, he was requested to report on weekends for completion of special assignments. His place of employment for thirty-five years was Koppers Coke and located next to a railroad siding in Clifton, New Jersey.

The original facility was a large pole style, corrugated, sheet metal, building that was constructed over a cold, dirt floor. The structure was used to house and repair red dump trucks that transported coal products throughout the vicinity.

On occasion, he took care of me on a work Sunday. So, I accompanied him to the job and was allowed to play in the garage or in a big chain link fenced industrial yard. While there, Dad's several coworkers became my new friends and these relationships endured well after he retired a few decades later.

From time to time, I was invited to supper at the local diner and then remained to attend the evening company bowling league games. It seemed that I was a major attraction who was the recipient of excessive amounts of attention, affection, candy, soda or ice cream.

Each summer, a fantastic corporation picnic was scheduled at Bertrand's Island Amusement Park in Lake Hopatcong. There, the wives of these fine men would take me on rides in the recreational area or enjoy swimming in the lake. During morning activities, I remember serving as team batboy, cheering for Dad who was the players' captain and catcher.

Over time, Father's workplace surrounded me with a marvelous large circle of very outstanding, attentive, adult acquaintances that provided excellent entertainment, safe supervision and companionship. To this day and in my golden years, their names, kind deeds and happy images of their friendly faces are firmly engraved in my file of fond visual memories.

One spring day, while a preschooler I was playing on the sidewalk in front of our home, an "old" pal drove up in his huge coal truck and parked to say, "Hello". As the conversation continued, he invited me to go for a ride around the block. Imagine the excitement of jumping into the passenger side of a big powerful vehicle and squirming around in a seat that had a collection of deep, black, coal dust on the upholstery which had accumulated for a long time. My crisp clean clothing was quickly enveloped in a dark, midnight, powder that permeated everything. Only white eyeballs and sparkling shiny teeth were able to glow when contrasted to the background of fine, pulverized, particles that stored potential heat energy.

This driver quickly shut the door, released the brake, pressed down the clutch, shifted into gear, gently depressed the accelerator and encouraged the gloomy, grimy, covered crimson truck to jump into action. A commanding sound became louder as machine, man and fascinated, spellbound, captive turned the corner and swiftly sped out of sight.

Moments later, Mom moved to the front walk to check on the little adventurous son. He was gone! Imagine what went instantly through her mind when thoughts swirled at a speed of light as she searched surroundings for the missing child who had suddenly vanished.

Shortly, the sound of the dirty, scarlet, truck chugged around the corner. Through the front, grubby, glass and in full view, appeared the two messy, midnight tinted, black grubby smiling mugs.

By the standards of that era, this ordeal was no big deal. Mother's concerns were expressed to the innocent "kiddie kidnapper" and the story ended happily.

How many things have dramatically changed over my lifetime!

BLACK AND WHITE TELEVISION

I experienced a childhood during the early days of black and white television. The first set had a large screen of twelve inches which was contained in furniture that was so heavy, it had to be delivered by at least two gigantic men. Programming was simple in the "olden days". A grand total of seven channels was available. Variety shows, cartoons, sports, and an overabundance of cowboy movies corralled the networks.

The good guys wore tan hats, rode white stallions, packed a pair of pearl pistols, and ended up riding into the sunset with a beautiful heroine. To the contrary, bad boys wore black hats, mounted dark horses, and ended up shot in the arm. The stories were no more than an hour in length and finished with a happy ending.

A local friendly TV repairman visited the house more frequently than a family doctor. He charged a higher fee than the traveling physician. Due to the tremendous number of live actions caused by an incredible volume of steeds and steers that ran across the tube, my dad would always demand the fix included a thorough cleaning. Father insisted that every bit of animal debris be completely removed from the living room entertainment center.

KINDERGARTEN BANKING SCANDAL

  The local city elementary schools initiated a program to provide young children an opportunity to establish saving habits. Each Wednesday, most pupils brought money to the teacher who recorded the amount in their individual, student bank account ledger.

  As a kindergartener, I was escorted to School #10 in Paterson, New Jersey with upper grade youngsters who were neighbors. On one occasion, a seventh-grade member of the group asked to see the money that I was carrying to be deposited. We compared currency and the suggestion was made that my smaller, sized, piece of change be traded for her larger, shiny, silver coin. We agreed and the switch took place. In class, business was conducted as usual, and the transaction was recorded by the educator.

Upon my return home, Mom asked me to examine the bankbook. Low and behold, she sized up the scam! To this day, I do not know about the conversations that occurred with the other involved people. But..., as a five-year-old, I did get some valuable financial advice and other extracurricular lessons about money topics.

LUCK AT THE LIQUOR SHELF

Behind the large kitchen door was the family pantry. This alcove was used to store non-perishable food, domestic supplies and a collection of homemade alcoholic beverages. These various, colorful concoctions were contained in unlabeled bottles. Gallons of homemade red wine and small containers of different tinted sweets, sipping, tasty cordials were shelved to eventually be shared as an important part of our family culture. During the year and on special occasions, I liked what was sampled and served.

One day while alone in this room, I decided to sneak a swallow. However, before putting the unmarked, magical, mixture to my lips; a deep sniff was drawn into the lungs to prepare the developing taste buds for an anticipated treat. Wow! The flow of inhaled fumes was hot, burning and very distinctive with a dangerous smell. It was cleaning ammonia and not Sambuca.

Both eyes immediately watered. Labored, strenuous, struggling, gasping breathing was instantly stressful and extremely uncomfortable. Lucky kid… the drinking gods were present in that dark, secret, space of time to provide protection and enable me to enjoy another day.

CHILDHOOD CAREER CHANGES FROM SINGING COWBOY TO CLUB DATER

Aside from athletes and the New York Yankees; my boyhood hero was the singing cowboy, Gene Autry, who eventually owned a major league baseball team and became a multi-millionaire. I saw all his movies, followed his serial episodes and watched his weekly TV show. In addition, a favorite uncle took me horseback riding each Saturday. Resulting from these youthful fun experiences, it was very understandable why I wanted to become a country western vocalist who played a guitar.

My parents recognized this interest at seven years of age. They took me to a music store to select an instrument and sign up for lessons. The teacher was rather talented, demonstrating drums, horns, strings and keyboards. The last instrument presented was an accordion and my parents said, "That sounds nice and would you like to start instructions now?"

Accepting this arrangement had a major influence on this little boy's career path! To date, a singing cowboy riding a horse and playing a squeeze box has yet to hit the big stage.

Fortunately, this tale has a happy and successful ending! I played professionally starting at the age of fifteen and retired from that industry thirty-five years later. Over time, weekend travels took me on musical adventures all over the countryside and provided opportunities to play with some of the best in the business. In addition, I performed in many beautiful rooms and at some of the most prestigious clubs in the area.

Thanks Mom and Dad!

NAMED MACK

While returning from a Saturday afternoon movie as a young child, my father took me to a local diner for a snack. On the next stool sat a gentleman. Dad greeted him and said, "Hi Mack, how are you?" I was impressed that he knew the name of this stranger. On the trip home, I asked, "How do you know this person?" The reply was, "I did not know him, and this was the first time we had met. In an attempt to be friendly with men, Mack is used to addressing them". This was an important lesson that was learned and to be stored for future reference.

Sixty years later, I met a fine widowered elderly man while visiting Minnesota. In conversation he explained that he loved to dance and enjoy a glass of wine from time to time. He had been happily married to a very conservative bride for well over fifty years and she frowned at these specific, social activities. He promised to refrain from these pleasures and was loyal to that pledge. Unfortunately, she passed away within the last few years and he was left a very lonely person.

Friends and relatives suggested that he attend church social gatherings with the hope of making new acquaintances. As weeks rolled by, his level of participation expanded and he found his schedule soon involved participation in several dances per week. During this interim, a need to build a current wardrobe was recognized and he engaged the services of a professional shopper to coordinate proper clothing and attire for these functions.

He was soon identified as a respectable gentleman and an excellent dancing partner. However, this presented an interesting new problem as he traveled to various occasions. In time, casual relationships developed involving three separate women who were delighted to be in his company. Since they were at different functions and days, several dating arrangements during the week were easily arranged. However, he had difficulty remembering each lady's name! Immediately, the Mack lesson from Dad was recalled and the suggestion was made to use the same pet's name for all of his favorite females. "Sweetie" was the selection of choice to resolve the pleasant difficulty!

MEMORIAL DAY- A DIFFERENT PERSPECTIVE

Remembering when Memorial Day was a single date of celebration and it annually fell on May 30th. Because it was rotated throughout the week people generally remained home to relax, recall and reflect on the deeds of military personnel. Early morning was devoted to visiting the cemetery and placing geraniums at the grave site. My ritual was followed by standing on tippy toes and gently kissing the embedded grandparents' photograph displayed on the top portion of our family gravestone.

The return car trip home, later in the morning, involved decorating anything that moved. This was in preparation for the noon parade. Included in the beautification process were pets, bicycles, wagons, automobiles, and tractor trucks which pulled elaborately adorned floats. This marching pageant involved: scouts, little leaguers, PAL people, high school bands, drum and bugle corps, police, firemen, and ambulance squads. The customary finale was distinctly marked with a few young pretty girls wearing attractive western outfits, riding on horseback and carrying large American flags of thirteen red and white stripes and forty-eight stars on a field of blue. This signified the final ending. The procession was followed by an assembly in a town center to hear a few platform speakers pay tribute to all the past and present war heroes.

Later in the afternoon, families and friends gathered in local parks to picnic. The traditional lunch menu was charcoal cooked hot dogs or hamburgers plus fresh garden salads, beer and soda. The recreational activity was a mixed gender softball game. After the sporting event, pails of water were carried to the grill and spaghetti was cooked for the evening meal. This portion of the routine finishes with hot coffee and homemade cake. Then, the group rushed to conclude eating, cleaning up the area, pack the cars and move to the large open field just before dark to watch a lengthy, free, fireworks show.

Throughout the war effort, parents who had members in the services proudly exhibited framed military stars in their windows. Many of these folks had more than one child in the armed forces and they, therefore, very proudly displayed a separate plaque for each person.

Professional photographs of every family idol in uniform were prominently exhibited in their homes. While these troops were stationed on the front lines of danger, their relatives stayed back to keep the home fires burning with dedicated hope and prayer for their youngster's safe return to friendly shores.

I observed personal letters received from battle stations written on the inside of bordered red and blue lightweight stationery which was folded inwardly. On many occasions the message segment of this V-mail contained several neatly cutout spaces to remove potentially, censored, sensitive, information. This was a major government security procedure to prevent strategic information from being intercepted by the enemy. The outer envelope surface of this correspondence contained the recipient's address.

On two separate occasions, my grandmother sadly accepted an official Department of Defense notification stating that her son's ship was torpedoed while at sea. Although this news was very devastating; he, fortunately, survived both catastrophes and safely returned home after World War II to raise a family and participate in his children's weddings.

During this stressful period in history, Paterson, New Jersey quickly became identified as a significant industrial complex that manufactured an abundance of war materials and supplies. Residents went to work in defense factories that managed a three-shift work schedule and operated production lines seven days per week. Rail links throughout the municipality were lined with miles of steam engines pulling tightly, loaded, flatbed and box cars. These containers hauled important combat materials around the clock. This mighty transportation system carried enormous quantities of jeeps, airplanes, ambulances, ammunition, heavy armaments, medical supplies, tanks, and trucks. Equipment was generally painted a distinctive brown and had either a red cross or white star for identification markings.

As a result of these outstanding efforts, this urban center was always on alert. Many public schools had batteries of defense, antiaircraft, artillery on their roofs. Communities routinely experienced a barrage of surprise, wailing, warning, sirens that frequently resonated to announce the common occurrence of another fearful startling air raid drill. As an impressionable youth and, because of these circumstances, the numerous late night time and daylight civilian training exercises were extensive and very frightening!

Dramatic practice exercises occurred in the evening when a training procedure was implemented. House lights were turned off and we scurried to the basement for shelter. There, water, canned food and emergency equipment were stockpiled. In preparation, cellar windows were covered with special darkening shades.

My uncle, who was a neighborhood warden, would put on his white military helmet, report outdoors and patrol an assigned area for inspection compliance with the strict rules that required total darkness. While on watch, he took pleasure in rapping on the underground safety storeroom casement window with his powerful searchlight. Until he shared a secret, which was his message that everything was in order, this distinctive tap initially petrified us with very accelerated apprehension and anxiety.

On the way to school each day, a billboard sized Honor Roll was posted on the side of a corner grocery store. It was separated from the sidewalk and protected by a large single pipe barrier. My daily ritual was to grab the steel conduit and make two complete belly turns around the three-foot-high metal conduit. At the time, I thought this painted red, white and blue wooden sign was an announcement for students who did well in the city school system. Later, I learned this was a posting for local military heroes and their printed names documented the ultimate sacrifice each one made to preserve our nation's freedom.

My youthful contribution and compliance experiences were related to rationing and collecting old newspapers. Valuable dime size, red tokens were accumulated for use to purchase limited amounts of butter, eggs, meat or sugar. In addition, a large upper-case black letter of the alphabet was posted on the rear windshield glass to determine gasoline allotments. Purchasing new tires or automobiles were almost impossible. As a result of these restrictions, walking was a major source of transportation and, therefore, social activities were primarily limited to neighborhoods.

During times gone by in which international conflict resolution was a very central theme, people for a variety of reasons, have always remained behind to provide resources, inordinate amounts of energy, morale reinforcement and fabrication of military materials to support the overwhelming numbers who were in action and consumed by the enormous battle efforts to maintain world peace.

On this day when we should take time to honor, respect and say thank you; please reserve a few moments to consider the uneasy, distressful and uncomfortable feelings of those who maintained the home front and experienced their own complex, multifaceted, emotional, combinations of pain and suffering. It is these blends of patriotic citizens who have waited at home to show moral support, produce military materials, continue to deeply mourn and shed volumes of tears for their absent loved ones. These touching moments attempt to fill the vacant voids with fond memories of those who were serving on the front lines and in harm's way.

Throughout history, cemeteries around the world have continued to grow and fill with dedicated veterans whose average ages notably ranged from eighteen to twenty-two years. Their carefully white painted grave markers, which are precisely aligned, can be identified with Crescent Moons and Stars, Crosses and Stars of David. These brave souls in uniform committed themselves to protect the liberties, sovereignty and independence that we enjoy daily. Sadly, and many times, these profound sacrifices are frequently taken for granted.

Municipal areas all over the globe are graced with numerous monuments, museums, exhibits and statues whose purpose is to commemorate, pay tribute and recognize historical heroes. While much attention is devoted to the deceased, we must always honor and respect those who have returned less than whole and with permanent scars and a lifetime of injury and pain. On that list are the wounded who continue to suffer the severe psychological and physical permanent wounds that are associated with the combat zone.

Shortly after the Second World War, two very popular historical weekly documentary programs appeared on the black and white small television screen. They were *Crusade of Europe*, which depicted the ground battles, and *Victory at Sea* which presented the navel struggles. Both series were watched, earning a high level of recognition and respect. As a young child, these episodes engraved poignant and lasting memories that have been sustained through my lifetime. Dramatic programs later included *Combat*! and *12:00 O'clock High* They later were followed by several comedy presentations such as: *Hogan's Heroes, McHale's Navy, Sergeant Bilko* and *M*A*S*H*. Throughout this period, many movies and live stage presentations also covered the topic in significant detail using a variety of versions or interpretations.

In previous decades, I was emotionally touched and impressed with visits to some of the following historical locations: Boston Freedom Trail, Valley Forge, Washington's Crossing, Gettysburg, Normandy Invasion site, Freedom Train which toured the nation immediately following World War II, Washington DC, Arlington Cemetery, Second World War Memorial, Korean War Memorial, Vietnam Wall, Iwo Jima Marine Flag Raising Monument, Tomb of the Unknown Soldier, *Arizona* Battleship, Punch Bowl Cemetery, Hickam Air Force Base in Hawaii and Ground Zero in New York City.

All mentioned here have reflected times which were marked by too many wars, conflicts or police actions to count. As my years have passed, the prestige and respect of our young military volunteers has significantly diminished. Then, flag burners and desecrates did not exist. Is it because the population who remained at home was deeply and directly involved or consumed with a single target goal? The clear objective was to win and defeat the enemy who could be easily recognized by the uniform worn. While today, the worldwide foe appears in a variety of costumes and carries destructive weapons that are concealed in clothing or hidden under their flesh. They go underground in small clusters and are rooted in communities all over the map.

In my "olden days" the nation seemed united in defending our shores, protecting liberty, freedom and enjoying the pursuit of lasting happiness and peace. Of late, the pondering and reflection of past patriots is forgotten by many. Memorial Day is associated with the first summer weekend and a focus is on getting to the highway and out of town. Parkways are congested with bargain shoppers, seashore swimmers or amusement park enthusiasts. In essence, the line to the recreational resort is much longer than the lonely lane to the cemetery. Town parades of the past are currently rare events and military memories of previous performances have become sleeping shadows. Is it time to return to the Decoration Day concept and concentrate on remembering the many giants who have served before us to make this great nation the envy of the world? Please join me in a private solemn, serious moment or two of silence to reflect on the true meaning of Memorial Day.

WHAT A MISTAKE

I was raised in an environment where my parents spoke excellent English. However, when visiting many family members and friends, Italian was the primary language used in these frequent social situations. Rather than take advantage of those "golden learning opportunities". I consistently elected to find a quiet place in those settings and enjoy reading a favorite book. In retrospect, not learning a second language was a major mistake!

CITY CHILD TO FARM BOY

Due to World War II and the Korean Conflict, young men were scarce and unavailable for employment. Dad and I volunteered to help friends who owned a truck farm in Wayne, New Jersey. The season began in early spring when spinach and lettuce seeds were hand planted in cold frames. These mini greenhouses were constructed of glass and wooden sashes made from recycled old tired storm windows. While these seedlings developed, soil in the field was prepared by Dad who walked behind Fred, the workhorse. He had a plow handle in each fist and the reins around his neck. His strong body and skilled hands guided the stallion to pull the Vee shaped, single, shining, steel plow back and forth to till the loam and create absolutely straight rows.

After the threat of a killing frost passed, these tiny, matured, sheltered, sprouts were then transplanted into the carefully prepared ground. Once repositioned, hand tools and intense labor began. Activities included: cultivating, plucking weeds, removing bugs and replacing sick crops.

Later in the sequence of these tasks, his third-grade son picked and helped crate ripe vegetables. A fringe benefit of the job was the advantage of being able to eat fresh food, directly from the vine.

Gradually, daylight hours increased and the weather became warmer. These conditions required an adjusted and longer schedule. We arrived at dawn, went to the barn and gathered our tools. Lined up on the large door moldings were knives that were used to cut and prune produce. They were arranged according to the height of the worker. Only adults carried sharpening stones to hone a razor edge on the blade. The full sparkling new knife in early spring was reduced to the thin size of a coping saw blade cutting surface as the cool winter season approached. Constructed inside this tall, large, wooden barn was a huge cement tub that was used to wash all the harvested vegetables that floated. It was, also, a great place to submerge sweaty arms for a few short minutes to cool down an overheated body.

Connected to this very chilly water container was a pump that was attached to an adjustable pressure hose nozzle. While a fine spray was applied to delicately skinned crops, a stronger volume of liquid was used to clean the hardier vegetables. Finally, on every Thursday and Sunday evening, the powerful, green, flat bedded Mack truck was fully loaded, gently washed and wet down in preparation for hauling a full load of ripe vegetables to the farmers' market.

Generally, daily work began at sunrise, and continued until midmorning. Then, we stopped to rest and went to the house for refreshments which consisted of coffee and newly oven baked buns. The procedure repeated at midafternoon.

After this lunch break period, the young children were released from the agricultural chores and allowed to play. A favorite game was tag on the large high piles of empty wire and wooden crates. These stacked containers numbered in the hundreds and were extremely dangerous at best. It was a miracle that nobody was ever injured during these chasing, climbing, hiding and running escapades.

Stickball, using the pink Spalding ball, was popular. The city kids represented the New York Yankees stars and the home country boys acted as Brooklyn Dodger heroes. The batting orders were announced by the aspiring athletes as each player addressed the plate. They possessed a complete knowledge of the professional they represented. Verbal information supplied a statistical presentation of each modeled major leaguer.

Because of our small numbers, most fielders were imaginary as positions were adjusted for righty or lefty batters. The magic of the game was that all the young boys could hit the speeding, sweeping, curving or dipping fast ball with tremendous skill, power and accuracy. Regardless of the distance the ball rocketed into the outfield, a landing in the undeclared area was an automatic out.

The rear of the small equipment shed provided the backstop in which the catcher called balls and strikes. At the opposite side of this building was an old, overused and under-maintained outhouse. On one occasion, my curiosity led me to open the door. One whiff of this captured, contaminated space motivated me to control bowel functions for the entire day. This was an important stinky lifetime lesson to learn!

Over the main large barn doors was a flood light that illuminated our natural surface basketball court. The autumn night random rock playing surface was covered with dirt and an occasional small puddle of mud. Our uniforms were the same clothing worn all day. They consisted of work boots, sneakers, old shoes, overhauls or dungarees.

Because of these inherent obstacles on the ground, farm boys became superb off-balance shooters and excellent ball handlers. Some went on to earn official uniforms on high school and college teams.

A few times in the late afternoon, I went fishing in the irrigation collection pond at the rear of the thirty- five-acre farm. The deep murky water contained an abundance of large turtles, sunny and catfish. In my last early evening trip to the private secluded quiet spot, I experienced an encounter with a large, curled-up, coral colored, snake that was basking in the sun and enjoying the warm heated stones on the open tractor path. Upon eyeballing the long-coiled reptile, this eight-year-old put his rapidly moving PF Keds in high gear and made his last speedy exit from this remote sanctuary.

Generally, the long day ended as the night stars and moon appeared. We returned to the farm house to take a community bath. The male youngsters shared the large old tub and splashed water all over the room. This was followed by a full delicious supper that included frosty, creamy milk from the neighbor's dairy cows.

After the sumptuous meal, our payment for the weekend's work was a full trunk of freshly cut vegetables. On the trip home, we enjoyed the evening sounds of the changing seasons. A standard stop at the first corner candy store in sight was a tradition. Dad bought two sweet crispy cones which were filled with a favorite flavored double dip ice cream that was carefully wrapped with a large folded paper napkin. Frequently, the sandman prepared me for a well-earned rest before the car parked in our garage. Dad, then, gently carried me off to bed.

Time passed, the manpower demands were satisfied with new machinery, Fred the horse was sold, military men returned to their home shores and migrant workers replaced the volunteers. Eventually, the property became too valuable to farm and the fertile land was sold to land developers.

A few acres, near the house, were kept for a nursery business that supplied advice, shrubs, flowers and landscape products to the new suburban homeowners. The kids grew up, went to fine colleges and secured advanced degrees. Some turned out to be prominent business people, others earned PhD degrees and a few became college professors.

TAKE THIS BOY TO A DOCTOR

As a little boy, Dad and I would rise early on weekends and drive toward the country to help friends who owned a family truck farm. Their planting preparation process began long before the last killing frost. To ensure a head-start for early germination and the beginning of a new growing season, spinach and lettuce seeds were carefully placed in well labeled cold frames that were located in the proper sunshine. Within a few days the warm fertile earth blossomed to life with a luxurious carpet of green foliage. At the appropriate time, the young fragile sprouts were separated and relocated in a carefully well-prepared field to grow into beautiful, healthy vegetables.

In addition to the hard and dedicated labor of Fred, the farm work horse; almost all of the cultivating, weeding and harvesting was accomplished by hand. Once matured, the crop was cut, cleaned, crated and prepared to be marketed on Thursday in Paterson, NJ. Sunday, they were transported and sold in New York City.

Our compensation for this grueling volunteer labor was a weekly trunk load filled with fresh produce that was brought home at day's end. Using several preserving methods, Mom would then carefully prepare and safeguard this food supply for future and winter consumption. Towards the end of fall, cabbage was the major yield to be picked.

Again, our car was packed with this large, nutritious, staple and delivered home. My job was to bury these large, leafy heads in the soil leaving only the plant roots above the ground. During the cold winter, this approaching meal was carefully removed from the frozen dirt with muscle, sweat, a sharp pick and shovel!

Using a variety of different recipes, our family ate this wholesome product throughout the wintertime season at least three times a week. Around the arrival of spring one year, I complained of serious abdominal pain. Convinced their child had an acute case of appendicitis and preparing for the worst, my parents decided to take me to the doctor. After a careful medical examination, the physician happily reported, "This boy does not have an appendix problem, he has "gas".

HOT ROD

During one summer vacation in New Market, New Hampshire, I had the opportunity to be watched and entertained by a teenager who had a driver's license. Part of our recreational activities included fishing and swimming in the local cemetery creek. We shared the water with a variety of snakes, leeches and small animals. Part of the challenge was to stay clear of our natural friends and immediately remove bloodsuckers from our bodies.

One day we decided to build a race car using wheels discarded from a retired old baby carriage. The recycled axles were fastened to a long thick plank, A vegetable crate was nailed over the front tires to form a hood and the second box was secured to the board at the rear of the frame to create a sturdy back for the driver seat and a storage trunk for tools. The steering mechanism involved tying a strong rope to the front axles.

A realistic touch was added when a shiny stove pipe was found and bolted to the action, packed, simulated engine compartment. Bogus exhaust was produced when the tubular, silver, smokestack, was packed with newspaper, dried wood and set on fire. The tiny flame accelerated in intensity as the "hot rod" sped down the mountain.

The experimental prototype was modified for safety and the blazing red pipe was insulated with several soaking wet towels. Fortunately, the adventures associated with this test homemade vehicle escaped the dangerous hazards of downhill racing.

THE BIG ONE THAT SHOULD HAVE GOTTEN AWAY

As a young child and while spending a July vacation at the seashore, I expressed an interest in fishing. Shortly after arriving home, an old-fashioned hand-me-down, deep-sea pole appeared at the back door with a reel and a full spool of line thick enough to anchor a battleship. Several visits to local lakes were enjoyed as Dad and I participated in the new experience.

Essentially, my father dug the worms, drove to the watering hole and set the bait. Each outing brought hope to really catch a big one, as this youngster repeatedly cast the line into the water. Before the summer ended, both of us became very skilled.

During the season's final days, we visited a favorite spot for the last adventure of the year. In time, there was a strong tug on the tackle as it hit the water! Viewers gathered and claimed the underwater treasure was a large rotting tire. Interestingly, the reel let out plenty of extra cord.

An encounter began and it was eventually beyond the strength and capacity of the novice angler. Dad, who was the most powerful man in the world, took the pole and continued the fight. Electrifying excitement encircled the pond as the expenditure of energy hastened! Whatever was on the last part of the submerged string was no match for Pop, a telephone tower sized rod and a thick clothes rope fishing line.

Suddenly there was a stir in the struggle, followed by a gigantic splash of sparkling, soft, silver, spray. While the action mounted, an audience assembled. Swiftly, all eyes went airborne. To the observers' surprise, a spectacular, sleek, male Mallard Duck was at the end and quickly elevated into a commanding full flight pattern.

The sporting event finished with a victory for Dad! Our trophy catch was gently brought back to earth; the bird firmly placed under his forearm and a hook tenderly removed from the bill. Strong hands softly opened, and the liberated fowl's wings frantically flapped. This was followed by furious quacking and an escape route to freedom. The bird swiftly soared into a fiery orange, picturesque, fall sunset. The season ended, all signs of fishing equipment mysteriously disappeared and the career of the young fisherman came to a screeching halt!

HAVE LUNCH ON DAD

As an eight-year-old child, Dad talked to me about the importance of learning how to swim properly. Eventually, he suggested that I join the YMCA, take lessons and participate in their other scheduled activities. The annual membership was $7.00 which included using the facilities after school on Wednesday and all-day Saturday. Generally, a Public Service bus was taken to travel to and from the "Y".

On the first weekend, my father drove me to the building, walked with me to the registration desk, helped with the sign-up, waited to make sure that I comfortably settled in and was ready to become involved in the day's planned program. He then gave me the bus fare and seventy-five cents to buy lunch. This was a generous amount and more than sufficient to purchase a substantial meal.

At noon, I went to the cafeteria and proceeded to load the tray with several different desserts and a large container of milk. At the cash register, there was more than enough money to pay for the "gourmet" meal. While I suffered from the stomach gouging with the large variety of assorted sweets, this experience taught me that a sensible selection would be more enjoyable and healthier. As time advanced, I learned how to choose a properly balanced diet. The responsibility of eating correctly and choosing the appropriate assortment of foods matured with advanced age.

MY MUSICAL HISTORY

FOUNDATION

Selecting an instrument and taking lessons at seven years of age were the first steps in becoming a music student. A neighbor owned a studio in Paterson, New Jersey and was chosen to provide my training. His store employed several talented professionals who were available to provide weekly lessons. Unfortunately, the accordion specialist was seldom accessible. Therefore, I received lessons from a variety of other instructors.

My parents were perceptive and quickly realized this was not an optimum situation. They then began an intense search for a qualified accordion teacher. Within a short time, they located a highly trained person who was both a competent instructor and an active performing musician. I studied with this person until my college years and received an excellent education that prepared me to take on my own pupils and provide the tools to play for hire.

CHURCH AND ELEMENTARY SCHOOL PREPARATION

The local church conducted a summer recreational program for neighborhood children who lived in the parish. One of the several offerings was an annual talent show for parents to attend. In addition to playing before small family members, these annual August programs allowed youngsters to demonstrate their varied developing talents. During the academic year, the public school conducted talent shows for pupils to share young emerging entertainment skills for an audience of peers.

FORMATIVE PERIOD

My first professional engagement took place in a local neighborhood tavern. As a fifteen-year-old, I responded to a newspaper advertisement to provide music on Saturday night. I got the job! Dad drove me to the saloon and we unloaded the music stand, library and accordion. The evening went very well and in addition to my fifteen-dollar wage, a generous number of tips were collected.

This five-hour experience was the start of a lucrative career. While in high school, there were many opportunities to meet a variety of students with similar interests. The shared goal was to form a small band. After several rehearsals, over months, with various different emerging musicians; three other teenagers and I came together. We seemed to properly blend and eventually formed a combo.

The group included: accordion, drums, guitar and saxophone. We practiced each Sunday night in the drummer's basement and developed the skills to perform a wide variety of music. The ever-growing assortment of selections included: most top forties, standards, and ethnic favorites.

We became very popular while attending Eastside High School and were hired to play many of the Friday night dances. The three-hour engagements paid sixty dollars per "gig". Within a short time period, we moved to other city schools, entered the social club network and banquet hall circle.

Before graduation, the quartet's popularity grew and were able to play a club date almost every week. During the summer weekends, we played steady at a Greenwood Lake nightclub. Because of our ability to provide an assortment of music, we frequently received tips which were split evenly between the band members. While in high school, I frequently earned more than thirty dollars per week from band jobs. This additional sum was combined with income generated from teaching accordion, working as a shoe store sales person and painting apartments

FRAMEWORK

Before high school graduation, I became a member of the American Federation of Musicians, Local 248 and now had access to many performers whose name, specialization, telephone number and address were listed in the BOOK. My inner circle of the original "CROWN FOUR" now multiplied to include several hundred players and I began to network with numerous additional groups.

As my skills and show business horizons expanded, so did my clothing wardrobe. Performance attire matured from sports jackets to navy blue suits to matching band coats to tuxedos. The apparel transition was directly related to professional advancement and increased monetary compensation. New opportunities on the journey to the upper levels of talent provided exposure and experiences with exceptional master artists. During the college years, this profitable activity enabled me to purchase two new automobiles and a home before marriage. We lived in that happy home for thirty-eight years and raised two beautiful children.

FINISHED PRODUCT

During the prime years of this musical occupation, I had booking engagements and contract commitments that were two years in advance. Some individual banquet performance routines had me in the limelight for six continuous hours. The affair started with strolling music during the cocktail hour. It then transitioned to four hours of dinner and dance music with the combo. While the band took an intermission, the accordionist sauntered around the floor to play melodies that guests requested. This segment was generally rewarded with generous gratuities. The party continued after the band finished and I concluded the entertainment with a one-man band "overtime" presentation.

Eventually the sophisticated equipment and the soloist began to perform as a single. The music produced closely resembled the sounds of a small orchestra. This phase was a very productive and profitable portion of my career! My stage, then, moved to private parties in gigantic, beautiful homes and mansions.

FINALE

I enjoyed a great run and was able to generate a second income to supplement my salary as an elementary school principal. This, however, came at a price! Hours were devoted to preparation, daily practice, and detailed business demands.

The melodies of this era were beautiful and enjoyable to play. However, times were changing and so was the music. It was quickly moving in very different directions and it was no longer fun for me to play.

At this time, our children both attended Trenton State College and this resulted in us becoming empty nesters. For many reasons, it was time to end my thirty-five-year career as an active professional musician. I closed the date book and stopped contracting new engagements.

FINAL CURTAIN CALL

We retired, moved from an active, exciting and congested Bergen County to a beautiful, quaint, rural, socially busy Four Seasons Community in Mansfield Township, New Jersey. The sophisticated, tired, accordion was withdrawn to a storage space in the garage. I then struggled, once a year, to play popular holiday songs at an annual clubhouse bowling luncheon and a fresh air spring open driveway concert in preparation for their season ending bowling banquet.

During this painful outdoor, pavement, practice, experience; I labored to resurrect old professional skills and to remember the beautiful melodies of the past. Throughout this rehearsal session for their restaurant, cocktail hour performance, a neighbor reminded me that I sounded better the previous year. Very funny...but sadly true! However, after the next year's outdoor recital she rewarded me with a beautiful bouquet of spring and summer flowers.

ENCORE

A change of snowbird address to Sun City, Florida has created a potential voyage to the past and an accordion reintroduction. While sipping a nightcap at the clubhouse, we became involved in a conversation with two ladies. The discussion keyed around music and ultimately resulted in an opportunity to borrow a squeeze box for the three- month period.

That evening, we were invited to their home to play music together. This magic moment occurred and I was again hooked. The women gave me the equipment, encouraged me to attend the Accordion Club's monthly meeting and, also, furnished a solo performance before the members at their informal gathering.

Now, laborious preparation was necessary to activate dormant techniques. Long, enjoyable, challenging hours were committed to revisit: scales, chord structures, triad patterns and melodies. It has been a very interesting, amazing, transitional, experience to observe how latent skills were being reestablished and remembered. The standard song selection library expanded and benefited from several, stimulating, recollection and revitalizations sessions.

An important component of the harmonious rebirth was the mastering of both instrument keyboards. The left side contains 120 buttons which are not visible to the player and the right hand manipulates 41 notes. In combination, both sets of fingers - when coordinated – produce beautiful music. Since the long course to perfection was introduced at the beginning of that year, substantial progress has been noted. Significant success occurred, which has enabled me to entertain on two separate occasions at the Accordion Club and for a King's Point lounge cocktail party.

Shortly after, I met a new accordion playing comrade, Frank Cimmino, who was a very active performing musician for many years. Ultimately, he invited me to his lakeside home to meet his wife, Madeline, and play our instruments together.

Eventually, we talked about the new technology that has evolved with our 120 bass mechanisms. After several conversations on the topic, I purchased a new electronic state of the art Roland FR-8x. This musical device incorporates over 1400 different sound voices which can be played separately or in combination.

Another challenge! An additional layer of skills is in the process of being developed, mastered and very much enjoyed! As a rebirth reward, I was provided the opportunity to entertain at a local Sun City, Florida restaurant for three years. Tips were excellent and I donated all of them to a lovely and extremely grateful waitress. During my last performance at season's end, two young teenage boys were leaving the restaurant and stopped to place a few coins in the tip jar to help the "poor old accordion player".

ONLY RATS EAT CHEESE

My favorite uncle was a widower at a young age. Because he did not have children, his abundant love for kids was devoted to his three young nephews who he took out on weekend entertainment excursions. Since restaurant meals were not a part of the family routine, lunches were made at home and packed in a brown paper bag. Our mothers would prepare an interesting assortment of delicious sandwiches for us to eat and enjoy.

Uncle Phil was a hardworking man who would bring a peanut butter and jelly snack for lunch. Unknown to the youngsters, he loved all kinds of cheese. However, he told us that only rats ate this food! With this morsel of information, the trap was set. Now, the innocent boys were more than willing to trade their mouse's meal for a tasty peanut butter and jam combination slathered on two pieces of fresh white Wonder Bread.

Sadly, he passed before age fifty and much too early for him to bring my taste buds to maturity. However, a smile is brought to my face each time Mickey Mouse's bait is inserted into my mouth.

MY LAST COWBOY

In the early days of my childhood, westerns were a major television program entertainment offering. Because of this influence, playmates devoted many hours to cowboy games or activities. My brown and white bicycle was ridden while wearing retired military Cavalry boots, plus a pair of brown World War II army holsters that were packed with a matched set of white, plastic handled cap guns. To complete the outfit, a lasso was fastened to the two-wheeler's seat.

Within time and in one magical moment as I rode up to a neighborhood factory to say hello to a worker who had become a friend, I became embarrassed to be attired in this make-believe outfit, playing cowboys and riding a large customized "two legged" bicycle.

In that brief instant, a mental transition occurred and the western imaginary heroes retired. The play direction moved to a new venue and sports activities took center stage. With this growing interest; coaching, instructing and teaching became activities that were shared and enjoyed with Dad. Another new chapter in my life opened for me to collect fond memories of my father and best friend.

PASSION FOR ROSES

My mother's name is Rose and this may be the primary reason for my infatuation with this beautiful blossom. The passion for this special selection was cultivated as a young child on the daily walk to and from elementary school. While choosing one of several routes on this journey, I passed through a neighborhood that supplied an abundance of vegetables, fruit and flower gardens.

In essence, these were established by proud talented, metropolitan, mini-farmers during World War II out of necessity and they lived off the land. It was interesting to observe that each property parcel was surrounded with a different distinctive fence. While most urban folks created excellent backyard produce for sustenance, many also used front and side yard areas for entertainment. Here they grew colorful collections of flourishing, fragrant flowers. The multitudes of sweet-scented blooms decorated their city homes with a prolific explosion of vigorous varieties of fantastic colorful flowers and stunning well-trimmed shrubs.

Resulting from hard work and very persistent care, extremely healthy yields matured and extended over their property enclosed boundaries. It was impressive to observe the magnificent transition that occurred between spring and fall as these yards came actively alive with numerous, large, nourishing and healthy blooms. As a young participant in the basic commercial agricultural chores of cultivating, weeding and harvesting, I developed a deep appreciation for efforts expended on these high-volume plants.

My favorite bush was the lovely rose with its beautiful assortment of aromas, dynamic showings of spectacular shades and huge abundant blossoms. It was easy to pick a mixed bouquet of sweet-smelling, large hybrids on the way to school. A lunch paper napkin that was carefully folded and placed in a shirt pocket to provide the wrapping package containing the freshly cut, bursting, scented, buds and petals. Shortly after arriving to class, the perfumed prizes were placed on the teacher's desk for her to open, enjoy and gain her favor. Through the passing of grades, the sequence of educators never knew the sources of the bountiful, secret, special, supply.

Years later and as a homeowner in Bergen County, I planted several varieties of this treasured flower in my garden. I developed an intense appreciation for the inordinate amount of attention to detail they demanded. The laborious task list expanded to include: proper placement, careful watering, specific fertilizing, skilled pruning and regular specialized spraying. These procedures were essential to create outstanding specimens and to prevent fungus, disease or insect infestations.

A few years ago, I began a growing rose garden in Four Seasons and plan to expand the collection in the future. Once again, the excitement has continued and much success has resulted from sustaining a very rigorous maintenance schedule. The ultimate reward remains when new cuttings are brought in to brighten the home each day. This joy will provide the motivation to expand the developing flower garden into the future.

MISS PEEK-A-BOO

Living in the city encouraged creative street play for young athletic children. Homes were situated close to the curb, on tiny plots with traditionally small grass front yards. Each owner constructed a fence to identify and outline their four property boundaries.

While we played touch football, roller derby, lamp post basketball and softball, in this neighborhood setting; batting accuracy was extremely difficult and challenging. A threat of breaking a window was an ever-present danger and chipping in to pay for shattered glass was the unwritten rule during those years. An additional incentive was to thump the telephone pole at third base on a fly for an automatic home run. Because of these restrictions, we developed skills in place hitting.

In spite of these constraints, retrieving a misplaced ball over the fence added an interesting dimension to this demanding part of the contest. On the first base side of the street field lived Miss Peek-A-Boo, who took delight peering at the children through an opening in her window blind. The instant a wayward ball traveled to her lawn, a race began between her and a speedy child to retrieve the errant projectile. In most cases the young legs arrived at the leather sphere before the old lady opened the door. On rare occasions, she won the race and the object was retrieved and added to her collection.

Years later we moved to a new locality with a more sophisticated Miss Peek-A-Boo. Her interest was perching at the front window and accumulating gossip to share with the community. Whenever seen at her hiding spot behind the drawn shade, the children would wave to her and watch the curtain quickly change position. With all the interesting things available to spend time, these unique individuals selected to squander their minutes and watch the world pass by through their own private portholes. This certainly was a very narrow, limited view of living and a waste of valuable precious moments!

TELEPHONE CALL FROM THE PRINCIPAL

The telephone was answered by my mother one afternoon when I was an eighth-grade pupil. The person making the call identified herself as the school principal. Mom immediately responded, "I'll break his neck and what did he do?" The administrator calmly explained in detail how her son was the hero for the day as he risked his life to bring a young child to safety.

This incident was reported by an automobile driver who almost hit a youngster that darted into traffic. The motorist stated a potentially fatal accident was avoided by the quick actions taken by this brave young man wearing a safety patrol captain's belt. He wanted to be assured this deed would be recognized and properly acknowledged by the authorities.

How times have changed!

FIRST FIELD GOAL

I attended an elementary school in a tough working-class neighborhood and was forced to quickly learn the necessary skills to survive in difficult situations. Although very tall as a seventh grader, there was a classmate who exceeded my height and that was probably due to the fact that he drove to class. While my sports interests were in baseball and football, I received a basketball for Christmas that had laces and a rubber air bladder to maintain its shape.

The ball was also too light for outdoor play during windy weather. Before the holiday recess ended, a homemade steel rebar rim fastened on a plywood sheet appeared in the backyard. This was mounted on a street lamp for night time games. Dad, who was a baseball, football and soccer player took his first shot which was an under-hand layup. During winter months, snow was shoveled off the road to enable the competition to continue. Gloves were worn while guarding on defense and removed for offense.

The local church team needed an additional player to complete the squad and I was asked to join the club. Before the first game, however, my rowdy, hoodlum, hoopster, pals were thrown out of the association for foul mouths and poor conduct. I was the only member who endured the cut and was fortunate to be assigned to another team.

The new group met on the court prior to the opening game of the CYO league. My job was to get rebounds, control the boards and make the out-let pass. Early into the first quarter, the opponents executed a press during an out of bounds play. I broke loose near the back-court line, and was thrown the ball. The basket was in sight as the dribbling accelerated. Once under the net, the projectile was fired to bounce off the rim, a rebound was made and the second shot was unsuccessfully launched.

The third attempt, through watery eyes, scored a two pointer. Instantly, there was a scolding and swift kick in my rear end as a reward for scoring at the wrong basket. The outcome of the contest cannot be recalled…**butt,** the memory of my first field goal in league play remains remarkable and unforgettably painful.

RAILROAD REALITY

Since history evolved over time, the impact of railroads has continued to serve as an important fabric in the growth of the world. Development of the United States is a prime example. These steel threads seamed the land and helped stitch the countryside together.

While at the exact same time, they segmented growing nations into new neighborhoods and pockets of society. Communities and localities were identified by the side of the tracks in which people lived. Interestingly, my mother was born into a home that was on a large property bordering the track fringe strip. During the Great Depression, she, along with playmates, walked the rails to pick up coal which fell from the steam locomotives as they shuttled merchandise and supplies to and from industrial centers.

During their chilly wintry search, several sympathetic, understanding train operators tossed coal from their feisty iron horses to help these children as they rummaged around to find fuel to heat their cold-water flats. Several years later, I was born into a home that was only two doors away from her birth place. Fortunately, this address had central heating and a reserve of precious potential black energy that was stored in a dark, dusty, bleak, basement bin

The freight and passenger coaches meandered through an open valley conduit at the rear of our backyard. Because of the sloping terrain; this soot and smoke, smoldering, cargo pulling, machines were out of sight from our four-room residence. However, their loud whistles were heard during all hours of day and night.

As a small child and during World War II and the Korean Conflict, I was able to observe the transportation of brown, army colored, military supplies that were being hauled on flatbed rail cars. This equipment included: folded winged fighter planes, ambulances with big red crosses, long gunned artillery, jeeps, tanks, trucks, and tons of medical or food provisions. In this lifetime I have experienced and observed too many wars to count.

As years passed over many decades, I moved three times and at each new location, further removed me from the ties associated with thunderous trains and their powerful impact on civilization. I currently use high velocity sleek, diesel or electric muscled steel wheeled passenger vehicles for recreational purposes.

In addition to frequent visits on popular routes towards Philadelphia and New York City; two Amtrak vacations, across the United States of America, were enjoyed. These two adventures were added to a collection of excursions throughout Asia and Europe. In essence, railroads built our united country and provided the resources to expand it from coast to coast and continent to continent.

The blended influences of living in the metropolitan corridor, linked with world touring and combined educational experiences, have acutely developed an awareness of the vast differences that are woven into the present complex world. This landscape resembles a technicolor tapestry that blankets our multicultural globe. While the harmonies of tolerance and tranquility have become some of today's leading objectives, misplaced tussles over terrorism have combined with traumatic, territorial toils. That torment has continued to result in augmented destruction of nations and lasting conversations which are button-holed, around long-term geopolitically correct comments, statements or deeds.

As we journey into and past the twenty-first century, reknitted recent patches of dialogue and redesigns are being tailored to alter the complex travel garments of today's international tablecloth. This confusing trend seems to produce fashionable, fancy communication engines of swift, sophisticated expressions to modify the routes or pathways leading to accelerated deception and exploitation of the planet's growing population. In essence, has a sophisticated society and fast-moving social order compromised politically correct statements for freedom of speech?

In my childhood, America was identified as a "melting pot" that welcomed people from all parts of the world. Blended together this mixture created the world's greatest nation in history. Recently, this migration has been defined as a "mosaic "and each component has its own individual identity that will have a major impact on our country's future.

WHAT SIDE OF THE TRACKS?

As a small boy, our first city home was in a residential parcel engulfed by a significant industrial complex of factories which were on two sides of the property. The railroad tracks were in a valley behind the rear yard. On the large, inclined slope between the backyard and the rails was an overgrown hill with tall grass, wild brush and native, natural foliage.

While identified as off-limits and dangerous, it was an intriguing environment that captured the vivid imaginations of young children at play. At the top of the ridge, was a well-worn, short-cut, foot path to and from school. Against parental permission or knowledge, this very well-established pattern was secretly walked four times a day.

On one secret trip as an adventuring seventh grader, I miscalculated the leap over a barbed wire fence and severely injured both legs with deep bloody cuts. The scars still remain as a painful reminder of penalties associated with disobeying the rules.

West of this sloping gorged transit route, was the wrong side of the tracks followed next by the worst patch of town. To the east and on a hill, lived people from the middle class. The public school was in the center of this configuration and provided scholastic programs for all the children in that district.

Needless to say, the pupil population included a wide range of learners that extended from the very good to those who were extremely troubled. Fortunately, the educational staff was exceptional, recognized these variations and made the necessary adjustments to provide an outstanding program for the children who were interested in being taught.

The environment was academically oriented, well-disciplined and in a safe setting. The religious, economic, ethnic, and social profiles of the student body represented an assortment of America's working class that seemed to be uniformly struggling to establish a much better life for their youngsters.

While it was very easy to identify racial differences, other dissimilarities and potentially controversial neighborhood issues were absent from student relationships. Youngsters seemed to study, play and interact in a peaceful and harmonious setting. Most shared a common goal which was connected to mastering English.

GLORIA

School Number Ten is a three-story building housing kindergarten through grade eight and is located in one of several industrial areas in Paterson, New Jersey. It serviced several classrooms assigned to each grade level. The brick building and cement surface playground is the size of a half city block and is surrounded by a tall, black, steel, picket fence.

At each end of the recreational area are huge gates which remain permanently in the open position. Children gathered there before school hours, during morning and afternoon recess sessions and after returning from home following the traditional long lunch period. Outdoor physical education classes also used the hard pavement for gym instruction.

The facility was immaculately polished and enjoyed the clean aroma of a sanitary, safe, healthy, educational environment. Students and staff were sincerely focused on successful skill development in academic, art, music, and vocational education. The facility had an appropriate library, large auditorium with a projection booth, full sized gymnasium, music facilities on each floor; an oversized well supplied art center, a home economics room in which cooking and sewing were taught (girls made their own lovely graduation dresses), wood shop and printing press instructional areas. In addition, there was a nursing station and a complete administrative suite to accommodate a principal, vice- principal plus a secretarial staff.

Many parents supported private after-school training for youngsters interested in additional music or dance lessons. While the theater area was used for weekly assembly programs in which children learned to sing patriotic, religious and holiday selections, it also provided a platform for these talented performers to share their gifts with school mates. There was an assortment of pianists, accordionists, ballerina and tap dancers, guitarists, violinists and vocalists. In addition to after school motion picture activities, the playhouse was occasionally utilized for professional performers who made sporadic special appearances for the youngsters.

Periodically, a talent show was scheduled to allow the artistic, entertainment-oriented boys and girls a venue to demonstrate their musical or dancing abilities. Two very gifted stand-out sisters, who played guitar and sang country music, earned center spotlight each time they appeared in front of the dark wine-colored stage curtains. Their musical genius was dramatically enhanced by their spectacular western outfits. Their resume began in elementary school and they continued to make my toes wiggle until they graduated from Eastside High School.

To this date, I vividly remember their white ten-gallon hats centered on the backs of white vests which were trimmed with long fringe that covered light blue silk shirts. Their shimmering blouses were tucked neatly over cowgirl boot length white skirts. Fancy white western shoes finished the picture. Their selections included: *"Cool, Cool, Water", "See Them Tumbling Down", "Your Cheatin Heart", "I Wish I Had Wings of an Angel", "Lady of Spain" and "Bye, Bye Love"*. Recently, it was learned that their dad was the teacher, electrified their instruments and excused the young ladies from after dinner chores to practice daily. He also recorded some of their selections as part of his instructional method.

During the early years of settling into Four Seasons, residents were eager to greet new neighbors. A shared community goal was to make acquaintances and establish future social fellowships. Clubhouse activities were numerous and well attended. At one party, my path crossed with this former friend. I experienced an immediate and exciting flash-back as a rush of warm sensations surged through my soul.

This is the glamorous multi-talented youthful starlet who wore stunning western outfits and made my young toes tingle as she and her sister sang cowboy tunes. We chatted about mutual historical connections to our hometown and I was thrilled to revive a sequence of previous, precious, magnificent, memories.

Once again, she knocked my socks off as it was confidently stated, "I don't remember you". What a shocking revelation for I was well known and the tallest thirteen-year-old boy in the entire building. Fortunately, we have revived this kinship and Gloria Gervasio can still make my feet flicker.

BICYCLE BUSINESS BOY

While progressing from a tricycle, I was taught that two wheeled bicycle riding was potentially dangerous and required advanced abilities. Safety conversations occurred frequently. Under the able direction of Dad, performance and proficiency in essential skills were eventually mastered. Once accomplished, the bicycle was accessorized to include a battery-operated front light, a rear fender reflector and a large handlebar basket. Unknown to me, I was being groomed to enter the business world as a young entrepreneur.

There was a neighbor who worked in a large supermarket, food warehouse and was responsible for processing fresh eggs. She found a way to liberate these valued tiny treasures from her place of employment. Pieces of the puzzle now fit as the new customized bike was ready and put into action as a working vehicle.

Wow! I quickly learned the importance of the special equipment. As evening arrived and cover of darkness set in; my skills were engaged to ride to the supplier who lived a distance of several blocks, fill the carrier with the frail product, return without cracking a shell and depositing them to the home distribution center in grade AA condition.

The next day, on the walk back to school after lunch, I was provided the addresses of people who were scheduled to receive the delicate merchandise. The return to studies in the afternoon was selected because my arms were free from carrying books and available to transport fragile bagged eggs.

At about the same time, my dear aunt went into the holiday, cookie, baking business. Mom and Dad volunteered to help support this hottest venture and they worked "gratis" several evenings per week. I fell asleep most times on her living room floor to eventually be aroused for the drive home in an unheated car on the coldest winter nights.

Ultimately, job responsibilities expanded and I was charged with the tasks of transporting both delicate commodities and collecting money. The very real challenge, however, was to avoid hitting pot holes or falling and placing the frail precious cargo in jeopardy. While the ramifications of damaged commodities were profound. I was soon labeled the egg/cookie boy.

Inevitably, that fatal day arrived during a lunch recess transfer. The delicate parcels were placed in a well-traveled grocery bag that should have been retired several trips ago. Ultimately, the bottom ripped and some eggs escaped through the torn opening. Upon striking my ugly hand- me down corduroy trousers, they cracked to spew several yokes and much clear yellow liquid.

I entered the customer's kitchen very upset and she quickly attempted to clean me up before being ridiculed upon returning to the classroom. A failure! While the garb spent much time in the washing machine, I stunk that day and every time I wore that memorable article of clothing

Fortunately, I was in one of my growth spurts and the hated egg delivery uniform was passed on to some poor, unknown, innocent victim. While there was a new memory owner for the well-worn garment, the episode remains a stinker.

BULLY BEATEN BADLY BY BALLERINA BOY

Featured players in this saga were two eighth grade children who represented very opposite sides of the social spectrum. The first youngster grew up as a member of an intact family who owned and operated a successful neighborhood grocery store. His parents were supportive of all academic and cultural activities. Their boy participated in private piano, dance and vocal lessons. The young man was an honor roll pupil who skipped a grade at the elementary level.

His counterpart lived directly across from the school and was associated or influenced by the fringe of local, small, gang groups. Unfortunately, his parents were strangers to the educational process. Once identified as a troubled child, he was retained in the primary program Talents seemed to be in the areas of streetwise events which enabled him an opportunity to provided tutorial information to peers on romantic procedures with a different sex. His reputation elevated him to the boss of our steel, picketed, fenced and concrete paved playground. He was captain of most recess teams.

The pecking order of pupil power was well established, and the young students seemed content and able to function comfortably within the parameters of this accepted structure. However, one spring day, bully boy pushed the unwritten rules and taunted the placid accomplished, docile dancer. Teasing escalated beyond words and a first punch was launched.

A growing circle gathered around the opponents and excitement elevated to a loud cheering level. Ballerina boy immediately took command of the conflict and disco danced all over his fallen foe. Within a few seconds and a tick of the clock, the entire student population knew the former king of the old tranquil schoolyard had been disgraced, dishonored and dethroned.

This pupil audience yelled and applauded their newly appointed hero. The tall toe tapper retired to his conservative posture of refined intellectual and artistic searches. Our tough thug, however, sauntered to a skeleton of silent solitude.

Predicatively, our new champion's future moved to bigger and better spotlights. To the contrary and within a few years, the town newspaper's headline reported that the juvenile ruffian had been killed in a failed, attempted, armed, robbery of a local liquor store.

DAD HAS A BOY AND BUILDS A MAN

While visiting a close family friend, my parents were introduced to a couple who were interested in selling building lots in a lovely area in Paterson, New Jersey. The property was on a piece of land that contained a demolished factory. Because the old walls were partially exposed, the purchase price was affordable and within a few months, the land changed ownership.

The project began in the Spring of 1952 and I was twelve years of age. Task one was to outline the building dimensions by marking the parameter with string and wooden stakes. Portions of the former factory sides presented a barrier in the initial measurement phase. The solution was for me to firmly hold a ½" x 18" inch steel, star, chisel with a thick leather protective glove while Dad pounded the drill with a mighty sledge hammer. After several hours of massive walloping and no mishaps at the concrete wall, sufficient space was cleared to position the cord outlining our building footprint. As a result of this accurate preparation, a remaining portion of the old structure could be covered by a lawn when the new home was completed.

An excavator was hired to hollow out and prepare the cellar hole. Used 2"x 6" boards were purchased to build forms for the footings. My task was to bicycle to the new address after school and remove bent, rusted nails to create smooth surfaces. Once completed, these planks were put in place to build the footing frames. Hand digging with a pick and shovel was used to establish precise levels and proper depths.

Once completed, a cement truck arrived to pour the new footings. After hand troweling and curing, the planks were removed and stored for future use as scaffolding to provide a secure, working surface as the walls increased in height. At lunch time, Mom drove to the new site with hardy gourmet sandwiches and beverages.

Shortly after the first cinder block was set, it began to rain, Dad pumped water daily from the hole and we worked several consecutive week-ends in heavy thick, soil slop. I transported all 840, 12"x18" cinder blocks from the curb, delivery spot to the basement hole. While the individual blocks were heavy, I learned to carry them, two at a time wearing thick protective safety gloves.

I worked as the chief laborer: moved blocks to the amateur masons, hand mixed mortar, carried filled buckets to the bricklayers who were building the eight-foot walls. In my spare time, my additional responsibility was to keep the area clear of construction debris. At the top of the walls, cap blocks were set and sill bolts were installed to anchor the upper structures. The chimney and basement steps completed the block work. A final test was passed when a variety of string leveling lines were set to determine plumb and square measurements. Amazingly, the project dimensions were within ½" margins.

The completed outer foundation structures now required plastering and an application of two tar coats of waterproofing. A next step was to have the plumber install the sewer pipe and make the connection to the city system. Upon completion, we covered and tamped the shallow ditches that contained the pipe.

Shortly, heavy rain fell to further compact the disturbed floor surface. The carefully removed old footing boards were again recycled to create braces to support the four new basement walls during the backfilling process. As a safety precaution, loose soil was hand shoveled around the outer border of the foundation to establish a soft earthen layer of protection.

A first delivery of building materials arrived and included all the windows and lumber supplies. In addition to keeping a safe area and maintaining a level working surface plus removing construction debris; my after-school job expanded to paint all new windows plus sashes, inside and out, before installation. Once the wooden, first, floor deck was completed. our attention returned to the foundation. A truck appeared and dumped several tons of coal ash. This had to be wheeled into the basement to cover the earthen raw surface to establish an even drainage depth of four inches.

After this task was completed, we were ready to attack the next phase of the floor project. A ready-mix cement truck arrived and we prepared to pour several cubic yards of very heavy, wet concrete through the raw open cellar windows and on top of the smooth ash sub surface. Large stainless-steel coal shoots were used to direct and disperse this very dense cream. substance.

Eventually, my young muscles became fatigued and the fast-moving, dense, soupy material accidentally dropped to cover my feet. Fortunately, tall safety protective boots were worn and a very serious accident was avoided. Dad immediately stopped dispersing the dense liquid substance and ran to my rescue.

After a short recovery period, the next procedure was implemented to evenly spread the thick, soupy, mass by using rakes and a long plank to level the dense, semi-solid stuff. Next, wooden hand trowels were engaged to even out this thick beige substance before it began to set, cure, harden and dry. The ultimate goal was to create a solid, smooth impenetrable surface.

While framing and roofing were being finished, Dad and I worked on the rough grading. This task involved pick, shovel and wheelbarrow skills. These basic tools were used to move many tons of dirt from the backyard to the front of the emerging dwelling. The land was sloped from the back of the property to the street for drainage purposes. In addition to land contour concerns, a five-foot terrace was established to finish the sloping towards the road.

The project was progressing nicely once the cedar siding was installed. Now all the nails had to be countersunk, covered with putty and painted. The 25-foot dormer was too high to reach and I was elected to stand on top of a 55-gallon steel drum. A plank was positioned on top of the barrel and Uncle Phil placed and held the extension ladder while this twelve-year-old Picasso spent the day beautifying the tall addition with two coats of white color.

The dwelling was now enclosed and Uncle Louie and I completed the electrical wiring. He gave me the job of using young muscles and pull the cable through the walls. Later, and once we moved into our home, he presented my parents with a gift of a payment in full. At the same time, the plumber completed the rough piping. Simultaneously, Dad and his eighth-grade son made hand mixed cement to float and finish the rear yard sidewalks.

After the sheetrock was installed, we prepared the walls and ceilings for painting. This involved: sinking all nails below the paper surface, taping the seams and applying spackle. The messy job of sand papering to produce a smooth surface followed. Our lungs were saturated with fine dust for several days. Once this messy process was completed, all interior surfaces had to be dusted and vacuumed. Finally, two coats of paint were applied to the walls and ceilings followed by two coats of varnish applied to doors and wood moldings.

A professional landscaper was hired to finish the final grading and prepare the site for lawn seeding. He also planted foundation shrubs at the front porch. A new after-school responsibility of daily watering was added to my list of responsibilities. I rode the bicycle to the house at 322 East 26th Street. Fortunately, all the new plantings and grass seed successfully grew.

Finally, we moved into our brand-new home in the Fall of 1953. During the holiday season, I won the contract to install all the attic insulation. Using the hedge clippers to cut the long fiberglass battens to size, a hand stapler was manipulated to fasten the material to the roof rafters. Several decades later, all these items were added to my growing tool collection.

The Franchino & Sons Construction Company then began the project to finish the basement. The, now, thirteen-year-old partner earned the job to apply two layers of green water proof paint on the interior walls. Once completed, we finished sheet rocking and painting the ceiling. My old friend and "pseudo" grandfather, Uncle Sam, helped us install a downstairs bathroom, second kitchen and a laundry area. The next step was to frame, spackle and paint the bathroom and large storage area. A pantry closet was created under the staircase.

My last construction job on the house cellar project was to sandpaper, polish and shellac all the exposed copper plumbing. Dad finished his project by constructing a large work bench with a vise and several shelves. It was painted dark green and used to store hand tools. Many of these implements have remained in my collection and are in the process of being passed to the next generation. While I lived in this home for ten years, my parents remained at that address for another fifteen years.

There is a strong parallel between the construction of a house and the building of a young son into a man. The home and little lad began with creating a deep perfect foundation. Upon this base, a long and enduring structure was assembled with much care, patience, guidance, love, admiration and luck. While Mom and Dad have passed, the impressions imprinted on their first child have endured and guided me throughout my lifetime.

Several years ago, I parked in front of this old castle and shed a handkerchief full of happy, sad and very emotional TEARS!!!

HOLE GANG

The scheduled, winter, children's, religious activity was finished; lingering good night conversations were cordially completed and most pupils left for their warm bedrooms. The neighborhood church was in the process of erecting an elementary school and the excavation for a basement had just been completed. Surrounding the endless cavity were massive very high piles of soil that had been freshly removed from the cavernous chasm.

It was early evening on a freezing, February, Friday night and the frost was glistening on the glacial, looking ground as a full moon shed shimmering light and sinister shadows on the scared, scary site. As my childish, crusty steps approached the construction zone, a group of local boys moved off the towering mounds and towards their potential evening's entertainment and the next victim.

Voices, volume and body language sent an undeniable message of immediate danger, difficulty and confrontation. The forming of a contentious circle converged as a tightened tension intensified around this target! Their objective was to pull this preteen prey up the pile of dirt and push me over the high perimeter and into the deep, dark, bottomless abyss. Instantly, a stream of adrenaline surged through my threatened body as a ring tightened. The combinations of energy and strength resulted in a swift, slippery, skillful and harmless breakaway. This conflict was not over!

While pondering a plan for payback, this incited, angry butt of battle sprinted to the security of home. Darting through the house and down into the cellar, a three-foot piece of hardened rebar was removed from the locked door. A jog up the stairs and through the living room began the retaliation, returning to the combat spot. Dad followed me onto the porch and then towards the place of worship. Realizing difficulty was in the air, Father asked for and received an explanation while accompanying this warrior back to the battle zone.

Bad, boasting, boys were still there wallowing in a celebration of their victorious humorous escapade and bizarre intimidation. The bragging adversaries now saw the pair of approaching, foe and awesome ally. Their tone immediately changed as they observed fuming, flaming, fiery eyes on the face of their recently terrorized target who was armed with his two devastating weapons of choice. As we moved forward, the gang drew back. Once within striking range, Dad removed the lethal rod from this angry fighter's firm fist and the forward movement accelerated.

At that moment, their tune changed, as the rivals rapidly retreated. They swiftly retired to the top of the earthen ridge and ultimately realized they had run out of room with no reasonable pathway of escape! I was excused from participation in the potential conflict. Father asked me to back off. Next, there was a short conversation between Dad and the junior henchmen. They were instructed to be grateful, told to disperse and go home. They never again confronted me!

The few words exchanged at the hilltop summit were stronger than the steel stick of substantial, and sustained devastation. Thanks for this very timely intervention; for the consequences of this event would have been permanent and severe!

MY FIRST BAND JOB

My musical experience began with taking private accordion lessons at the age of seven. Each week, Dad would drive me to the studio for a scheduled appointment. This was followed with a daily minimum practice session of thirty minutes and this routine continued for more than a decade. As skills developed and matured, I began to perform in school and at church talent shows. Frequently, family and friends asked me to entertain them at their social functions.

One day, a neighbor appeared at my home with the newspaper classified section which advertised an immediate opening for Saturday night entertainment at a local tavern. A telephone call was made and an interview was scheduled. At the tender age of fifteen, I got the weekend job to provide music for five hours. The club date occurred during the winter months at a period in which outdoor temperatures were well below freezing.

The squeeze box is essentially operated by forcing air through a series of complicated Swiss, stainless steel, slim reeds that are secured on several carefully shaped, wooden, tone chamber blocks. This air travel action provides the energy to make marvelous, mellow music.

Prior to being driven to the establishment, the family attended a February high school graduation party for a cousin. The precious, precision implement was placed in the car trunk which was parked outdoors. After being stored for several hours in this hostile environment, the subzero temperature had an impact on the internal mechanism of the instrument. Collections of condensed moisture formed thin ice particles which accumulated and adhered to the delicate inner structures.

Unknown to the teenage, inexperienced artist who was about to make his first professional presentation, the combination of adverse weather elements trapped inside the instrument created scores of considerable complications. The first set began with the production of strange sounds as the cold and frozen air circulated through the magnificent hand-crafted machine. Once warmed up, however, things settled down, and the evening became a total hit, earned generous tips and launched a successful and profitable career that endured well over thirty-five years.

HITCHHIKER

By the time I was permitted to walk to a local barber shop as an independent child, neighbors paid me small coins to pick up and deliver to them minor grocery orders. Their parcels were small and easy for me to manage. Items purchased were recorded on a tab and settled at the week's end.

As my height, weight and strength matured with time, the income producing efforts expanded into winter snow removal and summer grass cutting. Revenue increased from coins to paper money. As an early teenager, my backyard neighbor hired me to be a gas station attendant at $50.00 per week.

At the age of fourteen, I went to city hall for working papers. These documents enabled me to work as a caddy for Orchard Hills Golf and Country Club in Paramus, New Jersey. On the first Saturday morning, I was employed by a very patient golfer who taught me the essential skills of the job. I carried his full set of clubs and located his treasured ball after each shot at the green. He was pleased with my performance and paid me the basic fee of $3.00 plus a $0.50 tip for the standard 18 holes.

Within a few outings, I graduated to carrying a double set of clubs and earned $6.00 a round and a $1.00 tip. On some days, I did two rounds at double the rate. Because of my physical structure, I was, at times, hired to tote three bags at $21.00.

Transportation was an issue and Dad volunteered to drive me to and from the course. Within a short time, I connected with an older adult who also caddied at the club. Morning rides were resolved while the homebound journey remained Dad's job,

As a backup when my pop was unavailable, a bus ride was accessible. After a long day's work in the hot sun, this mode entailed a mile-long walk along a high traffic, rural road. Reaching the end of this journey was a potential hour wait at the transit stop. In the meantime, this was an ideal location to hitchhike an auto ride to my home destination.

On several occasions the hitched ride opportunity occurred long before the public transportation arrived. The combination of commuting arrangements was successfully implemented through the three- year employment period. My caddying career ended with my last ride from a stranger! A young man driving a current model automobile, picked me up at the standard stop.

The route home was a straight drive along Fairlawn Ave. As we approached the destination at the red traffic light on the Fifth Ave. Bridge, he inappropriately placed his hand across my lap and uttered a distinct suggestive statement. This bold combination of jesters quickly activated my limited previous training in judo. Instinctively, both my hands were wrapped around his neck in an inescapable choke hold. As he gasped. I firmly explained that this was his last lungful unless he let me out of the car. Without expressing another sound, the potential dead man stopped the vehicle and I quickly opened the passenger door to escape while he was gasping, desperately for air.

Interestingly, that was not my last hitchhiking adventure. Several years later and while on a trip to Hawaii with my wife of fifteen years, we were successful in hooking a ride up the side of a famous volcano to the Punch Bowl Crater Military Cemetery. We were with a retired, overweight couple who could not complete the trip to the top. As a joke, I resurrected latent skills and put out a talented thumb.

A young widow on the way to her veteran husband's grave site stopped the car to give us a ride. Before exiting the auto, she insisted that we coordinate our time schedules so that we could be driven down the hill. This tale certainly illustrates that normal people around the globe are thoughtful, considerate and compassionate.

ADVICE AT A PRICE

While a high school sophomore, I had the opportunity to work for a neighbor who was the proprietor of a gasoline station. Before starting the job, Dad instilled in me a very important work ethic. It was, ``never stand idle". This wise guideline provided excellent motivation throughout my employment career. It was easy to keep active through the day. Duties included: pumping fuel, checking fluid levels, washing windshields, checking tire pressure and general housekeeping chores.

Responsibilities soon expanded to encompass: detailing used cars which were being prepared to be sold, changing or mounting tires and taking cash receipts for daily deposit. The employer presented a second important principle that provided an honesty standard which was incorporated throughout my lifetime. It stated that everyone could be bought and sold at a price and be sure to establish a value that is beyond approach. These policies have always been at the top of the priority list.

ON THE WRONG SIDE OF A GUN

The high school schedule was designed to permit students appropriate time to visit their lockers for the purpose of exchanging instructional materials for later classes. As long as assigned rooms and storage cabinets were in the same shared corridor area, this opportunity was available several times during the day. During a travel period, I stopped, applied the combination, opened my long, narrow metal door and prepared to switch books.

A fellow student approached me, placed a small revolver in my abdomen and pulled the trigger twice. Fortunately, the silver-colored weapon misfired at the same instant a warning late bell sounded. This distinctive gonging alarm encouraged all to scatter before the late bell resonated.

A few weeks later, the potential gangster repeated the routine! This time the targeted victim was prepared to deal with the matter. Within moments, his gun game was over, the teenage hoodlum was neutralized and future firearm conflicts were never duplicated. This case was permanently sealed and closed.

JELL-O JOKE

Dessert was a standard component in our daily dinner menu. While we enjoyed ice cream, most treats were homemade and included an excellent variety of pies and cakes. Jell-O frequently augmented the meal with creative additions of assorted fruits and heavy cream which was collected from the tops of pasteurized, refrigerated, milk, contained in glass quarts.

In the early days of Redi-Whip products, Mom purchased the new item to decorate the Jell-O serving. The chilled container was brought near the table and the lady of the house was rather timid as the first depression of the nozzle portion of the aerosol can was applied. The result of this conservative pressure caused a highly liquefied, ashen, dairy product to slowly ooze a trickle from the tin spray potential weapon.

My brother swiped the receptacle from her hand, vigorously shook the can and aggressively pressed the tiny, red, release button. A lathery jet stream of delicious, white, whipped cream was liberated. Since this was a trial run, an oversized bowl was used to demonstrate the technique.

The rapidly moving torrent hit the front portion of the dish and sped across the bottom of the plate as it changed angle to gush up the opposite side of the bowl. The tasty projectile cascaded to crash into my mother's now masked, surprised, concealed face! As the three male members of the family laughed hysterically, the female target and victim of the mishap foamed with anger.

Dad immediately escaped to the bathroom to hide and conceal his hardy, uproarious, hilarious laughter. He took cover from the angry verbal barrage. Eventually, the funny mess was cleaned up, the atmosphere cooled down and the magic, delightful, yummy Redi-Whip was retired as a one-shot deal.

TRAGEDY ON TRACKS AVOIDED

One day, as a new licensed driver who mastered the techniques of managing a standard shift, I was given the car to drive to high school. After dismissal, I offered a young lady classmate a ride home. As we drove over a multi-track railroad crossing, the car stalled as an oncoming train appeared in the distance.

Sizing up the potentially very dangerous situation the female passenger panicked. Skillfully, the car was restarted and slipped into first gear. We made it safely to the other side with much time to spare. She never drove with me again.

WISE GUY

While in high school and during an evening snow storm, my brother and I returned home from our part time shoe store job. Entering the neighborhood after dark, we heard the impact of an ice ball hitting the side window of the car. A young boy scampered between two apartment buildings as our automobile came to a safe stop.

There was a toy pistol in the glove compartment that was pulled out as the chase to find the juvenile "criminal" began. We ran in opposite directions around the building and quickly converged on the delinquent who was hiding in a doorway. Instinctively, the toy cap gun was put to his head and a strong verbal warning was given.

As the years have passed, I wonder how this snowball throwing imp has remembered this incident.

PARKING PRANKSTER

My home, while I was a college student, was located on a quiet street in Paterson, New Jersey. In addition, it served as the headquarters for weekly jam sessions. Young musicians that were within driving distance from my finished basement would collect their various instruments and assemble to produce an assortment of interesting, innovative and original melodies.

The range of proficiency extended from local aspiring stars to students attending Manhattan and Julliard Schools of Music. All were at the beginning points of their professional careers and earning income from area establishments. My parents supported this productive weekly activity that helped many talented people connect and eventually advance to perform on several prominent world-renowned stages.

Since Wednesday nights were reserved for informal rehearsals, the other evenings were available for grown-up family, friends and card playing activities. The home was situated on an attractive, tree lined, residential street with an abundance of private driveways. Therefore, parking spaces were never a problem!

However, a prankster moved into the neighborhood who worked evenings. He took delight in pinning cars by placing his automobile against the rear bumper of the vehicle positioned in the front of his. While my folks communicated the difficult problem with him on several occasions, he would look at them, display a slick smile and shrug his slumping middle-aged shoulders. His tune did not change!

Emerging musicians have evolved from a long history of taking lessons, studying, following rules and practicing for several hours per day. Finally, the time had come to broadcast an important commercial jingle to the car clown. After an evening session, a young colleague approached his auto to observe that it was trapped in a very tight, demanding parking place.

Much time and effort were expended as he severely struggled to liberate the trapped vehicle. Once free, a mischievous, devilish twinkle sparkled and appeared in his creative eyes. The musician's artistic, magical, fancy fingers masterfully and tenderly removed the valve stems and allowed the air to escape from two tires. Within a few silent seconds of soft hissing sounds, two flat tires occurred as rubber caressed the pavement.

Our next-door comedian worked a second shift. Therefore, his day began at mid-morning. At that hour, my innocent Mother backed out of her driveway to observe the jokester rolling a pair of deflated wheels down the avenue. In an innocent, friendly manner and speaking in a helpful melodious voice, she asked if assistance was needed.

While his refusal was staccato, curt, clipped and less than kind, he continued the task of walking to the gas station. Obviously, the trickster was a good student and a quick learner. For, overnight, the complicated parking problem he orchestrated was satisfactorily transposed and permanently resolved.

KIT KAT CLUB CATASTROPHE

As a nineteen-year-old and member of the American Federation of Musicians; my name, address, telephone number and instrument specialty was listed in the union directory. This information appeared along with hundreds of other entertainers. One evening, I answered the phone and was offered a three-night, weekend band job at a local nightclub. The voice at the other end of the conversation asked if I could recommend a saxophone player to complete a pick-up quartet. Since my home was the center for weekly Wednesday evening jam sessions with the finest young performers in the area, this was an easy request to fill.

I was instructed to wear the standard uniform, tuxedo, and meet at the front gates of a Paterson hospital with the reed player. At the prearranged time and location, two very old men appeared in a beat-up car, waved and instructed us to follow them to the job. After twenty minutes, we arrived at the night spot and began unpacking the equipment.

Their gear was the same vintage and condition as the dated automobile. As a youthful professional, I learned that there was a correlation between the condition of the cases, instruments and the quality of the entertainer. The set of traps included the biggest bass drum I had ever seen and it appeared to be the newest addition to his ancient apparatus. The trombonist opened a very tired and torn container to expose a dull, dated and dented horn.

Before they assembled their tattered tools of the trade, I formulated a fairly accurate theory about the music this "original" band would produce. Sure enough! The first tune we performed fulfilled my expectations. While the young players made mellow, modern music that was suitable for the night club stage, the senior ensemble struggled! At an intermission, my partner and I slithered off the stage and slipped out doors to share hilarious, hysterical laughter. We knew this group should be "fired" on the spot.

Collectively, we somehow managed to put our talents together to survive this sad situation. After three evenings of acoustical agony, the club owner paid my partner and me and expressed his appreciation for managing this difficult situation. After providing an appropriate explanation to the other characters, he refused to compensate them and our paths, fortunately, never crossed again.

BAND JOB OFFER FOR MY COLLEGE MUSIC PROFESSOR

A number of music courses were required to graduate and obtain a teaching certificate. Because of my background as a professional musician, I volunteered to help classmates learn how to read music, play the piano, master the flutophone and conduct a chorus.

One of the college music professors was enamored with his academic training, knowledge, and aptitude. He took pride in using the lecture hall and podium to satisfy his ego. As a current active performing member of the international musicians' union, I would arrive to class on a few late afternoons dressed in a tuxedo. Wearing this standard formal outfit or uniform allowed me to immediately leave school and drive to a local band job.

In an attempt to take the air from his inflated self-image, I occasionally offered him a Local 248 club date opportunity to supplement his teaching salary and a chance to play in the real world before a live audience. Needless to say, he always found a variety of excuses to avoid the actual stage. Ultimately, he considered these propositions a challenge and a serious declaration of conflict. Each class session provided a forum to place me in the spotlight and allow him the opening to potentially give me the theatrical hook.

In essence, the college instructor mastered the book skills, had the training and knowledge to successfully offer and provide excellent textbook and intellectual information. But as an eighteen-year-old, my forte was performance and entertainment. Both of us realized we were in totally different venues and there was no match or need for competition. We eventually found peace, developed a mutual respect for each other's skills and talents.

As a result of many instructors' orchestrated efforts, I do appreciate that my abilities were recognized, developed and honed through the combined efforts of more than my fair share of outstanding professors and teachers. I am totally grateful for all the wonderful opportunities that have been presented, experienced, enjoyed and internalized by me.

CLASSIC DATE
The First Girl I Dated; I Married

In addition to being a full-time college student, I was connected in a variety of rather lucrative business ventures which demanded a complex schedule. Therefore, breaks between classes were committed to serious study sessions. Minutes were too precious to waste on social speculations.

On one wintery, windy March Day, a research block of time was free and available to complete several academic assignments. There was only one pair of unoccupied chairs at the rear of the crowded media center and the table was occupied by two girls who seemed consumed with talk rather than task.

My classmate and I asked permission to join them and they extended an invitation. Books and study materials were spread out in preparation for a few hours of concentrated work. The youthful ladies were noticeably attractive and seemed to be intent on shared conversation. Within a few moments, the boys became fascinated by their flirtatious and engaging chit-chat.

During the repartee, a textbook belonging to the better looking of the duo was opened and her telephone number, which was written on the back cover, was examined. This was quickly memorized for future reference. That evening, a phone call was made and a Friday night date was planned.

During the wee hours of the next morning, snow began to fall and it accumulated enough to close the school for the remaining week. Plows ran continuously around the clock and, eventually, the roads became passable for the weekend. As a consequence, snow, several inches in depth, was piled next to the curbs. While driving was difficult, walking was nearly impossible!

Because most main streets were safely cleared, the rendezvous could take place as arranged. Upon my arrival to her address, the bell rang and an eager younger sister opened the hefty front door. Instant havoc was sensed! Obviously, a communication misunderstanding had occurred and my appearance at her home was an hour too early.

My date ultimately emerged from the dining room clad in a bathrobe with a head loaded in bobby pins and tight curlers. Her complexion, although minus make-up, was an interesting shade of crimson. Instantly I thought, "Was this the pretty girl who was in the library?"

After a quick greeting, she introduced her parents. As the father welcomed me, I said, "The chauffeur is in the automobile, and I hate waiting for a woman". In the meantime, I suggested they finish their interrupted dinner while I wait in the living room. They excused themselves and returned to complete their disrupted meal. There was an indistinguishable undercurrent of low whispers, however, and the sister excitedly exclaimed as she looked out of the window, "It's a big black Cadillac!"

Shortly after, I eased into a comfortable sofa, a quick scamper up the stairs occurred with the leading lady at the front of a home, beauty parlor posse. Later, I learned that daddy was accustomed to his little girl bringing home youthful looking, fair haired, unshaven, boys, who were from either church or college.

His assessment of this mature, over six-foot person was that he was well groomed, appropriately dressed in a suit, tie, and wearing a full-length black top-coat. This is a man! In what seemed like a flash, a magnificent transformation occurred and a stunning, beautiful, woman graciously sauntered down the staircase to make a stylish, sophisticated entrance. Her fashionable, cosmopolitan attire included: a gorgeous gray cashmere sweater, black skirt and a pair of borrowed, dark leather, spiked, high heeled shoes.

A silent, inconspicuous, but noticeable, glance was exchanged between mother and daughter as they both went into the kitchen for what appeared to be a last-minute adjustment. The pair, however, left to discuss the possibility of suspending the dating rules for this occasion. Upon their return, it was carefully explained that my name, telephone number and address must be written on the family blackboard. Compliance was easily attained and a business card was confidently presented. As it was exchanged, I asked, "Will this do?"

As we departed from the front porch, the driver opened the car door to liberate a blue glow which originated from under the seats to sensuously illuminate the passenger area as the azure radiance elegantly ventured into the cold, crisp evening. Once settled into the vehicle, he asked if the temperature was cozy and if the heavy classical music was to her liking. While both questions received a quiet "Yes" response, the puzzled lady was deep in thought trying to mentally catch up on current sophisticated scientific space search conversation. Dialogue appeared to be over her head. By this time, her mind was spinning at the speed of light as thoughts soared among other solar systems in the Milky Way. *Interesting*?

The movie, *Yellow Submarine,* which she saw three times and knew the appropriate scenes in which to laugh, was chosen for the evening's entertainment. Because the parking lot was full upon arrival, another theater was selected. As the car headed in a new direction, the young woman was asked if she would mind giving the chauffeur the evening off and driving him home.

Automatically, the answer was a resounding "Yes", and she felt this strange situation would now become a normal typical "one on one" experience. The shiny but soiled sedan approached his home, and before exiting, the employee was requested to clean outdoor windows, headlights and make an appointment to have new side view mirrors installed. The directives were efficiently executed; he assisted the couple into the front seat and then was dismissed for the night. "*Phew!*"

Road conditions made finding a parking place rather difficult. However, one was located a distance from the cinema. During the careful walk towards the box office, the gentleman assisted his frustrated companion cautiously over each snow bank. There was a correlation between his giant size and muscular strength.

A firm grip placed securely under her arm easily enabled him to launch her over the high, white, frozen, mounds which were piled along the sidewalk. Each lift painfully propelled her skyward as her special, "on lend", shoes left the ground to enable her delicate, streamlined, body to take off and become airborne.

His long legs required an end chair in the theater and this presented some difficulty when considering this particular show was very full. He took her hesitant hand to begin the seat search, and they patiently pranced up and down aisles and across the front of the stage. He was tall enough to have his silhouette project on the silver screen as they sauntered past the first row.

Finally, the end places were located and they settled in to view the picture. During the movie, the couple seemed isolated and very little physical contact was established between them. At long last, credits appeared, lights came on and they followed the same rigorous strolling pattern back to the "limousine".

Without discussing the next adventure, they motored to a local diner. While she excused herself to visit the restroom, he ordered, without consultation; spaghetti, meatballs and cold milk. "*Revolting!*" When the meal was finished, he helped her put on a black dress coat and prepared for the trip to her home.

At the entrance door, his arm was extended and they shook hands as she was thanked for a lovely evening. Beyond the closed door, the family immediately appeared to begin their interrogation process. In depth details were disclosed while she removed the sweater to display the yellow, black and blue bruises which were forming on and under her upper arm. "There were no romantic maneuvers, boring scientific conversation, music appreciation compositions playing on the radio, no attempt at a good night kiss and we even shook hands to end the evening". She stated, with a firm conviction, "You will NEVER, NEVER, NEVER see him again!"

(To be continued)

SECOND ENCOUNTER
The First Girl I Dated; I Married

Although the last weekend experience was generally negative, curiosity provided motivation for the next episode. On Monday of the following week, the library ladies cut classes and posted themselves at each of the two college parking lot entrances. They then waited for the arrival of the black car. The all-day, secret, surveillance was unproductive for the special sleek sedan never appeared on the scene.

While at the school snack bar having lunch on the next day, destiny brought the hand shaking couple together for a second encounter. This time the pretty girl with the under arm of fading bruises was asked if she would like to join him for a cup of coffee. This opened a more comfortable entry for continued, casual conversation. Eventually, they discussed plans for the next Friday evening and an invitation was extended to a double date with his brother and girlfriend. To ensure that the getting ready phase could be leisurely implemented without engaging the emergency services of an onsite beauty boutique, times were carefully established and cautiously confirmed. Dinner reservations for four were made at an area up-scale supper club. As scheduled, three folks drove to her home for the final portion of the pickup. This time, all went well and the group proceeded to the restaurant in expectation of an enjoyable evening. As they entered the bistro, a warm personal welcome was extended to the two young men.

The dinner party was escorted to a choice table and it seemed that everyone in the place knew these two celebrities. Mid-way through cocktails, the girls left to use the powder room. While there, the brother's girlfriend chuckled, then said, "The boys pulled a snow job last week and explained that the limo incident was a farce". Suddenly, the perplexing, puzzling pieces came quickly into perspective, as; common family facial characteristics shared by the two pranksters were recognized as *brothers*! Now, her thought process was energized and a counter "get even mode" began to formulate.

The duped damsel acknowledged to the trio that she was a rather innocent victim of a practical joke and then meticulously proceeded to select the most expensive menu items for her meal. In spite of the previous sequence of capers, a good time was experienced by all four as they danced until the closing hour. In time, the blasé friendship progressed to a steady Friday night date and a more romantic relationship.

A close cousin of the young lady, who observed this developing situation, stated that any boy who takes a girl out on Friday must save the best one for Saturday. The response was, "But that's OK… because I always have a date for Saturday night!"

P.S. We were married three years later on June 22, 1963 and lived happily ever after!

THREE ENGAGEMENT RINGS

After a chance meeting with Bob in the library at Paterson State Teachers College, our first date developed into many over the next two years. Of course, we talked about our future together and discussed many topics such as: do we want pets, how many children to have, type of home to purchase, could I be a "stay at home Mom", and countries to travel in addition to visiting all fifty states.

So naturally, my mind started thinking about an engagement ring. While seldom shopping together, we looked at some jewelry store windows. This wasn't very often. Bob is NOT a shopper, he is a "buyer".

So, one day my future sister-in-law told me that I'm going to get engaged this weekend. She found this information out from Bob's brother, Mike. Needless to say, I was ecstatic. In preparation, finger nails were painted and a dress was picked out in anticipation of the big event!

As the night wore on, there was no sign of a ring. Upon arriving at my driveway, he said he had something to give me……. Here IT comes. He gave me a small white box, my heart pounded, my hands were sweating, I was thrilled. I opened it up and there was what he considered a 3-carat ring. There were three orange carrots on a gold band.... I did not think it was amusing. But with a brave face I felt my heart was breaking. My parents certainly did not think it was "FUNNY"!

Now we come to another weekend and my sister-in-law (to be) again tells me the same scenario. So being a believer, I polish my nails, got an outfit ready for the exciting special date. This time I didn't tell anyone. We had another lovely evening but no box. Once in my driveway he reached into his pocket and gave me a black ring box. This time I was not really as excited as I was the first time. I opened the container and there was a matched wedding ring set with ADJUSTABLE bands. The kind you would buy in Kresge's or Woolworth's 5 & 10 cent store!!!!!! That was equivalent to today's Dollar Tree! This time I was not as disappointed as I knew I would eventually get a ring. But my heart really hurt.

Guess what news I received a few months later? Bob was finally going to ask me the question!!!! I was ready!!!! The evening progressed and he gave me a bag to open. In it was a huge diamond baby rattle. The only good thing about it was that the ring was filled with beautiful sparkles. This time I did not take it kindly and I was really angry and upset.

I, now, drew a line in the driveway or sand and told him whatever you give me the next time, and I don't care if it's a rock set on a band, my picture and your name is going into the newspapers. Because that's what was done in the 60's. You announced your engagement. I proceeded to tell him that I did not think this was funny anymore and please don't do it again!

Quite a few months went by and I was figuring the engagement ring was not going to appear. But then one Saturday morning my Mom said to me at breakfast, "guess what?" Bob asked daddy if he could marry you! I was so happy, now maybe it will finally happen. I would get engaged.

The next day was Sunday, May 27, 1962, and my mother's birthday. As usual we went to Blessed Sacrament Church for mass. While waiting, Bob asked me to look at the ring I wore on

THAT finger. I gave it to him. Then when he gave it back to me, it was this beautiful diamond platinum engagement ring.

Finally, he asked the QUESTION. Because we were in church. I could not even say anything or give him a hug and kiss. I had to remain very quietly staring at my sparkling finger halo, Sitting, squirming, beaming and holding his hand. I just felt so loved.

When we got to my home, my Mom and Dad were waiting to celebrate. Mom helped me wrap tape around the band so I could wear it. I didn't want to take it off; it was so beautiful. I am still wearing it. I guess my last conversation on rings scared him! It was worth waiting for and so was he. I am so glad he chose me to walk through life beside him. We will be married 60 years on June 22, 2023.

THE BIG ONE THAT SHOULD HAVE GOTTEN AWAY

As a young child and while spending a July vacation at the seashore, I expressed an interest in fishing. Shortly after arriving home, an old-fashioned hand-me-down, deep-sea pole appeared at the back door with a reel and a full spool of line thick enough to anchor a battleship. Several visits to local lakes were enjoyed as Dad and I participated in the new experience.

Essentially, Father dug the worms, drove to the watering hole and set the bait. Each outing brought hope to really catch a big one, as I repeatedly cast the line into the water. Before the summer ended, both of us became very skilled.

During the season's final days, we visited a favorite spot for the last adventure of the year. In time, there was a strong tug on the tackle as it hit the water! Viewers gathered and claimed the underwater treasure was a large rotting tire. Interestingly, the reel let out plenty of extra cord. An encounter began and it was eventually beyond the strength and capacity of the novice angler. Dad, who was the most powerful man in the world, took the pole and continued the fight. Electrifying excitement encircled the pond as the expenditure of energy hastened! Whatever was on the last part of the submerged string was no match for Pop, a telephone tower sized rod and a thick clothes rope fishing line.

Suddenly there was a stir in the struggle, followed by a gigantic splash of sparkling, soft, silver, spray. While the action mounted, an audience assembled. Swiftly, all eyes went airborne. To the observers' surprise, a spectacular, sleek, male Mallard Duck was at the end and quickly elevated into a commanding full flight pattern.

The sporting event finished with a victory for Dad! Our trophy catch was gently brought back to earth; the bird firmly placed under his forearm and a hook tenderly removed from the bill. Strong hands softly opened, and the liberated fowl's wings frantically flapped. This was followed by furious quacking and an escape route to freedom. The bird swiftly soared into a fiery orange, picturesque, fall sunset. The season ended, all signs of fishing equipment mysteriously disappeared and the career of the young fisherman came to a screeching halt

MUSIC ASPHYXIATION CLASS

It was a clear, cold, crisp, cloudless day and the bright, warm sun's rays glistened off the freshly fallen snow. These balmy waves were magnified as they reflected into the music appreciation center through a set of large prisms like windows. This created a positive relaxed atmosphere for listening to and enjoying fine classical compositions.

My seat was located at the rear of the classroom and near the last row of chairs which were used to store heavy winter coats. An ambitious, highly motivated, well prepared, young, female professor was animated as she presented the full background of information that was appropriate and pertinent to the selection being studied.

As she proceeded through the relevant, significant and interesting material, each musical movement was carefully explained in clear detail. Eventually, the most current stereophonic system was activated and the audio segment began. In this peaceful setting, my eyes shut to help filter out unrelated distractions. This, then enabled me to absorb and internalize the fine, beautiful sounds that were tantalizing the tympanic membranes of both cultured ears.

In time and as the recorded symphony orchestra continued to produce delightful melodies, my closed peepers flashed open to a very dark, serene, cozy space. It seemed that I was enveloped in a layer of comfortable blankets that created a comfy, sweltering, snug and serene feeling. Gradually, the covering peeled off- one jacket at a time. Once unwrapped, a fellow student whispered that the garments were placed to absorb the creative, harmonious, snoring that resulted from my very deep restful sleep.

This was certainly an interesting and extraordinary musical asphyxiation experience!

A SHOOTING MACHINE TEAM

Because of many business activities, my basketball career ended in the second year of college. Fortunately, I was picked up by the Paterson Recreational League which had few demands. The only requirement was to show up for the game and be ready to play. The tallest team members of the squad were two white athletes who could jump. The remaining members were black boys who could run, dribble and shoot with phenomenal accuracy.

My role was to control the defensive backboard, get the rebound, make the outlet pass and wait for teammates to come back across the half court line. Because of the limited gymnasiums in the city, games were limited to four, eight-minute running periods. At maximum, we had a little more than a half hour to win the game.

This combination of well-conditioned, skilled young men, put together a perfect season in which we were undefeated. Within this time frame, we scored in excess of a hundred points in several of the contests that we dominated.

ENTREPRENEUR EVOLVES TO EDUCATOR

Motivation to make money was a driving force in my early life. The sequence of jobs included: farm worker, delivery boy, grass cutter, caddy at a golf course, gas station attendant, teaching accordion, painting apartments, soap dispenser assembler, music studio operator, musician and Cancellation Shoe Store manager. As time passed and a progression through employment activities expanded; duties, functions, obligations, responsibilities and income improved accordingly. While in high school my career path seemed to be carved for my future.

Advancement accelerated as responsibilities changed from shoe sales to store manager. This business venture had a potential for providing a lucrative future.

Returning home after high school one afternoon, Mom said she had something to discuss that was very vital. Apparently, there were frequent conversations with the local insurance man who had visited our home monthly to collect life insurance premiums. He encouraged her about the importance of my attending college.

Her message to me was convincing and a search began. Paterson State College was the school of choice for many obvious reasons. The application process began and all the forms were carefully processed. The final requirement was to pass a lengthy entrance exam. The results were reviewed at an acceptance interview meeting and it was reported that a near perfect score was achieved.

When asked to choose the area of specialization and a major, the most challenging course of study was selected. Three years later and at the age of twenty, I was eligible for graduation and a New Jersey teaching certificate.

I GOT THE JOB

Quietly behind the scenes, a recruiting team from Upper Saddle River, New Jersey visited the college with the purpose of selecting candidates to fill new positions for the coming year. They circulated through the departments to question professors and ask them to recommend exceptional graduating seniors who could then be invited to participate in an on-campus search.

Several instructors identified me as a very serious, conscientious, mature person who was on the dean's list and realized the importance of a fine education. In addition, student teaching, with an excellent mentor, had been recently completed and the evaluations were superior. While in class, a well-defined knock on the door summoned the lecturer. Upon her return, I was invited into the corridor for a brief talk with the visitors.

This resulted in a request to attend a meeting for a potential teaching position. The information gathered at this session was interesting and developed into making arrangements to visit the northern Bergen County district. This excitement was shared with the girl who eventually became my wife. She was asked to accompany me for a ride through the countryside and bring along good luck on that day. Located on the same winding rural road were two neighboring communities that had very similar names. In addition, the two separate district superintendents had last names of like spelling. As a result of this confusion, I drove into the wrong parking lot and went to an incorrect business office. There, a competent secretary recognized the difficulty and directed me to the proper township.

As a continuation to the preliminary activities which took place at the college, Upper Saddle River implemented an interesting hiring practice that involved: a lengthy tour of the building, a detailed examination of the facilities, a wonderful chance to meet staff members and an inspection of the beautiful two-hundred-acre natural wooded site. The walk through the complex concluded in an administrative office with an intense conversation that focused on the requirements of their learning process as it related to seventh and eighth grade children whose families were employed in government, international business or finance. It was obvious. These people insisted on excellence for their youngsters.

As the discussion completed, I was informed that the next step in the comprehensive procedure involved teaching a demonstration lesson. This experience would provide me an opportunity to directly interact with their pupils and gather a sense of my comfort level for the learning population in this community. At the same time, officials would be able to observe me actively teaching. The conversation concluded as the pupils' lunchtime began, and the instructional leader was requested to go to another part of the building. Before excusing himself, he encouraged me to complete the application, then wander through the school and become more aware of the offerings provided in this fine scholastic setting.

During the recess period a few eighth graders were deeply engrossed in establishing a band to entertain at their commencement ceremony. Realizing the difficulties, they were experiencing, I casually entered their classroom, gradually became involved and assisted them in resolving their musical challenges. Because of the concentration and attention devoted to the task, I was unaware of the growing number of faculty members who were drawn to the room to witness and enjoy the emerging sounds that were developing from this talented combo. Unknown to me, at the time, this forty-five-minute interlude qualified as the exhibition lesson.

Happily, the day ended with a signed contract, an opportunity to enter my own classroom at the age of twenty and the start of an exciting career of four decades. Within the next six years, I also became the youngest principal in New Jersey.

INITIATION INTO THE TEACHING PROFESSION

Immediately after graduating college in 1960, I was fortunate, at the age of twenty, to obtain a teaching position in a very prestigious school district. The assignment was to be a member of a three-teacher team. The responsibility was to serve as science instructor in a departmentalized setting for self-contained eighth graders. In addition to being the newest person in the group, I had the honor of working with the most demanding pupils at middle school level. Being naive and inexperienced, the challenge was accepted. Both educator and students bonded to enjoy a successful and productive term.

In the fall and at the first Upper Saddle River Education Association meeting, I was unanimously elected treasurer of the group. Although not eligible to earn tenure, I also became president of the professional staff in the second year of my new career.

The task was to represent my colleagues at faculty, administrative, township board of education meetings and negotiations sessions. Within six years in the district and at the age of twenty-six, I was fortunate to be appointed principal of the Robert D. Reynolds School and privileged to be the youngest principal in New Jersey at that time.

SUMMER
From age: 21 to 40

YACHT OWNER FOR ONE RIDE

As a college student, I had the pleasure of working with a very popular band that was booked well over two years in advance. While it was standard to play every Saturday, in many months the combo was contracted to entertain for three-night weekend engagements. We provided contemporary music, ethnic tunes, and an assortment of dancing rhythms to satisfy all requests.

The song library included: top forties, current popular selections and old-time favorites. Audiences ranged from high school proms to senior citizens celebrating their golden anniversaries. "The Top Kicks" was the name of the group and we were headliners through Northern Jersey. This financially productive stage enabled me to purchase two showroom new cars in a three-year period.

One member of this quartet asked if I might be interested in partnering in a forty-two-foot wooden yacht. This seemed to be an interesting adventure and the slightly used twin engine vessel was purchased. A result of this commitment, was more time was spent laboring under the craft than partying in it.

On a sunny February morning, I invited my future wife to spend some time where the new treasure was kept at a fenced in boat storage area in Peekskill, NY. Because of the winter season, the ship was elevated on special, secure chocks. This set-up enabled work to take place on the hull. While some of the nicest people can be found in this setting, out of water, boats are noted for being very unsightly. Upon arrival, I helped her out of the car, went to the trunk and I handed the lovely lady a scraping tool for the purpose of removing barnacles from the red bottom of the suspended cruiser.

My date was dressed in fashionable tailored, black, stretch slacks with stirrups that were topped with a matching turtleneck sweater. This ensemble was covered by a stunning gray, warm, white, paneled poncho. She was certainly not appropriately attired for a day's work in the fresh air.

The response while facing me and rejecting the tool, was that she will return to the auto, drive to a coffee shop, buy a newspaper, relax and pick me up in a few hours. I was abandoned with a sharp putty knife and the lone task of removing thousands of decaying sea morsels from the looming wooden structure. Unaccompanied on this cold shoreline next to a frozen river that contained chunks of floating ice, my work began. From that point forward, I went to the cold dry dock alone.

Eventually, the prized ocean craft was launched and made ready to coast down the Hudson River for a permanent docking place in Little Ferry, New Jersey. Restoration and redecorating activities continued until midsummer. After months of engine tuning, electrical checking, plumbing, scraping, sanding, scrubbing, caulking, and painting, the project was completed.

The beautiful finished product, named *Top Kick*, was ready for its christening voyage to the New York City Harbor. Proper sailing attire was worn, refreshments and safety equipment were carefully stowed and the group went on board to experience our first Sunday trip. For that memorable event, we sailed under the Verrazano Bridge while it was under construction. In addition, I responded to a dare by diving into the murky Hackensack River. This was the fastest swim that was ever experienced. Once aboard, immediate direct orders were given to report to the small shower for a combined sterilization clean-up, and to prepare for an afternoon of cocktails and dining.

Body language and facial expressions made it obvious that my date did not enjoy this special day at sea. In the car on the way home, I was presented with the most important choice of my young life. "Either the boat or me"! Fortunately, my brother was happy to assume my duties as the retiring captain.

After that complete commitment, this was the only pleasure trip I had to remember. Luckily, the decision was made to surrender the ship for bigger and better future things to come. Happily, an exchange of one maiden voyage for another journey provided a lifetime of smooth sailing that continues to swell and deepen with each passing tide.

CUTTING EDGE SISTER-IN LAW

Well after the presentation of our special sparkling ring, Evenings, visiting my fiancée, were dedicated to developing lesson plans for the next day's teaching while the special lady completed her important college homework. Because of our busy schedules, 10:00pm was the departure time to return home for a good night's sleep and rest for the next school session. My future sister-in law, who was four years younger than us and a high school student, took pleasure at being an unwelcome nuisance that enjoyed sharing the living room. She was a test for engaged couples' patience.

On a memorable evening, the young girl, once again, decided to occupy the same room and work on a lengthy social studies project. A devilish grin and gleam in her eyes clearly signaled that she was well aware of the anticipated good night romantic ritual and she planned to overstay her welcome.

In an attempt to encourage her disappearance, I moved the arm that was used to apply paint to paper. The slight nudge caused the brush to move off target. She then firmly fixed her position as an uninvited guest and the chiding continued at an elevated level.

Finally, she warned me that if her hand was pushed one more time, retaliation would be in order and my new custom suit would be cut. Temptation was beyond my control and war was declared as the artistic hand was pushed for the last time. Instantly, the enemy made a three-corner scissor cut on the jacket sleeve and the damage was done.

At the peak of battle in this dramatic confrontation, her father entered the skirmish to enact a truce. The crafty little girl exclaimed, "I warned him!" Dad quickly sized up the situation, resolved the conflict and made peace by having a replacement coat made by his tailor. Over the years, our relationship was mended, things were patched up and we all learned to live happily ever after.

"GOTTA" PEE MIDNIGHT MOONER

As a young married couple, we would frequently drive to our New England farm after a late-night weekend band job. The journey usually began well after midnight and continued for nearly three hours. During these labored excursions, travel facilities were long closed for the evening

On one memorable occasion, my lovely passenger desperately required the use of a bathroom. Except for a long dark dirt road that meandered into a lonely, bleak, looking forest; nothing was available. Ultimately, the car was driven off the road and parked in this secluded, desolate area to begin the squatting procedure.

At the "point of no return" a set of beaming headlights turned on to illuminate the beautiful glowing cheeks of a glistening full moon that was in a very compromising position. To my amazement, the fresh Mooner extended both arms to welcome an eclipse of the stranger's auto as it emerged from the woods.

I guess they were just as surprised to learn that there were two lunar bodies in the beautiful sky on this rare summer evening. At the intersection of passing cars, Nancy gave an enormous wave, a glowing smile and a wish for a safe journey.

MANY FIRST AID SAVES

I managed several emergency situations in the past by providing first aid care to people who have had respiratory difficulties. The earliest intervention occurred during my second year of teaching science to twelve and thirteen-year-old pupils attending Edith A. Bogert School in Upper Saddle River, New Jersey. The curriculum design was to present physical science to seventh graders and biological studies to students in eighth grade.

The older level participated in a concentration focused on human anatomy and physiology. As a wonderful bonus, many parents were executives in large corporations who were receptive to providing an excellent assortment of interesting supplementary supplies to augment the educational program. One father was the owner of a large food supermarket chain and volunteered to donate animal organs from his meat department.

These parts were delivered as requested and properly prepared for intense study in a classroom laboratory setting. Youngsters found the activities were very exciting, interesting, and informative. These samples helped them learn about the structure and function of anatomical tissues and systems. The instructional age was appropriate for animal comparisons and scientific relationships were made to the human body. In essence pupils had hands-on experiences with actual specimens and they became knowledgeable on these topics.

While preparing the science lab for the next lesson during a teacher planning period, an eighth-grade girl ran into the room and excitedly exclaimed that a classmate was in the home economics room and was choking to death. The young lady was followed to the troubled child who was seen gasping for air ...but breathing. In the meantime, the certified school nurse, who was summoned earlier, was at the rear of the room and in an uncontrollable state of shock.

This episode was caused by a hungry, curious, childish, victim who stuck her finger in the tempting, warm, mixture of rich, creamy, chocolate, cookie batter. In a sly, secret taste, the delicious morsel was swallowed, became caught in her throat and partially blocked the air passageway. The "medical" science teacher gently removed the "life threatening" treat, calmed the scared, dessert thief and treated the health expert.

While looking out the kitchen window on a sunny summer morning, the next episode occurred. I observed a blond haired, light complexioned, toddler face down in the plastic, and tube type, backyard wading pool. The water depth was less than ten inches.

I quickly ran out the door, scaled the triple terraced set of stone walls and pulled the lad from the shallow water. Fortunately, he was still breathing and fully recovered as I rang the bell and the father answered the door. Dad calmly took the boy from my arms and said thank you. In essence my shock was more severe than both parents.

Months later, I walked across the early morning frozen snow to visit a good neighbor. Upon approaching an above the ground swimming pool, I saw their three-year-old son face down in the partially frozen cover. Déjà a Vaux, the scene repeated and I again was shocked by the nonchalant reaction of the family. The rescued child is presently over fifty years of age and a parent of three girls. Years later, I told him about this event, he, his parents, older sisters and brother had no memory of the potential catastrophe.

During a summer vacation, my family toured the lovely Pennsylvania Amish country for a few days. While in a restaurant, our children were aroused by barking sounds coming from another part of the dining area. They quickly ran to the rear of the room to investigate the dog making these interesting sounds. They immediately returned to our table to report that a lady was observed to be on her hands and knees, making funny sounds and turning colors. I followed them to the scene, assessed the situation and applied the Heimlich Maneuver. The obstruction was liberated and comfortable breathing was resumed.

While a new member of the Washington Township, NJ Ambulance Corps, the rule was that on a scheduled duty day, the first aid radio had to be activated, carried and the volunteer had to remain in town for emergency calls. Being confined to the immediate neighborhood, we decided to go to a food shop at the local supermarket that was opposite headquarters.

On the way to the store, the warning signal sounded, a problem defined, address provided and patient identified. At that instant, my automobile was directly in front of the distressed person's home. The car was parked and I ran into the house to observe an infant who was not breathing. Before duty crew mates arrived in the ambulance, respiration was restored and the child was comfortably placed in the parents' arms.

I rode back to the squad building in the emergency vehicle for the customary debriefing session. Once the detailed report was completed, the officer in charge reprimanded me for not reporting to the station and riding on the rig. The scolding also included that I appeared on the scene without putting on a uniform. Taking this dialogue into careful consideration, I responded, "Please explain this policy with me to the mother and father. Then, carefully listen to their conversation and observe their reaction".

The most important save in the family occurred while babysitting for our two-year granddaughter. Nancy went to the nursery on the second floor to check on the sleeping little girl. There, she found a struggling little lass with an ashen complexion, high temperature and rolled back eyes. She yelled, "Bob"! I immediately rushed up the stairs to the child's room. The situation was evaluated, and infant pulmonary resuscitation was implemented.

After the third gentle puff was applied, breathing began. In the meantime, the ambulance was telephoned and quickly arrived to prepare the little youngster for the hospital ride. Fortunately, the emergency first aid training which I experienced saved the day and the story enjoyed a happy ending. In essence my little grandchild will never remember this incident and I will never forget!

BOB CHINO BAND SIGN

I was an active club date musician that entertained in local cabarets. Nightspots required signs to advertise coming attractions as well as the live entertainment that currently appeared in their establishment. It was important to have signs that generated interest for potential customers. I contracted a professional artist to create portable durable advertising announcements to be displayed in these cafés. They did an effective job and were successfully used for several years. As time passed my career moved in different directions and the posters were stored in my parents' basement for future use.

One day, Dad needed a durable wide piece of wood to make a home repair. One of my business band notices was put into service. He cut the miniature billboard to complete his renovation! It was the most expensive lumber he had ever used. Fortunately, my musical path progressed in other directions and the custom commercials were permanently retired. A second sign is currently on display at a Rob's family room museum in Minnesota.

PAPER SHIRT UNCOVERED

In my accordion career, the standard uniform for a performing professional musician was a tuxedo, formal pleated shirt, suspenders, cummerbund, bow tie, shined shoes, shirt studs and cufflinks. To reduce laundering expenses in 1960, I purchased a gross of stiff, rigid, thick, paper shirts and separate matching formal collars. The large front white portion was a dickey that was connected to the neckline collar and covered with an appropriate bow tie. The lower segment was fastened to a trouser button and covered with a satin waistband.

Because of my extra tall stature, the unique attire, which was worn over a standard tee shirt, required some modification. Two holes were punched at mid-point on both sides of the cardboard dickey and connected over the back with a long sneaker, shoelace. The suspenders then stabilized the design and the jacket completed the ensemble to create a formal picture of perfection.

Since the article was other than conventional shirt material, it was rather firm and starched. However, within the first few moments of performance on stage and the production of perspiration, the garment absorbed significant moisture, softened and was very comfortable.

A band job scam was used to get me to my surprise bachelor's party. While getting dressed after loading the equipment into the car, Nancy appeared at my home. She and my parents unsuccessfully attempted to convince the well-dressed musician to wear a regular shirt. I stubbornly insisted that this make-believe garment was part of the routine. Confidently, I drove to the restaurant and got ready to play.

Loading and unloading of instruments and equipment was always a responsibility that was equally shared by all the combo members. While my arms were loaded with heavy paraphernalia, the sax player carried a small clarinet and the drummer transported a light weight high hat stand. Subsequently, I asked why the keyboard man was the only beast of burden. The question was quickly answered when the banquet door was opened and the guest chorus of friends shouted, "Surprise!" Now it was clear! The tux jacket came off; we celebrated in my custom made, deceptive, masqueraded, wardrobe and the last party as a single person was thoroughly enjoyed.

DREAM HOME NIGHTMARE

The advantage of working full time while attending college provided an opportunity to save money and be in a position to purchase a home prior to marriage. Once engaged, the long, formidable, house hunting challenge began. The initial process included: devoting extensive quantities of time and much effort with both sets of parents, real estate agents, banking consultants and attorneys.

This experience resulted in the ability to define housing needs, identify community settings, select neighborhoods, agree on building designs and establish an affordable price range. As time passed, we were qualified to clearly define our requirements and search for a comfortable situation that could satisfy these specifications.

During the spring recess, a potential dream house that fulfilled our requirements, was found. It was a young three-bedroom, ranch style dwelling that was constructed on a nicely landscaped, corner lot. It was centrally air conditioned with a full finished basement. Interestingly, the floors were completely carpeted with the exact colors of our choice and the selling price was within range. The real estate agent assisted with preparing the paperwork and an offering bid was made. The proposal was accepted and a sales contract was prepared.

An attorney reviewed the purchase documents and set an appointment to discuss the details of the agreement. Sadly, and because the sellers refused to accept a penalty clause that would guarantee the closing date, the lawyer recommended the process be terminated and advised we look for another residence. Now, this devastating news had to be shared with my fiancé who was at her home preparing a champagne celebration with parents. An effort to carefully disclose the distressing information was made. However, the response was tearfully upsetting.

In an attempt to provide comfort during this untimely, emotional, stressful, situation, a suggestion was made to search the classified section in the local newspaper. There, an obscure three-line advertisement appeared mentioning an eleven-month-old, sale-by-owner home that was in the same township in which our future fantasy failed and was lost. Immediately, a telephone call was made and arrangements were made to visit the address of this interesting listing.

As we drove down the street, the homes got bigger and better. Parked in front of our destination, there appeared a "mansion" that was theoretically beyond our means! As the front door opened, we were greeted and invited in to inspect the site. By comparison this structure, for the same price, was more than twice the size of the first place. It included an entrance foyer with provisions for a large sunken family room and a second bathroom. We came to terms within a few hours and, fortunately, this transaction proceeded flawlessly. Within one week before the wedding, we were able to paint and move into a dream house. In time, a family was raised and we happily lived there for thirty-eight years.

PS Due to extreme complications, two years passed before the latent nightmare home was sold!

HONEYMOON NIGHT

Prior to the big day, Nancy's dad arranged the house and foundation gardens in preparation for a very serious, photographic session. Flower beds were beautifully trimmed, weeded and mounded. Shrubs were precisely pruned and the lawn was meticulously manicured.

At that time, it was a common practice to sabotage the happily married couple's car. Therefore, precautions were made in advance to hide the automobile in a neighbor's garage. After enjoying a fantastic wedding ceremony followed by an outstanding and memorable reception, the newlyweds returned to the bride's home to prepare for the honeymoon escape.

As the departure time arrived, the apprehensive groom swiftly scampered out the front door to retrieve the hidden vehicle. He instantly stepped into the decorative shallow trench which defined the landscaping beds. Sharp sensations of pain radiated from a seriously sprained ankle that was shortly followed by swelling and a series of screeching, stressful, screaming sounds.

The new bride, weighing less than a hundred pounds, swiftly scurried to the scene in support of her injured groom. A surge of super strength was mustered as she carried the 6-foot 7-inch husband into the living room. Ice was applied to the injured ankle and they left to begin their marital adventure.

MARRIAGE FIRST MEMORABLE MEALS

After returning in July from a delightful two-week honeymoon, that included a motor trip to Canada and a seven-day cruise to Nassau; it was time to continue the decorating process of our eleven-month-old home. The summer vacation mission was to change the outside color from green to white. The first morning was spent in the backyard on a forty-foot ladder applying the prime coat of paint. At lunch time, a romantic appeal came from an open window that overlooked the job site.

The newlywed's girlish voice summons me. There at the sink, appeared a teary-eyed, new bride engaged in mixing the hamburger ingredients to make her first hot lunch. The combination included a recipe of chopped meat, bread crumbs, assorted seasonings and raw eggs. A quivery feminine voice pleaded for assistance to stir the blend and a request to be relieved of this complicated, culinary chore.

A concise, condensed, clear conversation followed in which the roles of a new husband and wife were carefully communicated. Unhappily, the cook of the house completed the task by placing her hands in plastic bags that eventually were replaced by rubber, galley, gloves and they have remained in permanent service. While this brief encounter was unforgettable, it set the tone for the future and a lifetime of many outstanding gourmet, gratifying, and gastronomical experiences.

Later that week in a conversation with her mom, "my fair lady" discussed size amounts required for two adult dinner portions. The cuisine under consideration was pork chops, mashed potatoes, vegetable varieties and salad. The recommendations were to prepare three chops, a potato for each person and one extra for the pot, a can of vegetables for each selection and a small fresh garden salad. As the food preparation adventure progressed, wonderful sounds and delightful aromas trickled from an assortment of unblemished, pristine pots and pans. A lovely table was set and the eventual call to supper was extended. While seated, the banquet was carefully placed on fine China.

The young chef peered into the eyes of her new husband and looked for a signal to indicate when a sufficient quantity of potatoes was parceled out. A gentle tap on the dish indicated that a little more was requested. Eventually, both sat down to experience their first home cooked supper. His plate was filled to the brim while hers was missing mashed potatoes. When asked, "Where are your spuds"? The polite response was, "You have all of them!"

Ultimately, the necessary adjustments were made and future comfort levels were well established. As a compliment to the affectionate, caring kitchen chemist, the first six months of a loving marriage forced my skinny skeleton to support and sustain an additional weight of sixty-five pounds.

BEN GAY

A lower back pain problem originated in my teenage years and frequently reoccurred over my lifetime. Eventually, I found that sitting and relaxing in a very hot tub for about an hour provided much relief. This daily procedure was followed by rubbing Ben Gay ointment to the sore tender area. A combination of these remedies and careful, guarded, movement resolved the difficulty and shortened the recuperative time. During the recovery period, all modified physical activities continued without interruption. Ultimately, the ache worked itself out within a moderately uncomfortable week.

As a child, I was taught to properly clean the bathtub when finished. This responsibility was well established prior to marriage. So…when the ailment reappeared while working around our new house, the treatment was automatically implemented. However, while leaning over the sparkling, empty tub, my bride entered the room. In a volunteering cooperative spirit, she methodically applied the creamy, distinctive, smelling, salve to the sore spot and graciously provided a prolonged, magnificent massage.

As a finishing touch, she gently gave the exposed hanging family jewels an affectionate pat. Forgetting that the heat, producing, rubbing, cream remained on her skillful hands and kind firm caressing fingers; she lingered for an extended moment. We both shared a broad smile which was quickly extinguished as a smokeless, flaming, fire accelerated in the delicate area. A vigorous, fierce, dance ensued that was augmented by a fast-waving towel that was used to circulate a supply of fresh air.

The cold-water faucet was immediately turned on and a quick return to the chilly liquid began the next sequence. The eager water entrance continued and was followed by an energetic, aquatic, disco type, butt, boogie. It seemed that eons passed before the coals were cooled and the sensitive equipment was returned to a normal temperature.

MISSING MOTHER MYSTERY

It was July 4, 1963, and the family converged to the Berkshire Mountains for their traditional weekly retreat of rest, relaxation and refreshments. Activities included an abundance of delicious, home cooked food, varieties of thirst-quenching drinks, imaginative games and the marvelous Mass. Mountain Music Men. It was common for our farmhouse and side yard to comfortably accommodate approximately seventy people. While Massachusetts folks drove out for the day, a New Jersey contingency was able to stay over for the weekend and sleep in our four-bedroom summer home.

After a splendid lunch at the picnic tables which were located under the apple trees; men moved to the horseshoe pits, ladies lingered at the tables for card playing and children gathered to have fun in the open grass field that was within plain view of their parents.

During the afternoon, Grandma Drummer would take her routine walk to the flagpole, circle the wild orange daylilies planted at the base of the mast, pass through the wide, white gate and proceed up the dirt road to gather a bouquet of native posies. Because there was little or no traffic on this winding, rural, gravel, lane that was centered in the middle of the woods; leisurely flower picking was a wonderful activity for this woman whose age was 86 years.

Our secluded tranquil sanctuary was named Shangri-La and it was a safe haven in a secure, serene, peaceful place. This unhurried quiet stroll would consume more or less than thirty minutes and she would happily return with an assortment of very beautiful blossoms that were artistically arranged in a vase and enjoyed by the guests.

On this occasion, the comfortable walk was interrupted with a slight, sprinkling, summer, shower. One relative took a two-minute recess from the competition and drove in the direction of her predicted path to transport the elderly lady and shelter her from the damp, drizzling, droplets. This, however, was not the case on that memorable, unfortunate and regrettable day. Gloom set in when the car returned without the elderly passenger who was our senior female, forest, florist. Grandma was gone!

A silent panic slowly spread as the shocked relatives scattered in search of the misplaced soul. Over the next few days, the volume of help extended to included police, military personnel, rescue squad, scouts, friends, family, neighbors and bloodhounds. It was amazing to note the number of professionals and volunteers who came to assist during these dark, depressing, demanding hours of the next weeks.

Radio, TV and newspaper media reported the events in detail as a fiasco and failure. Over sixty years have passed since that dismal, dreary date and the mystery, missing mother remains unsolved and continues to haunt those of us who have remained behind to worry, wonder, and grieve.

LIFT THE LONG LADDER

After returning from a honeymoon, we decided that the outside green color of our home should be changed to white. Supplies and a forty-foot extension aluminum ladder were purchased to do the job. The project required two coats and the work day began early in the morning. The front of the building was completed using a new four-inch brush and several gallons of clean, creamy liquid.

The sides which were on a hill were next. Because of the inclined terrain, the ladder had to be adjusted for safety to make accommodations for the sloping land contour. Once these three outer cedar shake surfaces were covered, the rear of the residence, which was three stories in height, was prepared and the ladder had to be relocated and extended to its maximum length.

Leverage was a key factor in securely maneuvering the tall ladder to the roof line. The double rungs were moved to their longest setting, and it was immediately realized that assistance was required. A friend was telephoned to provide an extra set of strong muscles.

This talented do-it-your-self skilled colleague arrived and assertively sauntered to the backyard to evaluate the situation. He looked at me, laughed and said that a person of my stature should easily be able to lift the ladder. He assuredly stepped to the foot, grabbed the sixth rung and proceeded to confidently lift the challenge. When the upper end was raised to approximately twelve feet off the ground, the combined impact of gravity, fulcrum location and weight became overwhelming.

My expert helper was embarrassed as the forty-foot object crashed into the grass. He now realized that this was a two-person project! Together the ladder was lifted and placed below the roof soffit. Once in place against the siding, it could easily be moved and adjusted as necessary by one person. When the job was completed, the same two workers took the ladder down and stored it in the basement.

AMATEUR OUTPERFORMS CONCERT PIANIST

Piano performance proficiency is a requirement to obtain a New Jersey kindergarten teaching license. Since Nancy had a musical background resulting from studying the accordion as a young child, the transition to an eighty-eight-note keyboard was less cumbersome. Her parents obtained a used upright and I provided the lessons.

An ability to read music was an asset. Implementation of the right hand, which played the melody line, was fairly comfortable. The challenge, however, was mastery of the left hand which provided the harmony and foundation for the piece.

Memorization of triad formations in the root positions were eventually learned and coordinated by the fingers. Eventually, she developed the knack of producing: the proper I, IV and V chords at the beginning of each measure. She pressed the correct three notes, held them down for three or four beats and repeated the technique for each separate bar in the song.

This basic method enabled her to pass the music test, secure a certificate and earn a teaching position in a very prestigious community. The five-year old pupils loved her and she was immediately their favorite! Near the end of autumn, she became ill with the flu and was absent from school for a complete week. A lovely talented, well experienced substitute teacher, who was also a concert pianist, was brought in to instruct her class during this period.

Upon Nancy's return after five days, the children complained that the replacement person did not play the piano nearly as well as their first-year teacher. The little students were either madly in love with Mrs. Franchino or tone deaf! In this story, the youngsters' affection could be described as both melodically blind and slightly hard of hearing.

HANGING A DECORATIVE CHRISTMAS BALL

Fortunately, as a single person, I was able to purchase a home prior to our marriage. Therefore, only one name appeared on the title of ownership. As our first Christmas approached, Nancy, the new bride, received a very large beautifully decorated, holiday ball from her kindergarten pupil.

She then wanted it to be displayed and suspended from "my" kitchen ceiling. This required putting a small hook in the freshly painted surface. Once removed after the New Year, an unsightly permanent hole would remain in the refreshed plaster finish. Concerned about creating this lasting blemish, I delayed and procrastinated in response to her repeated requests.

Late one evening while relaxing and watching television, the new wife entered the family room with a short, handled, five-pound, sledge hammer. She had a spike in one hand plus the fancy, large festive ornament in the other. In frustration, my gentle lady was determined to hang the gift and complete the project.

Sizing up the situation, I tenderly and calmly asked her to put down the dramatic tools of massive construction and leave the task to the man of the house. Within moments, the combination of red, white, green and glitzed covered ribbon that wrapped the huge lightweight sphere was hung for all to enjoy.

The discussion ended with, "… and you had better go to the lawyer and get **my** name on the deed!" Within a few days, I happily responded to this new female homeowner's requirement.

SCIENTIFIC APPLICATION FOR SARAN WRAP

Saran Wrap in the hands of an imaginative, inquisitive eighth grade child launched a research idea for an innovative science project. The known qualities of this common food packaging product enabled the young elementary school pupil an opportunity to design a new and original application for the item. It ultimately became a vital tool for examining the development of chicken embryos.

Through much reading and several library visits, he discovered there was a thin, unbroken, translucent membrane beneath the shell of a chicken egg that separated the inner structures of the white and yoke portions from the outer hard covering. By carefully leaving the transparent protective skin intact during the removal of a shell segment, the pupil thought he could cover the newly created outer void with an airtight seal of Saran Wrap. The crafted, secure, clear, sight porthole would now enable observations to easily occur on the growing embryo.

After completing the detailed examination of information, developing an experimental plan and applying the Scientific Method; dozens of fertilized eggs were purchased by his very supportive parents from a local hatchery and placed in a homemade well tested incubator. The experiment began.

Each day a new egg was selected for the delicate, surgical procedure of carefully installing the observation window. Success! The developing chicks continued to grow and change with each passing day. Through the study, detailed notes were taken to record the progress of the developing embryos as they matured.

The combination of these reported activities generated enormous conversations as the entire class eventually participated in the daily discussions and discoveries. In the short time span, most of the chicks hatched and grew to adulthood. Over the long period and years later, the boy was accepted to several medical schools and eventually became a very prominent surgeon.

FIRST ANNIVERSARY PRESENT

Our first wedding anniversary coincided with living in a new home for the same amount of time. A neighbor, who was employed by General Electric Company, offered me an opportunity to use his corporate discount to purchase small appliances. The understanding was the merchandise could not be returned once acquired.

Since the brand-new address was constructed with hardwood, oak floors in five rooms, inlaid linoleum in the kitchen, vinyl in the family room and ceramic tile in the bathrooms; it was decided that his connections could be utilized to purchase a floor buffing machine. The shiny chrome apparatus that operated a double set of forceful powerful brushes was delivered. It was then carefully wrapped in a large box and tied with a special ornamental bow.

The parcel was proudly presented on the morning of the special event with much anticipation and excitement! Enthusiasm filled the air as the pretty, decorative paper was delicately separated from the gorgeous package. Finally, the electrical, domestic, floor polishing device was liberated. The bride's response was immediate, nonverbal and ice cold.

In seconds, silence smothered the room! Stillness, lucid body language, that was unspoken, clearly conveyed unmistakable expressions of sadness and distressing, disappointment. A new profound lesson was learned in that instant! Any device that plugs into the wall to celebrate an important romantic occasion is the most inappropriate, inadequate expression of true love and affection.

After more than fifty years of wedded bliss, the power polisher remains in the talented, tender hands of the loving husband who is in charge of **all** floor responsibilities. And…he has happily mastered the task!

ASTRONOMY

As a science major in the Master's Program, an astronomy course was a curriculum requirement for graduation and state certification. To have the opportunity to observe actual real solar bodies, the class was taken in the evening during the fall semester. The observatory was located on the roof of the tallest college building. After a short lecture presentation on the names and positions of various visible stars, planets and constellations; the students were escorted to the top of a three-story structure for the practical part of the lesson and to identify or find the sky's illuminated nighttime treasures.

Cosmological, astrophysical or planetary spotting and recognizing solar bodies were listed low on my areas of interest. As we walked toward the staircase, I lingered to be the last person in line and out the door. In addition to these factors, there was a chill in the air and I elected to skip the evening's planned viewing and head for the warm comforts of home.

The next week there was a buzz of conversation in the building corridor before the students entered the classroom. Apparently, the automatic security lock engaged and the star gazers were trapped on the unprotected roof with the temperature dropping with each passing moment. It was near midnight until they were retrieved and rescued. Fortunately, the moonless dark sky and their concern for a safe return to the solid portion of warm earth protected me from being discovered as a missing body. I was lucky to miss this potential shooting star and was able to use other worldly skills to ace the course.

MONEY DOES GROW ON TREES

The family again planned to gather and celebrate the Thanksgiving Holiday at "Shangri-La" which is our peaceful, serene, sanctuary in the Berkshire Mountains. This annual tradition always attracted relatives and friends from the New England area. After a solid week's preparation, we traveled Wednesday night to this destination for the big event which would finally arrive.

At dawn the next day, a transported, ice cube packed turkey was washed, prepared, stuffed, patted and put in the oven. Around the large kitchen table, "GG" then served her standard, country, gourmet breakfast that was fit for royalty.

While the bird roasted in the warm toasty oven, women prepared the dining area for the big fall feast. At the same time, men worked in the yard to prepare for the coming long, cold, winter. Before noon, guests began arriving with their arms filled with lovely assortments of interesting things for the wonderful banquet. The remainder of the day was devoted to gobbling up the delicious homemade food and sharing God's blessings.

After a sumptuous dining experience, the party portion of the celebration began. Activities included card playing, kiddies' board games and music by the "Massachusetts Mountain Men". This unique band which consisted of an accordion, harmonica, trumpet and variety of hand-crafted instruments was supported by loud voices of the "Agony Choir". The more we drank, the better we sounded! This was a true old-fashioned country celebration.

The well-established ritual continued the next day, Black Friday. The girls piled into the cars, went to town and enjoyed a day of bargain hunting. Men remained behind, took care of the children, helped make winter wreaths using native foliage, shot clay pigeons, enjoyed eating Nancy's homemade vegetable soup and prepared to close the house before winter arrived.

While involved in early morning chores, a person drove up the winding, dirt road and through the large white gate. His truck was excited, introduced himself and asked if we were interested in selling the timber which was on our 140 acres of land. The mature weather-worn hard-working gentleman proceeded to explain the details and before the weekend concluded, we crafted a formal agreement. Essentially, he had until January 1, of the next year to complete his project, could not remove any tree that was less than ten inches in diameter at the stump and all the money specified in the contract would be paid in full at the arrangement signing.

Being a local resident, the wood cutter planned to harvest timber he bought that was a distance from his home. His decision was to save our plot from inclement weather and avoid traveling on twisting, unplowed, country roads that were covered with heavy accumulations of ice and snow.

To the contrary Mother Nature was warm spirited that year and did not blanket the area with a severe Jack Frost white, deep winter coat. Therefore, all of the cutter's energy was consumed in removing every morsel of lumber from the distant property. Shortly after the agreed upon deadline arrived, he was notified that the termination date had expired. He left more than 90% of the precious forest entirely intact.

This series of events repeated in the following two years with different buyers. On each subsequent occasion, the money was again collected in full each time a deal was made. This good fortune could certainly not go on forever and the last character sold the contract to a large company who removed every eligible piece of lumber.

Once again, favorable conditions continued. A neighbor expressed an interest in converting the slashing and limbs, remaining on the ground, into usable firewood. He offered to pay a sum of ten dollars per stacked cord and the compensation would be made monthly as he proceeded through the woods. The income received was related to the amount he was able to bring to markct.

Monthly checks were received for about a year; and then, they suddenly stopped! Detective skills were mustered and it was determined this was a common practice he had implemented with other suppliers of this recycled, raw material. With a bit more persistence, I was able to locate his hiding place at a very remote motel in the snow-covered mountains. Unexpectedly, his telephone rang at 4:00 am.

My response to how he was tracked down was "Send me the money. The last thing you want is me standing and knocking at your door!" While other clients remained unpaid, the final calculations yielded from firewood activities far exceeded the income generated from all the other standing timber sales.

MY THREE SONS

As a child, our family included my parents, two sons and a male collie. We lived in a lovely urban community at a home that I helped dad build. My younger brother and I were at that address until the date we married and then moved out to live with our new wives.

On the day we each left, Mom gave us a complete set of luggage, new underwear, a tearful kiss, and a wish for good luck. Several years later, Skippy, the pet dog died. My sad mother wore mourning black for two years!

HAY! LET ME SHOW YOU

The side yard at Shangri-La was more than two acres in size. The other grass areas around the house accounted for an additional acre. The combination of lawn and its vigorous, aggressive spring growth resulted in an extensive and challenging task when the first cut was scheduled for the Memorial Day weekend.

The available tool of choice was a push, steel, reel mower with a wooden handle. Because of the high, thick, wild flourishing green foliage, the amateur, guest, city farmers took turns during the few days to complete the project. Uncle Harold, the local forest ranger, lived at a nearby small house on a wooded country road. This precious, secluded, palace did not enjoy the common comforts of electricity, indoor plumbing, central heat or running water. For most of his life, he and his family lived off the land.

While taking my turn behind the old-fashioned, labor intensive, mowing machine, he said; "Hay let me show you!" The tall, trim, lean and lanky 75-year-old veteran who served as a professional park superintendent slowly ambled to the barn and took out two long handled scythes. After providing a fifteen-minute lesson on safety, blade sharpening and mowing technique, we went to work.

At the time, I was in my twenties, a former college athlete and in seemingly excellent physical condition. The fifty-year age difference was theoretically in favor of the young man. The scene was set and the standard scenario of youth versus age was in place. Let the contest begin!

I took the tool in hand and went to action like a stunned jackrabbit. His pace was similar to the traditional turtle. Instantly the senior competitor was outpaced. While my completed parcel was much larger than the adversary's; the end product was uneven, jagged and rough in texture. His by comparison, was neatly and skillfully manicured and had the appearance of a well-cared for golfing green.

While my burst of untamed energy expired within a short time, his experienced hands demonstrated precision, perfection and a meticulous approach that produced a picture-perfect product which could have been featured in a fine landscaping magazine. The senior's skills endured throughout the day and put the entire crew of sophisticated city slickers to shame. This favored relative, Uncle Harold Sattler, remains well revered as a legend and superstar in our historical family tree.

SEVEN MAPLE TREES

The Beech Street house in Washington Township, New Jersey was located on an oak tree wooded plot that created an appealing natural setting. While many of the towering trees exceeded one hundred years of age, two had presented a danger due to trunk decay and had to be removed. A few days later, my father drove from Paterson with seven beautiful tall replacement sugar maple saplings.

Because he did not want to soil his sparkling new car, the root balls were washed clean then wrapped in moist cloth and placed in plastic bags. In an attempt to appease him, we went through the process of expending energy and effort to prepare the holes to insert them in the ground. After a long afternoon, he was satisfied and I was tired.

What a wonderful gift…all survived and matured to become marvelous additions to the lovely landscaped property. Ultimately, the tall green leafy foliage matured to create a beautiful shade canopy that enveloped the large elevated deck that was entered through the double French dining room doors.

From this setting, the in-ground swimming pool could be viewed. This marvelous, relaxing scenery could have been photographed and printed in most home and garden publications. Thanks Dad!

RAILROAD TIES

Our Washington Township backyard consisted of three terraces. The various levels were identified by large stone walls that extended the length of the property. Because of the irregular lawn surface, grass cutting was tedious; trimming which required hand clipping was cumbersome and the chore was time consuming.

Through the efforts and business connections of a good neighbor, who had similar terrain, contacts were made to obtain replacement, retired, railroad ties. With this valuable resource available, we decided to build a wall in front of the large boulder barriers by using sturdy, creosote, saturated, preserved wooden beams. Once constructed, plans included backfilling and topping-off the new timber barrier with soil. This would result in a smooth level surface at the summit of the thick, sturdy rock covered partition, make turf care easier, more efficient and eliminate hand work edging.

While the railroad ties were well over fifty years in age, they were in good condition and able to provide excellent long-time service in the new application at this location. The project involved moving these cumbersome three hundred-pound, eleven-foot beams from trackside, onto a truck, off loaded, carried to the construction site on my property and installed.

A work crew of good strong men and my dad gathered at my home early one Saturday morning. After breakfast and a few hardy shots of whiskey, we traveled to the train tracks with a combination of rugged special tools, mighty muscle and youthful energy.

My father was the senior member of the team and probably in the best physical shape. In addition to his conditioning, he was an experienced master truck mechanic. One pick-up site was located in the center of a city. During the loading segment, the borrowed truck stalled and refused to restart. While we pushed the partially loaded vehicle down the street to the next log liberating area, Dad plucked and collected an assortment of curb debris.

As we loaded ties, he worked on the ignition system. While man power continued to push the free cargo to the next stop, he made progress on the tired motor. To the amazement of his younger colleagues, the old engine eventually came to life! It was much easier to complete the job when the escape means of transportation traveled under its own power.

Once loaded, six very filthy fatigued friends headed for home. On the way, the exhausted bunch stopped for lunch at a highway tavern. The grungy group sat at the bar and I suggested to the proprietor that he let the beers run because we wanted them cold. In the course of the spring project, the volunteers moved over seven hundred ties to complete a series of walls in the neighborhood. After five decades and to the credit of the weekend, workers, warriors; the structures still are serviceable and remain standing.

IS THAT THE DOCTOR?

While painting the outside of his home on a hot summer day, my friend's little boy fell off the backyard swing set and ran into the house with a painful cry. Mother quickly assessed the situation and concluded the child needed immediate emergency room attention! After working a full day, Dad had accumulated a large collection of paint on his clothing, face and hands. In addition, he drank a few bottles of beer to replace the moisture and salt that he had lost through perspiration while expending energy to cover the house with a new color. There was no time to clean up or remove an unshaven beard that was grungy looking.

Upon entering the hospital, Mother was assigned a seat in the waiting room. Father, along with his young son, was immediately escorted to an examining room. After first aid was administered and completed, Dad decided to report to Mom who was in another area in the building. He walked through the double doors and sat next to his anxious wife with the intent to carefully explain, in correct medical terms, what had transpired.

She was assured the injuries were not serious, there were no broken bones and the youngster would make a complete recovery without scares or need for further treatment. Confident that a properly communicated, accurate and compassionate message was conveyed, he returned to comfort his resting child.

Sitting next to his calmed wife was a young sobbing, distressed new mother who was on the edge of losing control. She cried and hugged the now reassured parent and asked in a trembling, apprehensive, nervous and frightened voice, "My little girl is in there, and is *that* the doctor?"

GREENHOUSE THESIS

The school system in which I was employed for forty years was located on a natural wooded plot of land that was approximately two hundred acres in size. It resembled a park type of campus in a setting on which three buildings were located. The instructional configuration, with an enrollment of approximately 2,000 pupils, housed a primary program, an intermediate facility and a middle school.

The learning complex was situated in the most northern segment of Bergen County and in a fast-growing area that was rapidly making the transition from a small, rural, agricultural oriented community to an upscale, residential, suburban municipality. Due to its close proximity to New York City, corporate executives and their young families discovered this as a valuable place to satisfy their relocation needs. Their points of origin extended from all over the world.

Because it quickly expanded and enjoyed excellent public support, opportunities for being on the positive leading edge of educational enhancement was always encouraged and readily available. As the science teacher and in pursuit of a Master of Arts Degree, I elected to devote the required thesis for an integration of a self-sustaining greenhouse which would be incorporated into the instructional program. If successful at that time, a hothouse would be a first for an elementary school in New Jersey.

Since this was a new and original innovation, research information on school related construction and curriculum concepts were scarce and generally unavailable. The college advisor, who served as director of research activities, was consulted for assistance and guidance. A very confident resource direction was provided with a recommendation to contact a person from Upper Saddle River who was identified as the most current and knowledgeable professional on this subject. With this information and a very strong suggestion from the chairperson of this graduate department, the rest was easy. Unbeknown to that professor, I was recognized, acknowledged and referenced to myself.

PS: The environmental center was funded by the local P.T.A, constructed in the early 1970's and still remains an extremely vital part of the district's course of study.

PREGNANCY AND WHAT SIZE DRESS?

Nancy walked down the church aisle on our wedding day as a slim, stunning bride, and weighing less than one hundred pounds. It was a wonder that she had the strength to support the weight of her beautiful, sparkling, beaded, Cinderella type full gown. Always having a sparse appetite, it was understandable that she easily maintained this slender profile. During the third year of our marriage, we joyfully became pregnant and looked forward to the welcomed arrival of the first child

Shortly after this announcement, my wonder woman developed a ravenous, craving for substantial amounts of food. The new baby was predicted to arrive on December 26, 1966 and during the nine-month period; the wispy wife accumulated a profile of an additional fifty-five pounds. In addition to the very dramatic change in eating habits, she developed a changed attitude that justified and centered around eating for two people.

During the waiting period, she continued to sew the bulk of her temporary new clothing. The skills associated with modifying patterns to accommodate a new body shape negated the concern for dress size. Essentially, the creative design was modified by adding more fabric to the garment being shaped.

On Christmas Day, my mother gave the expectant lady in waiting a large pair of royal blue stretch slacks that were designed with fashionable foot stirrups. Instinctively scanning the label indicated that the pants were clearly marked size 16. The disappointed, sad facial expression was dramatically displayed and the silent sounds that were restrained in her mind were deafening. Obviously, the expectant mother was distressed and offended. This emotion continued for the next few days. In the meantime, a six-pound ½ ounce little girl was born on the due date and this blessed event eternally changed our lives.

As part of the holiday celebrations, we were invited to a neighborhood New Year's Day house party. In a failing, frustrating, attempt to select a coming out outfit from her very, full, clothing closet, nothing fit. She then reluctantly asked me to search under the tree for the large royal blue slacks. We both struggled to force the elastic fabric onto the altered body shape.

Ultimately, this dramatic wardrobe episode provided the motivation to eat selectively and a return to her standard dress size.

Thanks Mom!

MICHELANGELO MYSTERY

Children in the intermediate grades of three, four and five were encouraged to take on increased responsibility for their research studies and are stimulated to become more independent learners. Individual projects and library exploring activities were some of the educational techniques employed to develop this instructional objective. During one of the research assignments, a fifth-grade girl steamed out of the library with frustration and anguish deeply embedded in her pretty, tense, red face.

When asked to explain her distress, she responded, "I spent the whole time looking up Michelangelo and could not find anything! First, I tried his last name, Angelo, and then I searched for the first name, Michael. No success! Her expression dramatically changed and a brilliant ear to ear smile appeared when she was helped with an explanation of the artist's name and the correct spelling.

BUNNY FUN FUR COAT

We were invited to attend a political fund-raising affair at a local, popular, prestigious, country club. Formal apparel was required. Nancy designed and hand crafted a beautiful gown and I accompanied her wearing a standard tuxedo. At the time, bunny fur coats were fashionable and she, therefore, sported hers to the elegant function. Prior to the occasion; this warm, full-length, stylish coat quickly earned a reputation for generously sharing its delicate, fine, long hair with anything in its vicinity.

We fully participated in all the planned festivities and enjoyed an excellent evening. At the end of the dinner dance, our winter wraps were retrieved from the hat check person and then, carefully placed over our fancy, smart, special attire. We then made ready for an exit into the chill of a crisp winter evening.

Before departing; a well-groomed, dapper dressed, ashen haired man, who seemed to be attracted to my lovely wife during the entire party, chatted several flirtatious remarks and aggressively moved towards my alluring bride who was mother of our two children. I suggested that she finally make the persistence pest happy! My lovely lady immediately responded by enthusiastically embracing him with both arms and followed with an extensive, energetic, bear hug.

For a few moments, she sexually wiggled her freely shedding and friendly coat over his total torso. Throughout his enchanting encounter, this distinguished looking, handsome gray headed, irritating nuisance obviously experienced ecstatic, euphoric, elation. He swiftly endorsed these emotions by flaunting a broad, bright smile on his well-tanned, gently creased, leathery, looking and mature face. Upon separation, his very beautiful, custom fitted, mohair, charcoal tuxedo was covered from top to toe with snow white rabbit hair.

This interesting combination created a new "first time presentation" in the fashion world. He now was able to prance and swagger in an original bunny fur suit which was stunning, exotic and surely spectacular. All that remained missing in the exquisite outfit were a pair of long, pink ears to match his changed, crimson complexion and a fluffy smoke colored tail accessory to augment his elegant ensemble.

FIRST EAST RUTHERFORD HIGH SCHOOL REUNION DRESS

I graduated from high school in 1958 and met Bob in March,1960. We were happily married three years later on June 22, 1963. During our wedding month, an invitation to my first East Rutherford High School class reunion was delivered. Naturally, I was very eager to attend and wear a stunning ensemble. The next Thursday while shopping with Mom, the hunting search discovered the perfect beautiful dress in Orbach's that was located in the Paramus Bergen Mall.

Unfortunately, I did not have enough money or a credit card to complete the sale. The clerk informed me of the store policy that required a dollar to place the merchandise on hold for a twenty-four-hour period and that was the procedure implemented. When Mom was driven home, Dad was at the door waiting to welcome us. Needless to say, he shared our excitement about the garment and reached into his pocket to give me the cash to complete the sale. I was ecstatic!

On the journey home, I stopped at the shopping center to buy my "dress". I was thrilled and could not wait to model it for my husband. It was a white satin dress with rhinestone buttons placed down the front. Added to the design was a cummerbund that wrapped around a full skirt. This was perfect for me and I knew he would love it!

When he came home from school, I showed him this gorgeous fancy outfit. He asked, "Where did you get the money?"

I replied, "From my Dad!"

His curt retort was that, "You are my responsibility now and your father is not buying your clothing. Take it back."

The answer was, "No way and I am keeping it!" The grumpy response was that he will return it.

In those days, parcels were wrapped with fine tissue paper and placed in a nice box that was carried by a sturdy wooden handle. While preparing dinner, the item was tied around my waist by the apron strings. The heated discussion continued through the meal and I finally thought the matter was resolved.

Now, the box has been relocated to the den. Quickly, he snatched it and left for the return. I was left home crying! Two hours later he returned and asked, "Where is Orbach's anyway?"

    Needless to say, the dress was worn and the look was absolutely sensational. Everyone clearly stated how lovely it appeared on me. Sadly, this memorable garment was the last one Dad ever purchased for me.

NEGOTIATIONS UNDER THE GUN

As a working college student, a substantial portion of income was generated from being a performing musician who frequently entertained in catering houses, country clubs and restaurants. I was fully booked for several years into the future.

After completing a successful three-night weekend playing engagement at a prestigious, local night spot, I went to the business office to collect the wages earned by the combo. Hector, the owner of the establishment, was sitting behind a solid cherry desk in a high-backed, swivel, dark, leather chair. At the time, he was a middle aged, medium built, curly blonde headed man who displayed a sly, smooth, slick smile. While speaking in clipped, short sounds through glistening, white, sparkling teeth, he firmly said; "I am not going to pay you or the band".

He appeared serious. With the passing of time, the dialogue became more heated as frustration fermented in my gut! Many more anxious moments passed as the conversation and negotiations deteriorated. Finally, and very dramatically, he slowly opened the center top drawer from this massive desk and pulled out the longest pistol I had ever seen. This appeared to be the beginning of a very dramatic end to a shortened life and promising professional career!

The gun was pointed directly at my head and although words were not expressed, his position was clearly conveyed. There was a flash in my mind, as I looked down at the barrel. There was a choice of either facing him or answering to the boys in the band. As insane as it might have seemed, the conflict of wills continued for more than an hour.

Eventually, his other hand reached a file cabinet. It was entered and his fingers carefully turned the tumblers of a hidden safe compartment. Slowly and meticulously, he pulled out a large stack of neatly arranged large denomination dollar bills and peeled off enough money to satisfy our contract. With an immediate about face, my trembling body in a perspiration-soaked band tuxedo gingerly left the room. By that time, the musical equipment was loaded into our cars and a speedy, but silent departure followed.

Several years later and while serving as a principal in a Bergen County elementary school, a bus was driven into the parking lot for a dismissal pick-up. As the door opened, I immediately recognized the "gunslinger". The yellow vehicle was entered, a door slammed shut and the former –now- elderly bistro owner was raised by the jacket lapels until his head hit the roof.

As his glistening, white, full head of hair lifted; I asked if he was the famous supper club proprietor, Hector. He said, "Yes". As he was gently returned to the driver seat, the tale was retold; we both enjoyed a hearty laugh as memory lane was revisited. He then stated with that same sharp smirk, on his laughing, cragged, and mature face, "I was the toughest person he had ever encountered!" The secret was kept and his new career continued as he remained on the job to safely transport our pupils for several seasons.

GOTCHA

Over the years, I have provided free entertainment for various charitable organizations. The range of audiences extended from young children to golden ages. Events were presented in clubs, convalescent homes, hospitals, meeting halls, parks, religious places of worship and schools. Affairs were scheduled throughout the year; however, they seemed to concentrate mostly around holiday celebrations. On several occasions, I brought our son along with the purpose of helping him develop an understanding for the less fortunate members of society.

On a warm summer evening, I volunteered to supply a solo performance for a dance in the psychiatric wing of the local hospital. After parking the car, I carried the instrument, amplifier and microphone to the building. An elevator was taken to the proper floor and directions to the ward were provided at the nursing station.

Numerous unsuccessful attempts were made to enter one of the several locked doors. Eventually, an access gate was found slightly ajar. It was carefully opened and the equipment was briskly carried across the threshold. Upon release, the check control mechanism immediately activated, energized and the thick, heavy, metal, entrance way smashed shut.

This sequence produced a specific sound of an electronic lock slamming into the safety deadbolt latching device. Instinctively, the strong knob was grabbed. It did not budge! A first instinct was that I was trapped, and my wife finally got me confined to a mental institution.

NEWBORN NBA PREDICTION

As the pediatrician presented our newborn son to us, he exclaimed, "He is going to be a tall basketball player. Just observe the size of his large feet!" The years passed quickly, and the future ball player's interest, height and talent grew. Finally, he was eligible to play on a recreational team in third grade. In preparation, we purchased a fine pair of expensive basketball sneakers that were to only be worn for indoor practice and games.

This pattern was established and endured throughout his entire playing career. In the gym, street shoes were exchanged for game wear in preparation for this athletic activity. During elementary school years, three pairs per season were incorporated into the annual family budget. While in high school and college, this costly expenditure was absorbed by the team.

The doctor's prediction was accurate and he excelled in the sport. The highlight of being a member of a team that participated in the championship game at the National Final Four Basketball Tournament will always be remembered. After graduating from Trenton State College, he invited us to the Hamilton YMCA to watch him play in a competitive adult league. To our amazement, he appeared on the court with tattered, torn, well-worn sneakers that were held together with gray duct tape. A deep concern for his possible injury accelerated as the contest progressed.

Fortunately, the game ended harm free. At dinner that evening, his response to the rat torn sneaker issue was that replacement is rather pricey and these basketball shoes have a few more game miles remaining. Needless to say, money exchanged hands for old time's sake and we returned home after participating in our last purchase involving a pair of shoes for him.

At this time, he is the proud and happy father of three beautiful children that are consumed with athletic and dance activities. I would imagine his yearly shoe supply bill cost is equivalent to a substantial mortgage payment.

SWIMMING POOL CONSTRUCTION

After three years of discussion, the birth of our second child and several visits from the Buster Crabb Pool & Spa Company representative, we finally made arrangements to have an in-ground pool constructed during the Easter vacation of 1970. The first task was to install a 500-watt quartz light on the third-floor roof soffit to enable immediate spring, nighttime, construction and future summer evening bathing.

To our surprise on Good Friday morning, the lawn was covered with several inches of snow that had to be hand shoveled and carted away before the rented, sod, cutting machine could be utilized. Once the white, winter blanket was removed, strips of thick dormant grass and soil were picked up and stored on a lower level of the property. These heavy, wet, turf. sections were 3" thick, 16" wide and 4' long.

The place in which a 16'x32' pool was to be positioned consisted of three terraces of land that ran the full length of the backyard. A 3½' high reinforced railroad tie wall, 30' from the house, supported the lawn and pool on the first level. The next 10' drop of elevation was supported by a combination of two additional and separate rock walls. These formed the lower double levels which were used for flower and vegetable gardens.

Once the 16,500 gallons of water filled the aqua, colored, pool lining; real work began. This project could not have been completed without the dedicated assistance, hard work and advice of Dad who was at my side throughout the entire ordeal. The sequence of tasks was as follows:

1. Install a temporary snow fence for safety.

2. Lay down 4'x8' pieces of outdoor plywood to serve as temporary sidewalks for the shallow and the diving board ends. Later these sheets would be used to construct a cabana under the elevated cantilevered kitchen on the second floor.

3. Return the sod to create a mature lawn which covers the construction site.

4. Build a 12'x48' redwood deck to provide a picnic and lounging area next to the water's edge.

5. Bury two 4" PVC tubes as a conduit for drainage, to protect water, gas and electrical lines.

6 The second pipe contained surface bell drains to remove rain or splashed swimming water.

7. Put in a 6' tall cedar stockade fence with a gate at the filter end.

8. Complete the 6' wooden fence at the very narrow sidewalk portion of the deep pool end of the site.

9. Install a 6' stockade fence along the outer edge of the redwood deck.

10. Set up a 6' chain-link fence and gate at the shallow end for access to the finished basement.

11. Run underground telephone wire to the side of a large oak tree that was at the center portion of the deck.

12. Stain all wood surfaces with preservative.

These jobs were completed to begin and enjoy daily swimming on Memorial Day. Within a few weeks, a ridge in the bottom, sloped, transition, region of the pool between the deep and shallow portions of the liner appeared. The pool engineer from the spa company determined this problem was caused by runoff water from the street side slope that found a path under the liner.

This action, hypothetically, eroded the sand base at this location. He recommended that I dig a 6' deep trench the width of a shovel from the basement wall to the property line which was about 25' in length. The excavation was then filled in layers. At the base was 5" of gravel; next was 4" porous drainage pipe which was covered with straw. On top of this was more quarry stone and then covered with 5' of concrete. At the terminal end was a 16" diameter, vertical sewer cement pipe placed in a plastic bucket which extended from the top grass surface to the bottom of the hole. This was designed to collect the runoff underground water. Several weeks later and after all this hard work no water was collected. Finally, the pool company agreed to lift the liner and refloat the sand.

A lot of work for nothing!!

The Franchino Cabana and Swim Club opened to a double set of two glass patio doors that enabled easy access to a finished basement, recreation room, potential 4th bedroom and 2nd kitchen. These placements provided a comfortable situation for walking to and between the house, pool and deck. Propagated Taxus Yew cuttings from the front shrub beds were planted in front of the shallow end of the pool fence and along the side yard wooden privacy fence. By the end of the next season, cement sidewalk decks were set, the cabana, with its curved circular roof, was built and the yard layout presented a pleasant setting that seemed to have been there forever.

In 1976 we decided to construct a 12'x 28' addition to our growing home. This extension created a large dining room and a soundproof office. This project included a set of double French Doors which opened onto a large, elevated, shaded, deck for picnicking away from the splashing children. This post card picture was completed by the natural mature foliage provided by the seven maple trees that were planted by Dad and me several years earlier.

SILHOUETTES ON THE WINDSHIELD

I was a principal of an elementary school in a district that had three buildings located on a 200-acre rural site. This educational park setting enabled the administrators several opportunities to share staff members and facilities. Due to this configuration, pupils advanced through a sequence and trio of separate buildings. The primary school, of which I was the principal, presented an ideal setting for an eighth-grade outdoor graduation.

The programs leading to a memorable commencement day were well shared, always carefully planned, coordinated and superbly implemented. Concerns about adverse weather conditions were always resolved. In the end, it was a pleasure to watch the last youngster complete the recessional march and bring the delightful ceremony to a very successful closure. After the informal congratulations and conversations were concluded, children, parents and friends left the complex to continue private celebrations at their individual parties.

Traditionally, the two administrators and their wives convened at a local lounge to dine, drink and relax. This arrangement provided a wonderful opportunity to celebrate the completion of another positive and productive educational year. The cocktail of choice, on this warm summer evening, was gin and tonic. After a few hours of eating, unwinding and enjoying several refreshing alcoholic beverages, we left the restaurant and headed for home.

On the road and halfway to our friends' destination, there were a series of strange sounds originating from the rear seats. This was followed by a fine, warm, spray of interesting partially digestive fluids that passed through tightly clasped fingers which were used to cover a mouth that seemed to be in the final full stage of a volcanic eruption. The high-speed shower spewed through the clenched hands which were used to block or filter the materials as they passed towards, into and through Nancy's high styled, well lacquered, Queen Victoria, coiffure hair style. The cascade stopped at the windshield and produced a profile silhouette which accurately resembled my speechless, stunned, shocked, spouse.

After temporarily recovering, we continued on to their home. On the way to our final Beech Street destination, beaming headlights from traffic behind us illuminated the front window and put on view two clearly crafted images of the driver and a perturbed passenger.

Finally, at home, Nancy, who received the brunt of the stomach blast, struggled to remove the partially liquefied solids from her tightly plastered head. I cleaned up, changed clothing and proceeded removing the embossed dual portraits which were clearly recognizable in the front stained-glass windshield.

Early the next morning our dear embarrassed friends telephoned to apologize and make arrangements to restore the car. They were informed that the job was done, all is forgiven and... we owe them one! Many years have passed since this incident and we still remain very close friends and traveling companions.

BICYCLE BOARDWALK BATHING BABY

Rolling Ridge Estates is a suburban Bergen County neighborhood located in the residential community of Washington Township, New Jersey. During the planning stage, local citizens decided to maintain a rural setting by eliminating sidewalks and the future potential creation of commercial or industrial zoning. Over time, property owners continued to enjoy the positive aspects of these regulations. In addition to homes being constructed in this wooded gently sloping area, they benefited from very little automobile traffic. Walkers, skaters and bicyclers enjoyed their street activities in this refreshing country setting.

As our young family grew, we decided to install an in-ground swimming pool and surround it with redwood decking. At the same time, our three-year daughter began to ride her red and white tricycle. She did not, however, have the strength or endurance to cope with the hilly topography. The long, flat, rectangular, boardwalk around the pool seemed to be a solution to her riding.

The recreational wooden bicycle track functioned very well as Rene's skills and confidence expanded with each lap. Then on one hot summer August afternoon, Gram and Mom were sitting on our lounge chairs chatting life-guarding and rocking our baby son in his black, shiny, patent leather, pram carriage. In the meantime, I was dressed in painting coveralls, heavy work shoes and focused on staining the six-foot pool fence. The three-year-old cyclist was practicing racing talents and concentrating on circling the pool.

Suddenly, there was a large splash followed by a screeching, shout which swiftly shattered the serene, still, summer scene. Although the Mom's screaming sounds were indistinguishable that second, the situation was immediately processed. The saturated 4" paint brush was thrown to the protective drop cloth and a flying Olympic record, shattering, dive across the diagonal pool length occurred.

While submerged at the end of this noteworthy gigantic leap, I saw a toddler in a green and white polka dot two-piece bathing suit peddling her underwater bike and reaching for the coping at the pool's edge. Within an instant, the bike and tike were lifted by me and she was gently placed into the shaking arms of a shocked mother!

After all, settled down, Mom put the bike away and returned the baby bikini bicycle rider to the refreshing water! Eventually, all things returned to normal and the fence was painted to completion. The pool was now and forever- more limited to only swimming activities

. Interestingly and many years later, our daughter's family built a new home and also installed an in-ground pool. However, their neighborhood was on flat land and came with sidewalks. Their children have grown to learn about proper bicycle, sidewalk and swimming protocols.

"MEASLE" PAINTING

During my career as an elementary school principal, I was fortunate to work with an experienced veteran staff of outstanding professionals. Located in a corridor opposite the administrative center were the kindergarten classrooms. Within a few steps of the central office was a teaching station for the department head of that grade level. She enjoyed years of highly successful experience and was well recognized by the community as a master teacher who was able to manage the many educational concerns that were associated with guiding children through the developmental process.

On a bright, sunny, fall morning, the school secretary flung open the door and stormed to my desk while stating there was an intolerable situation in Miss. Borneman's classroom. Realizing this was a very rare circumstance, all official matters stopped and the problem was addressed. The teacher was obviously and visibly distressed as she explained that the child was painting a multitude of various colored spots all over the designated learning center.

Being a rather verbal young man, he described in detail what had occurred to upset his instructor. In clear unemotional language, the blooming Picasso claimed that directions were carefully being followed and he was enjoying the "measles" painting activity. Obviously, he had heard "measle" rather than easel and therefore, proceeded accordingly.

In order to prevent hysterical laughter from escaping in the administrative response, my lip had to be bitten as the very serious conversation continued. Rapport was restored between the child and the teacher as the story was retold by the junior artist. Shared glimmers and masked smiles were exchanged between the grown-ups involved in the dialogue and an important lesson was learned by all. Obviously, and at that moment, the three of us were students with different levels of understanding.

SIMPY

Shortly after the birth of our son, a fantasy friend began to frequent our home. During a relaxing autumn afternoon, a favorite easy chair was chosen by the youngsters for their daily reading ritual. As the story started, shouting began. Rene` hollered. "Don't sit on Simpy!" We immediately moved over to make more space, allowing this invisible girl to be comfortable and, also, enjoy the story session.

One day, as our family took its weekly visit to the children's grandparents, our automobile passed the back of a house with a tall brown wooden fence. We were asked to slow down and wave to Simpy. Now and finally, her address was identified. This standard hand gesture tradition grew and eventually expanded to include a pair of two additional companions.

The new friends were Mr. Sover and Mr. Scisser. As the tales were related to our grandchildren, over their growing period, these three imaginary people became an important part of our extended family, and they were often referred to as the "imaginary playmates' '.

During a recent winter season while in Florida, we met a real young girl named Simpy. Resulting from this interesting conversation, we sent a postcard to our daughter and signed it: Love, Simpy. Recalling this interesting past enabled us to resurrect the fine recollections of Simpy, Mr. Scisser and Mr. Sover that have continued to bring joy and warmth to our hearts. Along with a multitude of other exciting adventures and fond memories, the fun filled eons of travel and spending valuable time with various folks have enabled us to meet many new, fantastic, fictional and factual friends.

UNIQUE CHAMPIONSHIP PET

As our romance advanced from a dating level to the point when my toes wiggled at the sight of my lovely future spouse, conversations became more serious as plans for the long, exciting future developed. We both came from families in which a dog was a contributing household member, and decided, before marriage, that our home would be without living animals of any type. Eventually, we were blessed with two beautiful children who continuously asked for a furry friend. Their parents' position was firm and the answer remained, "No".

After years of pleading their case, I decided to honor the request and went to the tool box and spent hours constructing two homes for their new pets. The matching finished products had white sides with bright shining red roofs. The floors were covered with an inviting soft green artificial grass. When finished, they resembled highly crafted pieces of fine furniture. The local stream was then searched for two water washed river stones that were to be placed in the new sparkling miniature homes.

While less than overjoyed with the pet rock gifts, they were reluctantly received and placed in their rooms. Later that year, the youngsters were enrolled in the township summer camp and entered the pet contest. Both were highly honored and surprised with first prizes for having the two most unique entries.

MAGIC KEY

Our neighbors decided to take a winter week vacation in the Caribbean Islands. On the way to the airport, they did not recall turning off the burner under the teapot. They telephoned and asked me to check out the situation. I picked up the box of collected unlabeled keys and took a morning winter walk through the snow to their back door.

While struggling to peer into the kitchen window through the sun glare and reflection, it was determined that a small flame was still lit. Unfortunately, the glass storm door was locked and easy access now became difficult. The only solution was to remove the aluminum frame. Before this was attempted, the police were contacted to witness the break-in. Under the watchful eyes of the local patrolman, a Phillips head screwdriver skillfully removed the casing.

Fortunately, a key opened the lock and the four gas jets were definitely observed to be in the off position and everything was in a safe condition. After reinstalling the metal molding, the wooden main door was closed, locked and the officer left to resume his duties. The holiday bound family was contacted and given the all-clear message.

Shortly after returning home, Nancy suggested that an old towel be taken back to their kitchen and used to pick up wet snow and dry the floor. Since the magic key was now labeled, this was an easy assignment. Not the case! Several attempts to liberate the lock failed. The lucky stars aligned once, determined that this was a single shot deal and Mother Nature would have to take care of housekeeping.

A FAMILY FANTASY ABOUT SANTA

It was a week before the final holiday of the year was about to happily arrive! Excitement abounded throughout the community as decorations, serious shopping, gift wrapping and festive celebrations appeared in school, on television and at our home. The children were highly active participants in all the joy and merriment that surrounded the family during this exhilarating season.

While at a rare downtime period before bedtime, our daughter climbed on her mother's lap and sadly expressed to her, "There is no Santa!" With that, Mom instantly replied, "Do you think your father would buy all the presents that will be under the tree and spend all that money"?

After scratching her head, pondering the point for a long theatrical moment, she deliberated and processed the information, shook her head in an overly dramatic no emotion and slid slowly off Mom's lap. Alas, our little girl was satisfied.

WHY DO ALL MOMS HAVE THE SAME NAME?

At the time we raised our family, the world seemed to be safe for youngsters, it appeared bad people had rules and values that did not impact small children. While on a shopping spree at a neighborhood department store, our three-year-old young man separated from his mother. Before a state of panic set in; he ran up and down the aisles shouting, "Mommy, Mommy, Mommy".

He then yelled; "Nancy, Nancy, Nancy!" Within seconds they found and comforted one another. Mother anxiously asked, "Why did you call me by my first name"? He answered with a profound confident statement, "I shouted at Nancy because all mothers have the same name!"

TINY TOMATO TRADERS

We had installed an in-the-ground swimming pool shortly after the birth of our son. As a result, the children eventually graduated from their small, round, blue, plastic, wading, tub. Once retired from summer duty, the large container could be converted into a temporary indoor hot house for propagating plants.

The unfinished walk-out cellar was constructed with a six-foot sliding glass door that was positioned to allow perfect filtered sunlight to enter the basement. A combination of proper exposure, natural heat, and a large leak proof container of fertile soil, created an ideal environment to germinate new vegetation.

Both youngsters enjoyed the tasks associated with being youthful farmers as they watched the tiny green leaves pop through the well moistened loam. Over one hundred little bundles of potential food sprung to life. A decision was made by the Franchino in-house family committee to share their tomato treasure with interested neighbors.

After distributing the wealth, fifty-eight seedlings were left and another vote had to be taken. The discussion revolved around the crime of destroying the remaining sprouts and the ruling was reached to insert the rest into the backyard garden. Surprisingly, all matured to produce a bumper crop of ruby red, rich, robust, round, gorgeous fruit.

Grandma suggested we set up a sidewalk table under an umbrella and sell the produce to passing buyers. Because of the small volume of cars or walkers traveling by the front of our suburban home, the mini commission reconvened and decided to peddle the product in their little Radio Flier wagon.

Each day during the harvest period, the ripe riches were cautiously picked and carefully placed in paper lunch bags. When full, each package had a weight of over three pounds and was marked to sell for twenty-five cents. Early in the day, Mommy watched the two tomato traders walk down the street to market their fresh vine ripened magnificent merchandise.

They would return home with an empty cart, orders for the next day and pockets full of green cold cash. This was a fruitful experience that delivered abundant pleasure to the youthful planters and their proud parents. We were fortunate to live in an area that enjoyed protective, supportive, kind, generous friends who were excellent and reliable customers.

A FOOL'S JOKE

Shangri-La was a comfortable farm located in the Berkshire Mountains on 137 acres of overgrown pastures and thick forests. It was a weekend gathering place for family and friends that extended from Memorial Day until Thanksgiving. Sattler's New Jersey neighbor was invited to spend a few days at the Massachusetts retreat.

After Saturday morning breakfast, the young married men walked deep into the back field to set up targets for rifle practice. While assortments of items were properly and safely placed, the next-door Bergen County guest followed a few minutes later. The elderly gentleman found a nearby clump of thick trees and planned to rattle the bushes to frighten us with strange sounds of a wild ferocious animal.

Knowing what the situation was relative to the old timer's warped sense of humor as a practical joker, the potential victims quickly decided to turn the tables on the prankster. Collectively, the well-armed hunters responded with fake excitement and enthusiasm. The atmosphere was set. While a rapid harmless volley of quick shots was fired into the ground, a few small stones were tossed in the direction of the trickster.

Instant panic was displayed as the creative clown scampered from his scary hiding place waving his arms and shouting strange shrilling sounds. He now realized that the circumstances were turned and the fool was fair game in this very dangerous adventure.

A NEW TWIST ON TAXES

While deeply involved in the annual task of working on various forms necessary to complete the state and federal income tax reports, my young son, Rob, entered the room to observe several piles of papers stacked on the desk and Dad vigorously pounding on an old-fashioned manual adding machine.

In an attempt to assist, he eagerly asked in an excited inquisitive voice, "What are you doing?" Without breaking concentration, the frustrated reply was made by a tense amateur accountant, "I am preparing income taxes". Quickly sizing up the stressful situation, a very common-sense suggestion was provided by the young child, "Why not hire a TAXIDERMIST?"

LITTLE LAD BUYS LINGERIE FOR A LOVELY LADY

The mother of our children has continued to enjoy a stunning shape that always looked good. The backyard pool and cabana served as a lovely showplace for her delightful swimsuits. It was common for Dad to come home with a lovely, decorated package that contained an enchanting ensemble for warm water wear.

During one winter holiday shopping spree, Father and a very young son visited a fancy lady's lingerie lounge to buy a pretty present. While the clerk carefully wrapped the wonderful, well-designed, sheer set of a breathtaking, flimsy, fabric; the excited little lad exclaimed, "Isn't that a beautiful bathing suit for my Mom"?

In subtle shock, the sales girl said in a theatrically toned voice, "Bathing suit, bathing suit, bathing suit!" With that, she looked up and saw a gleaming glow in Father's eye. She smiled, finished decorating the gift box and said, "It is a stunning suit and have an elegant evening and a Merry Christmas!"

HIP SURGERY MADE SIMPLE

Our children were fortunate to have both sets of wonderful grandparents living near our home. A total of four wonderful senior citizen relatives resided within ten miles of our backyard and provided us with frequent opportunities for them to visit. As a result, the youngsters participated in many activities, ideas, conversations, discussions, and problem-solving situations. Within a short period of a few years, we were involved in making arrangements for five serious hip surgeries.

During a major family brainstorming session focused on planning all the detailed arrangements surrounding this series of important decisions, a small boy's voice in the background suggested, "Why not use a HYPNOTIST?"

LIQUID ORGANIC CLEANER

The time arrived when our three-story house required a fresh coat of paint. With the exception of a brisk wind, the spring weather conditions were excellent to prepare and apply the first prime coat. Because Nancy's dad was a traveling salesman who was out of town for several weeks at a time, her mother was a frequent welcome guest and happily involved in weekend visits. This was always a pleasure for us and her two small grandchildren.

While at the top of a forty-foot ladder, the telephone rang, and I was called into the house to take care of business. Finishing the conversation, I returned to the decorating job and felt a sudden change in the wind speed and pattern. The accelerated velocity toppled the ladder and dumped the full can of white paint all over the cement swimming pool apron at the shallow end. While the coping and water escaped damage, the deck was covered with an abundance of paint.

A call for help was sounded and all responded. Before entering the picture, Nancy carefully wrapped her freshly styled beauty parlor coiffure in a fine, green, silk, scarf for protection. She managed the garden hose and I soaked up the large swathe of diluted milky liquid. At the peak of action, the high-speed stream of hose water struck my free paint hat that fell to the lawn and then spun to be propelled into the sky!

This was a very frustrating moment and my vocal cords exploded with a volume of expletives that were completely out of character. Next, the dining room window opened and my mother-in-law softly suggested that L.O.C. be used to assist in cleaning the messy project. The vulgar verbal tirade continued and our favorite lovely lady quickly closed the glass frame to be sheltered from the vicious and nasty noise.

Fortunately, a magical miracle occurred and every morsel of thick smeared paint was removed. The free old hardware hat was replaced; the ladder was cleaned and put away for a more appropriate day.

CRUISE FROM HELL

After enjoying a delightful honeymoon of seven days in the Niagara Falls area, we returned home, and then prepared to board the cruise vessel, *Italia*. The next destination was sailing to Nassau for the second week. This first sea voyage exceeded all expectations and we had a wonderful excursion. At the time, Paradise Island was still in its undisturbed, natural, beautiful setting. The only way to the delightful isle sanctuary was via a small ship or tender.

Because of this great experience, we returned to the same scene two years later and were joined with parents, brother and sister-in-law. We traveled on the *Oceanic* and the marine vacation was once again just as enchanting. As a result of these two pleasurable adventures, we were committed to this fantastic mode of travel.

A next third trip was planned on the *Sea Venture* to Bermuda. Based on our past history and descriptions of accommodations, food, drink, entertainment, weather, blue ocean water and the Caribbean atmosphere, we convinced two friends to accompany us. The *bon voyage* fan-fare party set the stage as several acquaintances partied with us on the deck and in the ship cabins.

This happy gathering occurred on a warm, sunny February afternoon at a New York City pier. As the sun began to set, an announcement was made that departure would take place before nightfall and guests could continue their farewell send-off while waving from the dock. Once out of sight of the land, we returned to our stateroom to settle in and prepare for an early romantic magnificent dinner in the sumptuous restaurant section. Completing this fantastic meal, we moved to the bow nightclub to participate in the dancing activities.

As the beautiful ship approached Cape Hatteras, a strange movement was detected as we gracefully glided across the floor. Not realizing that this was a preview of coming attractions as weather conditions worsened with each passing minute, we decided to retire for the evening and rest for the next day's schedule.

During the night, the craft continued to rigorously rock and roll. A passenger in a suite near us was awakened from a deep, dark, slumber by the tumbling, turmoil. While asleep in the turbulence, his portable, plastic cooler fell off the coffee table, capsized and caused the melted ice cubes to escape from the toppled container. He stepped on the cold soggy carpet, panicked and concluded that we were sinking. At about the same time, a cabin neighbor who used the ceiling sprinkling system detection device to hang clothing was awakened to a chilly liquid spray spewing on the satin sheets. This shocking shower and the screeching, scary, sounds coming from the next state room created an imaginary panic situation.

The culmination of these actions and a pair of vivid imaginations was activated simultaneously. Both frigid, frightened passengers ran through corridors in pajamas warning that we were in danger of sinking. This episode occurred at the time when the film, *Poseidon Adventure,* was a popular movie. Now, the entire deck was awakened and it was interesting to observe the crew as they masterfully calmed the aroused and anxious, drowsy dreamers.

The *Sea Venture,* which eventually became the television *Love Boat* continued to have difficulty in the stormy sea. Next day, on the walk-through passageways, staff members secured velvet ropes in open foyers to provide temporary handrails. Then, white thick paper bags that were Velcro type cases stood fastened to the richly wooden paneled partitions. Banquet table side rails were positioned to catch dining and crystal ware before items crashed to the floor. Sections of large thick plywood sheets, which were cut into the shape of the large windows, remained carefully positioned as we watched the violent water cascade over the gigantic, glass curved, bow transom panes. Struggling, strange sounds were produced as the massive propeller blades rose from the swift, moving, swaying seas. The sustained storm situation continued to deteriorate as this small, shaky, steel ship slithered southward.

Once settled into port, following these few frightening days, body parts recuperated and returned to function normally. Passengers recovered, seemed to be in great shape and able to enjoy beautiful Bermuda. Mopeds were rented and detailed maps were used to explore the superb sights around the charming island. It appeared that everything was painted in pristine, pastel, rainbow colors on the day prior to our arrival. At noon, we visited a local spot for lunch and a few drinks.

On the main street and on the way back to the cruiser, a car pulled from a parking space in front of our moving, motorized bike. The brakes were applied with full strength and we, unfortunately, hurtled to the ground. Immediately, the accident scene was surrounded by shop owners and villagers who came out to render first aid care and support. Once assured that Nancy and I were safe, the search for my treasured camera began. Someone in the crowd shouted that it safely hung around my neck.

By this traumatic time, we had fully recovered from the horrendous bout with the ocean and a distressed digestive system. While sitting in a ship cocktail longue, the duty nurse, who had visited us on two separate occasions during the previous nights, came through the swinging doors. She appeared to be exhausted, extremely tattered and obviously disheveled. Still in a white uniform and before returning to her compartment, she sat at the bar for a quick refreshing cocktail. Since her medical efforts were greatly appreciated, I sat next to her and offered to buy the lady in wrinkles to grab a drink. She looked at me with bloodshot, bleary, bewildered eyes and a blank facial drained expression.

I thanked her for the several pills, sea sickness shots and attempted to generate casual conversation by saying, "Obviously, you don't recognize my face and maybe it would be helpful if my pants are pulled down". The lady did not find humor in this statement, picked up her refreshment, gave the witty prankster a dirty look and speedily exited the bar.

That evening we dressed formally for a dinner show at the local hotel. My distinctive band tuxedo and colorful pleated, ruffled, shirt made an exceptional appearance. Because patrons assumed the unique suit identified a *Maître d'hôtel*, I quickly took advantage of the stolen identity and began seating theater guests. Before long, the attending staff responded to the instructions to move tables near the front stage row. The command of the situation was convincing. Several couples appreciated their special placement, thanked the impersonator and provided a crisp hand that contained a generous gratuity. Realizing this was a short-term career, my party was assigned to a choice placement and we quietly sat down to enjoy the program.

After the performance, we returned to the ship and continued the party. By this time a colony of new friends joined us in the extended evening celebrations. An older lady proudly announced that she was an amateur astrologer. Once provided the date of birth, she was able to accurately present the person's family status, personality traits and lifestyle profile. She was amazing and when selected for the spotlight, Nancy and I were accurately described to a tee.

The next day, we were provided with a box lunch and rode to the beach to join friends. Once the site was selected on the soft, silky, coastline; the group settled in to relax and the food package was opened. To our startling surprise, all the meal components were carefully wrapped in separate containers and we had to construct individual sandwiches. The wind and fierce flying sand made this mission impossible. Sadly, the gourmet ingredients were discarded and we ate at a local restaurant.

At that time in 1974 and while in town, each passenger was permitted to bring a gallon of duty-free liquor home. We carefully selected the most expensive assortment of bottles and then had them properly wrapped in two separate straw shopping bags. They were separated from the luggage, cautiously hand carried and secured in our cabin for safe keeping. Our visit to the tropical retreat was delightful but much too short for the pain and suffering that was endured in order to arrive there.

On the first day of our return trip to New York City, the wallowing waters returned to bounce and bobble the boat as if it were a wild, wine cork set afloat in a whirling, washing, machine. Fortunately, the toilet was next to the sink and we took turns voiding from each orifice. Because of the violent traffic in the bathroom, the shower had to be used to handle the emergency overflow.

In desperation and in order to get a formal picture from the photographer, Nancy pleaded that I dress and meet her on the staircase for a professional portrait. Knowing that she was dressed in a stunning, sparkling, pink full-length gown, my attire had to match with the same colored, fancy, frilly, shirt to accompany the traditional tuxedo. The demarcation line between my elaborate stiff, starched collar and face was indistinguishable as both were the same sickening shade of matched pastel hues. Immediately after the picture taking session, I returned to my cubicle to continue the unpleasant task of eliminating sour liquids. It could be compared to a colonoscopy preparation without the necessary stimulation of medication.

While I fully recovered on the last evening, Nancy remained confined to quarters. I dressed and headed for the lounge. For some unknown reason, people thought that I was a doctor. An attractive lady was brought to my attention and asked if her shapely leg, that was injured in a moped mishap, could be examined. A low table was cleared and the well-formed thigh was placed on the flat surface. She tearfully explained that the misfortune occurred when her bicycle collided with a shell encrusted wall which was alongside the roadway. Using gentle fingers, strong palms and talented hands, the full length of this lovely, smooth, well-tanned long limb was studied, scrutinized, slowly caressed and inspected by the medical pretender.

This scene occurred with a growing full audience in an open public arena. The procedure was conducted over ten minutes and the appendage was tenderly returned to its resting place. In the meantime, the cooperative patient was told to rest and arrange an appointment with her family physician once she arrived home. Then, the boyfriend stepped forward and stated that he was in the same two wheeled accident. The response was that his evaluation would cost $50.00. All of a sudden, he stepped backward and my therapeutic consulting career came to a hasty halt.

The last morning of the trip was devoted to preparing for disembarking. Nancy remained devastated, very sick and completely exhausted. She definitely needed help in packing and dressing. After each article of clothing was put on her weary body, she collapsed on the bed and fell into a deep sleep. Eventually we struggled with the burden to go ashore. Somehow; I managed all the luggage, the straw liquor bags, and a limp, lethargic lady who labored with each footstep.

Unbelievably, the customs inspection agent decided to examine the suitcases that she sat on to support her spent, sinking, body. The scary, severely sick, condition was described to the government official. It was explained that my poor wife was very ill for the full week and in all probability, she could easily throw up all over the entire area and he would most likely be included in the volume of vomit. Wisely, he asked that we move on.

The carefully protected liquor containers developed an equipment malfunction, ruptured and deposited two gallons of valuable fluid on the porous pavement. Fortunately, the magnificent merchandise was purchased from a reputable company and we were, later, reimbursed for the damaged commodities.

We arrived home and the unloading began. The good wife was still suffering and went directly to bed. Upon checking the refrigerator, it was determined that it had broken down shortly after leaving for vacation. A serious sterilization and scouring process commenced and all items had to be discarded into double thick sealed plastic trash bags.

Once completed, I drove to Elmwood Park to pick up the two children. All this excitement occurred while mother struggled to regain her stability and health that was caused by a cruise from hell. This trip took place in February, 1974 and this disaster tainted our thinking about ocean travel for a long time. It was not until October 2010 that we mustered the courage to resume sailing excursions to distant ports. This next adventure was very positive and we planned several other sea voyages which were both a pleasure and very enjoyable.

SEW GET A JOB

Our children have been surrounded by a family that has experienced a long prosperous association with the fabric, sewing, clothing and interior decorating industries. Several close relatives have successfully earned prominent recognition in the international business world over the years.

So, when our teenage daughter expressed an interest in working at the local lady's dress shop, it was natural for her younger brother to suggest that she "applicate" for the job.

FROM GO CART TO SERVICE MANAGER AT LEXUS

My father was a mechanical genius who was educated by living life, hard work, gaining practical experience and attending the school of everyday competitive existence. He could repair anything If Mike couldn't fix it, then throw it away. Over a rewarding career his large nimble hands, smiling face and creative mind identified him as a professional, productive, master mechanic. As an example, we were the first family to have a gas powered, self-propelled lawn mower which was designed and constructed by him.

When this tool was retired from grass cutting service, the engine was modified and used to operate his grandson's vintage go-kart. My seven-year-old boy proudly drove the special vehicle throughout the rural neighborhood until a policeman's siren sounded. He immediately abandoned his minicar, ran into the house and hid under his bed.

The understanding officer appeared at the door, rang the bell and kindly explained the law and legal situation to our boy. The four wheeled motorized miniature road car was then transported to our remote New England farm where he had the opportunity to freely drive around on our several acres of private property.

This joy riding continued for several years until the barn was burglarized during the winter. The prized possession was stolen. His young teary eyes, broken heart and shaking quivering tender voice expressed, "Dad, I have a strange pain in my stomach that I can't explain".

Since we were the youngest parents in our neighborhood, Rene's and Rob's friends tended to be a few years older than our children. Some high school students drove automobiles, others had mopeds and some had motorcycles. Our son was buddies with the good bigger boys who were rather skilled in many mechanical activities. In this environment, he developed the knowledge techniques and patience necessary to diagnose complex repair challenges.

Assessing this situation and realizing that his parents did not want him to develop an affection for motorcycles, I presented him with a long-term plan which involved the purchase of a non-running dirt bike for a few dollars. The goal was to provide him a frustrating encounter to dissuade and discourage him from these activities as he approached adulthood. He accepted the proposal and spent several months and long struggling hours attempting to make the bike operational. Eventually, it ran in the backyard.

The true test occurred when it was driven on a rarely used high school field. While it functioned properly at home, it failed under real off- street conditions. This unsuccessful trial analysis test required a two-mile walk pushing his small motor bike back to the basement repair shop. Finally, the problems were solved and the bike operated perfectly. By this time, he had grown in stature and his two wheeled vehicle was too small to support his weight and frame.

Luckily, a Harley Davidson motorcycle was For Sale in the neighborhood. Knowing this full-size bike also had difficulty, he agreed to make an exchange. While the story was repeated for the second time, my goal to make him despise motorcycles was achieved. By the time he got the Harley to run properly, he was now a young man and eligible for a driver's license.

We purchased a used muscle car that ran flawlessly. With the skills inherited from his grandfather combined with firsthand practice and extensive research activities, he customized the car body and was able to install a super powerful new engine. He drove this automobile until college graduation and never received a traffic ticket.

As a technology major at Trenton State College, he obtained a fine part time job at a local Lexus automobile dealership. There he successfully designed, installed and maintained their computer system. Upon graduation, he earned a full-time position as a service repair writer at a very substantial salary.

WORRISOME WEEPING WILLOW TREE

Within a few years after settling in our new Washington Township home, a spa salesperson was invited to help us plan for an in-the-ground swimming pool. He made several suggestions for a complete layout which included: location, cabana, decking, fencing and landscaping. Eventually the outdoor entertainment center was installed with all the essential accessories.

In time an insignificant small weeping willow tree, which was just behind our rear property line, sprouted to become an ever-growing obstacle. Aside from being a beautiful source of shade, it produced an abundant volume of messy tiny dirty leaves which dropped throughout the entire summer. This compounded the chore of maintaining an inviting clean, clear, sparkling pool. Surface skimming became a full-time task.

This backyard neighbor had a young talented baseball pitcher with aspirations of becoming a major leaguer. While practicing daily with his son, he served as the catcher and also called balls and strikes. In a few seasons, this powerful developing competitor matured with astonishing speed and an assortment of sophisticated deliveries. Interestingly, the aging father was forced to keep pace with his promising athlete.

One day while attending a local picnic, the boy's father expressed a concern about the difficulty he was experiencing following the young right-armed speed merchant's blazing, curving white projectile as it swiftly rocketed from the sunny mound to the tree-shadowed home plate. My response was that I could easily solve his potentially dangerous problem and save him from serious injury. He asked, "How"?

Automatically a spacious smile formed on my face, "If your wife tells me to cut the tree down, I will gladly do it!" Within moments after he chatted with her, she came to me and requested the problem be removed. Making sure this statement was heard by several people; I put my plate down, excused myself and went to my basement. Equipped with a trusty, experienced, well-worn chainsaw and in front of a full audience, I heard, "Timber" as the thirty-foot willow safely fell to the ground. Done deal!

Returning home after the party Nancy asked, "Why didn't you wait for tomorrow"? Again, a broad grin was flaunted." They both had consumed several cocktails and I did not want to give them an opportunity to change their minds". Once the leaf manufacturing machine came down, I could leisurely cut, split, move and stack the new source of firewood. In this game, all players were winners.

MASS. MOUNTAIN MEN ON ELECTION DAY RALLY

Throughout the years, family and friends gathered at Shangri-La in Tolland, Mass. to share and celebrate good times. Participants' ages ranged from infants to very senior spry, golden citizens. Generally, men's daylight hours were consumed with farm chores that included: fetching water from the outside Jack and Jill type well, general repairs, grass cutting, maintaining the fires, and preparing future firewood. At the same time, ladies took care of household duties and prepared sumptuous meals. Breakfast was outstanding, lunch was hardy and supper was always memorable.

During the day, Gramp made sure the shots and beers, which were served in proper drinking glasses, flowed continuously. Considering there was no running water and lighting was supplied by antique, fragile, kerosene lamps; we worked, played and cooperated in a safe, comfortable, close setting of beautiful harmony.

After dinner and clean-up, the sundown schedule was reserved for merriment and partying. Essentially, the festivity folks, country relatives and acquaintances were a collection of amateur musicians who played an assortment of homemade gadgets. Some inexpensive, hand-crafted contraptions included: paired spoons, a washboard and a galvanized, steel wash tub with a single rawhide bass string that was fastened to a long narrow board. Drum sticks were engaged to bang on assorted dented pots or pans, metal lids and cow bells.

Original rhythms were drummed using all parts of a wooden chair. Store bought instruments were an accordion, harmonica, maracas, trumpet and ukulele. This loud conglomeration provided the background for card players who joined in the singing. Between the hilarious vocalists and the hodgepodge of musicians, very original tunes emerged! The self-entertaining ensemble performed, laughed and rocked into the very late evening. Children, too young to participate, snuggled in sleeping bags and provided the arcade that enjoyed the actions, silly sights and sounds of the grown-ups. Eventually their tender eyes became too heavy for the racket and they fell asleep.

With the passing of time, the home spun band became proficient and their library of "oldies but goodies" improved to become more interesting. A regular visitor to the weekend parties had political aspirations and was eventually nominated to run for mayor in the city of Holyoke. During the campaign, he scheduled a rally at Mt. Tom Amusement Park in Massachusetts and vigorously encouraged the farm group to provide entertainment for this gathering. The troupe accepted the invitation and was advertised as The Mass. Mountain Men.

While I had club date bookings on Friday and Saturday, That Sunday was open and reserved for this special occasion. However, it was a long, tedious drive on the morning of that extraordinary show. Traffic was heavy, and I was tired. As the starting time grew near and because of the travel delay, my fun-loving friends became increasingly nervous and highly apprehensive.

While they were the stage stars, I was the only member with cultivated professional talent. I arrived fifteen minutes before showtime. They eagerly helped me unload the equipment and set up. The grandstands were filled to capacity and their surge of pre-performance jitters settled as my sophisticated electronic machine was combined with ten trained fingers and put into action. My job was to accompany the way off- Broadway colleagues. Fortunately, it was the right music for the right voters and, ultimately, the right time to elect the right person. My contemporaries basked in the limelight and took full credit for a fine performance. I was delighted to share in their extended moment of glory as I sauntered to the curtain wings to observe their celebrity reception and witness the abundant audience applause. This was their day to shine, and I was delighted to be a part of this shared experience. Also, the winning candidate continued to successfully serve as mayor for several terms.

WHEN I GROW UP, I AM GOING TO BE A DENTIST

Many parents devote years to conversation with their children as they discuss: career plans, job opportunities and future college study considerations. Over time, our dialogue involved several topics which included the standard occupational choices for consideration. Teachers, policemen, astronauts, rock stars, and sports players were frequently on the potential selection list.

After an annual dental check-up visit, our son stated what he wanted to be when he grew up. "I want to be a dentist because they are rich." The youngster's explanation was, "Dentists get a lot of money for collecting the teeth they pull. At night, they are placed under the pillow and the Tooth Fairy replaces them with money".

BEECH STREET ADDITION

In time, the number of relatives, friends and playmates from a growing family challenged the available space of our original dream home. While the den, kitchen and living room were large enough to accommodate our needs, the dining room was much too cramped or tight to satisfy holiday meal sitting requirements.

Nancy and her mother began searching for a larger place to live. Once the children became involved in the conversation, sides were polarized. The youngsters did not want to relocate and change schools. An obvious solution to the facilities dilemma was to build an addition to include a banquet size dining room, a deck overlooking the swimming pool, a sound proof office to practice my accordion and a storage basement plus an increased attic area.

At the end of the street, a neighbor with the same model had just completed a renovation. Their design seemed to be able to satisfy our desires. The outdoor structure had an attractive aesthetic appearance and blended nicely with the original home. We visited them, enjoyed a guided tour and asked permission to incorporate their design in our project. Eventually, plans were drawn up by me, and the bidding process began. Early proposals were accepted and the anticipated costs were beyond our budget.

A friend's general contractor was invited to our home to discuss the blueprints. During an extensive conversation and inspection to prepare an estimate, he observed the work that I had completed and realized that it was of a professional level of quality. Before a quote was presented, he suggested that I become a subcontractor with responsibilities for the following jobs:

1. Tear down gable wall
2. Build deck from dining room
3. Hire on as a laborer
4. Plaster outside basement walls for waterproofing
5. Tar plastered walls for additional waterproofing

6. Mount heating duct work

7. Install electrical work

8. Break portion of foundation cinder block wall to create a doorway between the new and old cellar

9. Hand backfill excavation site

10. Install roofing

11. Landscape and restore grounds

12. Apply outdoor cedar shakes

13. Paint all interior and exterior surfaces

14. Before the project began in early June 1976, a variance was approved, and construction permits were obtained.

On the day on which the groundbreaking occurred, the first problem was unearthed. The excavator, digging the basement hole, exposed a boulder which was the size of a Volkswagen Beetle. He left the obstacle in the center of the future basement and vacated the job. Several suggestions emerged which include hiring a blaster. While his language was shaky and unclear, I comprehended his outlandish price and statements of no damage coverage responsibilities caused by the dynamite blast.

Everything was on me! During this agonizing problem-solving process, Nancy searched the Yellow Pages. In the telephone book, she found a backhoe operator with the equipment to do the job. His machine had a long arm that was used to dig a hole in front of the gigantic stone. Within a few moments, the obstruction was quickly buried beneath the future cement cellar floor.

Once the foundation was completed and on an early Sunday morning, Dad and I began backfilling with a pick and shovel. Luckily, on the way home from church a friend stopped to chit chat. He had just obtained a used backhoe and offered to change clothes and return to practice developing skills in my front yard. Within a few moments and a minimum of muscle, the big job was finished. The rest of the day involved hand raking to prepare the ground for landscaping.

By Labor Day; furniture was arranged, a two-tier crystal chandelier with fifteen candles was installed and we were ready to enjoy our first large family dinner party in the new dining room. There was more than enough space for all to comfortably sit around a sixteen-foot-long table. Presently, the extravagant gift of a magnificent formal, lavish, ceiling candelabra that was provided by our parents was moved and displayed as a focal point in our Four Seasons home.

ROMANTIC BOB WHO

We were in the process of finishing the basement which was an extensive, interesting project. Some of the challenges included the removal of a major house support column and installing a full bathroom which was to be positioned on the opposite side of an unfinished cellar. Placing the lavatory in that desired location, twenty feet away from the sewer connection, demanded the use of an industrial sized air compressor and a jack-hammer. The messy, dusty work took place in an enclosed area and on a hot, humid, summer day. It was a two-man job which required one person to operate the 135-pound hammer and the other to shovel the broken concrete from the future waste pipe trench.

The air sledge was maneuvered by Nancy, who wore cut-off jeans, tank top, double hair pigtails and diamond earrings. Bob was attired in plain old working clothing, and he removed the broken debris. This toiling, energy intense, grueling, labor of love consumed several nonstop hours. As late afternoon approached, both were grimy and soaked with salty sweat.

Before evening, a florist truck parked in the driveway and a person walked to the door and rang the bell. The lovely lady of the house, in her fully tattered grungy perspiration-soaked outfit went to the entrance. To her surprise, a delivery man presented her with a long slim box which was wrapped with a wide pink bow. At the same instant, her male co-worker appeared around the corner of the construction site and listened to an interesting conversation.

The slim white package was opened with dirt, stained, soiled hands and a bouquet of long-stemmed red roses was separated from the green waxy paper. The same filthy fingers nervously pried open the gift envelope to read the enclosed card. On the formal parchment was written, "All my love, Bob" Knowing the tight financial situation at that moment, she exclaimed, "Bob who?"

Thank you, Nancy, for a job well done!

ROMANTIC SATIN SHEETS

A house addition of 500 square feet was constructed in 1976 and incorporated a large expanded dining room and a comfortable office. The new portion was erected along the full side of the dwelling and featured a two-foot extension which was beyond the original front structure. This component created an attractive exterior architectural break. This room aligned with the front entrance foyer at the opposite side of the residence.

The workplace included a large bay window which overlooked the street side of the building and provided a view of our daughter's beautiful pink magnolia tree which was located on the lawn. A desk was placed in a position to see and enjoy this lovely scene as the seasons changed.

This sanctuary was designed to be soundproof and fabricated with heavy insulation and thick carpeting on the walls and floor. This, set-up at the remote end of the home, enabled me to do school work and practice the accordion without disturbing family members.

At the rear of this study was a fireplace which was decorated with a mantle constructed with wide pine boards that were two hundred years old. The antique inner facade sides were edged with marble and trimmed with eye-catching, colonial, moldings. A pair of matching leather Queen Ann chairs, on the gable wall, centered on a drop leaf folded table. The opposite interior partition backed the living room and was furnished with a love seat that transformed into a single twin bed. A small end table and lamp completed this arrangement.

A ceramic tile floor hearth was installed to align with the top of a shag rug. Above the fireplace was an oil painting winter scene of our snow-covered Berkshire Mountain Shangri-la farm house. The remaining walls were decorated with personal memorabilia that was collected during my professional career. An entry pocket door opened from the dining room into the study. Book cases, file drawers and storage cabinets completed the project.

To celebrate the baptism of the special place, a neighbor gave us a set of dark, navy blue, satin, sheets for the convertible bed. On the first snowfall, we decided to share a romantic evening. Once the logs began to take on a red, orange, yellow and lavender color cast, the room became toasty warm. Bed coverings were turned down and we snuggled in for the night.

Needless to say, the tight sleeping quarters and the slippery, silk bed coverings did not create a situation for much creative movement. More energy was consumed in remaining in the small sofa bed than enjoying the adventures associated with this potentially passionate interlude.

CAMPING AT FORT WILDERNESS

Using the offers of kindness, generosity and great gear borrowed from family and friends, we were able to use a large cargo van and portable sleeping unit that converted into a comfortable sitting area. This combination created an efficient temporary traveling recreational vehicle that was easy to drive and park. Advanced reservations were made in Disney World, Fort Wilderness, Florida for the February school vacation.

Before packing for the southern sunshine, adventure; the vehicle windows were decorated with sliding homemade privacy curtains. We left immediately after dismissal on a frigid Friday afternoon. It was extremely cold until we traveled deep into Georgia. Frozen ice crystals lined the inner walls of the light truck. This situation, mixed with a two-day collection of snow on the road, made driving very interesting.

Fortunately, we rested at night in motels and the room heater warmed us up while traveling the interstate highways. At the final destination, Nancy and the children slept in the conversion bed and I relaxed in a portable hammock placed on a strong movable steel pipe stand. There was sufficient space for the four of us to snooze at the day's end.

Our compact four wheeled temporary home was located in a small lot that was surrounded by very large sophisticated and luxurious camping vehicles. These had numerous tires and several interesting pull-out living sections. The sides also had movable attached shade canopies for outdoor entertainment.

By comparison, we were paupers and midgets in a neighborhood of enormous expensive, exclusive and elite equipment. Interestingly however, while they spent many hours involved in household chores and cooking, we were the first to arrive at the Magic Kingdom in the morning. This four-some also dined at many of the fine Disney restaurants throughout the vacation.

Our group played in the park for most of the day and returned to the campgrounds for the well-planned youngsters' evening activities. Rob, who was seven years of age, and I took on all challengers at the outdoor basketball court and we remained undefeated for the week. Years later, our grown children still claim that this was their best vacation ever!

FARCE IN THE FOREST

Nestled on a winding dirt road in the Berkshire Mountains is the location of our picturesque country farm. Situated across the road are more than 10,000 acres of rolling hills and sprawling woodlands. This is all a part of the state forest. Our children have spent several weekends, summer vacations, family reunions and the Thanksgiving Holidays at this beautiful retreat. Frequently, the youngsters and I would leisurely meander through the timberland and enjoy the beautiful scenery and abundant fresh air.

In the dense foliated area, we would find an old dead tree that was about to topple in the next small wind storm. Dad would then flex his muscles, go through the entire Olympic Team warm up routine and bear hug the lifeless sapling. At the end of these dramatic gyrations, the tree would be pulled from the ground complete with decayed roots and a small ball of soil.

The kids thought their Pop was a real Super Hero who should be on television or in the news. Regardless of how many times they observed this spectacular feat of strength, they continued to be amazed. Of course, they eventually did grow up to realize the facts related to this father's farce in the forest.

THE IMPACT OF A SINGLE PHOTO

A single photograph of our son playing basketball, while in the third grade, has had a profound influence on me and its impact has continued throughout an entire lifetime. The lone image taken by a team mate's mother, several years ago, remains vividly embossed in my memory. Our child's facial expression, uniform color and posture taken in preparation for shooting a free throw from the foul line is as clear in my mind as the day on which the scene was captured.

While viewing the poignant film, I vividly remembered immediately experiencing excitement and a warm sensation that surged through my energized emotional system. This picture keepsake continues to be placed in a lofty position in my assorted collection of personal mental treasures.

Shortly thereafter, it was realized that a camera in my hand would provide opportunities to extend this marvelous gift to my acquaintances as we, together, traveled along life's spectacular corridor. Over the years, snap shots preserved major family milestones, athletic events, vacation visits and historical occasions.

Thousands of photos were supplied and, hopefully, through this medium exchange, a significant nostalgia was preserved for all to enjoy. Over the passage of time, people frequently reminded me of the joy associated with the pictures they accumulated through my efforts. Their expressions of genuine gratitude, appreciation and thanks have continued to be my reward over time.

FADING FAST FEET TO FLASHING PHOTOS

My active competitive basketball years ended when I realized my hands became faster than my long legs and arms. There was a pair of my pointy elbows which became lethal weapons that were successfully implemented over my playing career.

Renewed efforts were directed at our son's recreational sports for the next few seasons. Coaching and managing satisfied the need to be in the action as an active participant. However, this avenue of involvement ended when he made the middle school team which was run by a member of the teaching staff.

My family made a very wise decision to give me a professional camera set which included most of the essential equipment to do the necessary job. My new focus required concentration, eye hand coordination, physical conditioning and knowledge of the game.

There was no time for the Funtographer to become verbally or critically consumed in the competition that took place before his very active fast lens. Taking contest pictures, processing, sorting for delivery and passing them on became a passion that I continue to enjoy. Magic occurs when the recipient views the photographs, smiles and says thanks. Sometimes expressions of gratitude include a hug and a kiss on the cheek. WOW!

STAY AND STAB

Throughout elementary school, our children were charged with the responsibility to do well in school and complete all study assignments accurately and on time. Their afternoon schedule was full of play, athletic and recreational activities. Homework tended to be scheduled around the dinner period so that it could be casually supervised around the kitchen table.

At the day's end, our son, Rob, and I would retire to the bedroom to relax, talk and watch TV. Generally, we viewed a sporting event and discussed game rules, strategies which included professional, specialized, techniques or skills.

Commercial long breaks were filled with one of two contests. We played stay or stab. The goal of the first competition was for the little boy to remain on the bed during the entire advertising segment of the program. Dad's objective was to gently remove him from the wrestling platform before the sporting event continued. The mini struggle lasted during the full break period. Just before the show continued, the child found himself gently deposited on the floor. As the years passed, our son became much stronger, however, he inevitably ended up on the carpet.

The second pastime was played in the same padded arena with a rubber hunting knife. We alternated turns holding the toy weapon. The purpose of this match was for the person lacking possession of the knife to ask for sympathy before the dagger was used to stab and cause a lethal fake wound.

Many times, Dad would hide the soft plastic blade under a pillow and use a finger to duplicate the point as it touched the youthful victim's tender back. He had difficulty realizing that Pop was so skillful in quickly maneuvering the replica dagger that it required him to yell, "Mercy, mercy, mercy". During several battle moments, he never saw the swift scalpel.

Weekly lady Mah Jong players in the kitchen, asked Nancy about the loud racket coming from the second-floor bedroom or arena. Once the careful, creative, ventures were explained to the girlfriends; they were comforted with the knowledge that this was an original, innovative, fun activity between a father and son.

Let the games continue and they did for several years.

SNIPE HUNT

One of the most memorable rites of passage for children occurred at Shangri-La, which is our summer home and farm in Tolland, Mass. The event is a beautiful memory that is permanently etched in the minds and imaginations of the young relatives who are now parents in their own families. Over the years the little boys and girls were entertained by the adventure stories associated with snipe hunting.

They were told numerous frightening yarns about the vital precautions and procedures that had to be used to trap this legendary bird. Pictures appearing in reference books, descriptive information in resource materials were provided for them to study. The documented literature was used for them to learn about the dangers associated with capturing this famous fowl. After many seasons of hearing about these encounters, the youth were properly informed, motivated and prepared to participate in the special pursuit.

Necessary safety measures were carefully presented and reinforced. The junior hunters knew the prey was fast, dangerous, and were described to cluster on the ground to hide in bushes and tall grasses. Since the aggressive flock was skilled in attacking the whites of tender eyes at night, they were specifically warned to keep them tightly closed to protect against damaging pecking.

While assembling for the expedition, silence was essential and the stalking strategy involved precise planning, a very high degree of organization and specialized assignments. The grown-ups remained at the outer fringe to chaperone. Chasers formed the next inner circle and made noise to move the winged creatures to the center. Baggers, at the middle of the group, were equipped with large empty grocery bags and instructed to hold the brown paper traps open at maximum width and in contact with the dirt.

The trackers were primed to carry out their specialized assignments and anxiously awaited the directive to begin the encounter. On this pitch-dark fall moonless night, stars were obviously absent from the crisp, cloudy, covered, black sky. The painstakingly orchestrated mission was set to unfold. All the players were properly tuned-in and precisely positioned.

At the optimum moment, a signal was given, and the well-coordinated team sprang into action. The adults shouted superficial auxiliary directions and insisted that all lids remain tightly shut. Chasers made a variety of original shrieking sounds as they tightened the human oval cage. Baggers were ready and were warned to snap the sack quickly and firmly to avoid escape and a potential lethal counterattack from the sharp beaked frightened captured victims.

The evening was filled with a wholesome assortment of sounds and motions while the entertainment became more involved and intense. As the past hunters moved about, the crashing of body limbs and collisions with wild natural field vegetation elevated the excitement and intensified imaginary fear factors.

Supervising parents on the outer fringe of the area enjoyed tapping the safari staff with long twigs to augment the anticipation and anxiety components to higher levels. At the end, our birds escaped because the youthful energy could not contain the feathered game that was temporarily captured in the hand-held containers.

Memories of this single successful escapade involving small explorers remain the topic of conversation as these, now, parents are mature tale tellers who happily relate these sensational stories to their own youngsters. It continues to bring smiles to the seasoned generations as the stunning legend continues passing to the next sets of impressive ears.

SPECIAL SALES SPEECH

A lifetime love of fishing was introduced to our little son by his grandfather and relatives. Many days after returning from school, the young angler would put his books away, eat a snack, pick up his pole and run down to a neighborhood pond. There, he would carefully bait the tiny hook, cast and practice his developing skills.

At an appropriate age, his uncle invited him to enjoy a complete day on a chartered deep-sea party fishing boat. This, eventually, became a weekly and costly activity. Therefore, and as time passed, he was charged with the responsibility of earning the funds to support these expensive excursions. He was a resourceful youthful entrepreneur who became involved in several business ventures. Included were: snow shoveling, lawn care, leaf raking and curbing.

Painting address numbers on curbstones involved a front door promotional pitch, an agreement which was then followed by producing the finished product. Before the fee was collected, approximately ten minutes had elapsed to complete the task. He instantly was engaged in a profitable enterprise that easily supported weekly, seashore summer trips. When visiting family or friends, he would inevitably take the curbing bucket with him and travel from home to home to practice a rather profitable trade.

One day, however, his good fortune dramatically changed, and his confidence quickly ebbed. In a strange new neighborhood, he experienced a consecutive string of refusals. Nervous anxiety accelerated as he prepared to greet the next potential consumer. Between the time the bell sounded, and the door eventually opened, the stress and thoughts of rejection mounted to a maximum fear of another disappointing denial.

Readying his vocal cords, he prepared to give the well-rehearsed proposal. The young tense mouth opened and stammering, stuttering, sounds were squeezed through his tightly drawn lips. The person at the listening end of the conversation must have been a caring, compassionate, understanding lady. For, she took this difficult dialogue to a logical conclusion and immediately directed him to paint the numbers in black and white.

This pivotal moment introduced him to a new technique for successfully completing and improving sales averages. This young flourishing business venture enabled him to easily support his weekly deep-sea summer fishing adventures.

SEE THROUGH BATHING SUIT

Summer attire was determined by the school vacation and the swimming pool. During most sunny, hot and humid days, the family and friends collected on the deck to circulate in the cool invigorating water. While the boys wore the same standard cut-off outfits, the young ladies enjoyed collecting and accumulating an assortment of various attractive bathing suits to adorn their young attractive bodies.

Mom, on one of her very frequent productive bargain hunting searches, purchased a lycra, silky, yellow, one-piece bathing suit for our thirteen-year-old daughter. The first wearing was christened by a striking grand entrance off the diving board.

She gracefully proceeded to the ladder at the shallow end and made an impressive exit. The splendid shopper ran to meet her with a long fluffy beach towel and escorted the child into the house for a speedy change. To their distress and disappointment, evident dark shadows appeared in strategic locations. The nonreturnable item was brought back to the store and a refund was obtained without argument.

THURSDAY NIGHT RITUAL

While living in Bergen County, we were fortunate to reside a short distance from both sets of parents. My Mom and Dad established a tradition which began early in our marriage. Thursday evenings were reserved to visit them for a weekly, family, Italian dinner.

The menu was generally the same. It consisted of macaroni that featured specially prepared homemade tomato gravy which bubbled on the stove for several hours. The rich, red, thick sauce contained: meat balls, spare ribs, braciola and a variety of chicken parts.

The first course of rigatoni was followed with a garden salad that was dressed with Dad's delicious homemade wine vinegar. To the frustration of Mother, the dishes never left the table to be replaced. They were wiped clean at our places and were diligently polished with fresh Newark, Sicilian, Italian bread. The plate refreshing process was repeated between each course through the dinner. During the entire feast, a generous amount of powerful, tasty, basement, brewed red wine was consumed.

The participants remained consistent and included the gracious hosts, Nancy, me, our two children, Uncle Jerry, and Aunt Margaret. Since my father-in-law traveled on business trips and Nancy spent the same day with her mother, Lena was also invited. After a gourmet meal was completed, the table was cleared and the cards came out. The standard simple game was called Blitz and it was easy enough for the youngsters to play.

The evening ended with coffee, new saucers, freshly baked cake and a healthy portion of ice cream. Generally, the children put on their pajamas to prepare for the short ride to Washington Township. On the way out the door, a heaping bowl of left-over food was provided. This treat was sufficient for us to enjoy over the next few days. The youngsters quickly fell asleep in the back seat of the pre-warmed car and their evening was completed with an early start for a well-earned sleep.

A MACHO MAN'S ATHLETIC MASSACRE

I was fortunate to play competitive basketball until the age of thirty-eight. During these years, I enjoyed being with excellent players and with a few teams that frequently scored more than 100 points per individual game. With these athletic experiences as a solid background, self-assurance was well established and the stage was set to take on all challengers.

As a student, an early test was presented when the intercollegiate female fencing champion invited me to participate in a contest against her at the annual campus carnival. Prior to the performance and before a full audience, she carefully assisted me in putting on and preparing the necessary safety equipment.

Seconds after the charade started, her swift saber slashed my psyche into smithereens. The spectators' silent smiles quickly segued into stomach screeching and hilarious laughter. As the match ended, their sympathetic applause enabled this defeated swashbuckler to take a gracious bow and slither off the stage

Years later and as the school principal, I volunteered to have a good time in a scholarship fund raising tennis match against a young member of the girls' high school team. After a friendly warm up period in which the ball gently crossed over the net, I was able to muster confidence for the show. She was selected to serve first and begin the social competition. As this young poised female athlete stepped to the serving line, the ball was firmly grasped, body muscles flexed with the racket slowly swirled in a powerful hand and her eyes fixated as the yellow projectile was tossed into the air.

The rocket launcher attached to her strong well-defined arm instantly ignited, fired a neon payload at the velocity of light and the missile soared towards an innocent defenseless target at the opposite end of the court.

Ace!! This single shot was a preview for the following events. The cloudless clear blue sky came into my focus and thoughts of mercy, mercy, mercy was visualized! Eventually, the vicious persecution ended and the tattered victim was commended for having fun being a good sport.

As a resident of Four Seasons, I was encouraged to join the mixed bowling league. During the first year, I was receptive to guidance from **all** veteran players. There are a multitude of lessons to be absorbed and advice depended upon on the expert providing the instruction.

While each person presented a different approach to the simple game, the outcome was confusion and it was soon realized that most ladies recorded scores better than mine. In the meantime, three goals were established by me and they are:

1. Keep the ball out of the gutter.

2. Maintain an average equal to my body temperature

3. Because of these difficult economic times and to get my money's worth, throw the ball down the alley twice in each frame.

I did learn, however, that lunch is the highlight of the day. Women are better than men. In baseball, three strikes - you are out, and, while bowling, three strikes are a turkey! Most importantly, this activity is a community function, and it should be enjoyable??

WHERE ARE THE CHILDREN?

While the children were growing up, we implemented conversation and discussion when family matters had to be resolved. At times the dialogue concerned parents only and therefore, the youngsters were excused to find space in another part of the house.

Late on a warm, sunny, summer day the telephone was answered and a date for a band job was scheduled at a local catering restaurant. Over the years, this establishment hired me because I performed as a one-man band and was able to produce the full sounds of a tight small combo. The electronic accordion combined with a sophisticated rhythm mechanism created the easy listening effects which ranged from a full church organ to complete sections of strings and horns. These instruments and devices were combined with a little talent and much luck. This situation created a rather lucrative business that was beneficial to the entire household.

The conflict, however, was that we committed to attend a dinner party with friends and the restaurant owner, employer, was in an emergency situation. Being a business person, and realizing all the ramifications of this potential conflict, I accepted the band job. Now, I had to accept the challenges associated with this unfortunate poor decision.

The positions were immediately fixed! To resolve our strong differences of opinion, the children were asked to sit on the deck outside the dining room and enjoy the afternoon sunshine. In the meantime, although nothing was cooking in the oven, the heat in the kitchen dramatically increased. Ultimately, the issue was resolved and harmony was restored. I canceled the band job!

Mother set up the card table and prepared the den for the arrival of female friends who were scheduled for a night of Mahjong. Dad retired to the home office to prepare his schoolwork for the next day. The ladies arrived on time and took their places to begin exchanging clanking game tiles.

Early in the second match, a player said the house was noticeably quiet. In the middle of that sentence, Nancy leaped from her chair and ran through the house and onto the deck to observe the two little children tightly embraced on the outdoor couch cushions. The older daughter was comforting her small brother whose tender cheeks were encrusted with deep dark tear stains. Upon seeing his mother, he asked, "Are you and Daddy getting a divorce?"

Years later and after our children were married, the question was asked of them to recall a most memorable event of their childhood. Instantly, both young newlyweds shouted out in unison, the deck argument incident. Both senior parents were amazed about their combined unison response. Of all the wonderful vacations, trips, parties and entertainment we experienced as a family, this is what they both remember as the number one experience.

KEY CAPERS

Since the moment when our son was old enough to carry his own front door key, a problem of safe keeping this important device began. This is a responsibility that continues to plague him on an almost daily basis and consumes an inordinate number of valuable minutes. Through the years, the ritual of searching for the misplaced tool has involved parents, sister, friends, and neighbors. Now, his wife and children are consumed with the project. The mystery of the missing metal opener has always been the fault of someone other than himself.

An early relocation challenge occurred when he was ten years old. The escapade occurred on a very hot summer morning. It involved his immediate family and two visiting cousins. Before father left for work, the little boy announced that the elusive item had once again disappeared. Dad responded that the swimming pool would be closed until the lost object was found.

While the young children began the search, Mom stated that she had to drive to the supermarket for milk and groceries. The sly smart lady slipped into the hardware store and had several duplicates made. She returned home and secretly scattered the replacement treasures on the front lawn.

In the meantime, neighbors came out and asked what the children were about. Hearing the news, they joined the search site and shortly reappeared with many copies of the lost item. Instantly, his small hands were loaded! By the time the sun went down, his pocket was filled with several missing treasures.

Recently while visiting from Minnesota, the father of three stated that our car keys were misplaced by a family member. Because of his convincing tale of woe, this search lasted several days and involved everyone. As we left to drive to the airport, the phantom item was found in a compartment in his backpack. Once again history is repeated and how long will the saga continue?

RENE IS FINANCIALLY INDEPENDENT

As an eighteen-year-old daughter, Rene had been a long part time employee with Burger King in Park Ridge, New Jersey. During one busy week, scheduling permitted her to work several extra days. These hours were reflected in a substantial pay of $85.00. The young lady proudly displayed the check and clearly exclaimed that she was now financially independent!

My response was to have us turn around in the child's bedroom, scan the walls and look at the floor space that was provided by her parents. We then walked to the front door to observe her car which was parked in the driveway. She was quietly asked to take out the family gas credit card which was in the youthful capitalist's pocket.

At this point in the conversation, she suddenly realized, after banking the required 50% of her income, this tidy sum of money was certainly less than sufficient to even consider supporting her comfortable lifestyle.

YOUR CAR IS FOR SALE AND MAKE THE SIGN

Within a short week after our daughter's seventeenth birthday, we returned home after attending a late night post New Year's party. As the dwelling was approached well after midnight, both parents observed that this driver of a few days did not have her vehicle parked in the driveway. Since her work schedule was posted and she volunteered to remain at Burger King until closing at about 11:00pm, panic quickly set in as we entered the house.

Within a few short anxious moments, a search plan was developed. Her girlfriend was telephoned; it rang dozens of times and was never answered. This was a devastating sign that something very bad had occurred. However, and unknown to us, the bell was turned off for the evening.

Next, the local police department was contacted and the officer alleviated our nervous feelings by clearly stating that if an accident had occurred, the department would have been immediately notified. A mistake was made when the grandparents were phoned and awakened from a deep sleep. They provided a serious scolding for not knowing the location of their first grandchild.

It was then decided that Mom would remain home to wait for a telephone call while Dad could drive to the hamburger restaurant and then search the favorite teenage hang-out spots. As he approached the family car, the missing girl drove around the corner and her vehicle had many passengers that were obviously in a party mode. Before she stopped and opened the door, Dad announced that there had better be a good explanation or her wheels would be put up for sale and she would make the sign.

Her description was that she was asked to remain after closing to clean up and prepare for the next day's business. As the coworkers locked up and set the timed burglar alarm, the store phone rang. She instinctively knew that it was her parents who were calling and this is now a very difficult dilemma. Her store manager could not reenter the building without knowing the code, so he volunteered to follow her home to explain the situation to the parents.

On the way, he got a flat tire and did not have the tools to make the repair. So, he also had to pile up in our daughter's car to continue the trip. These facts were accepted, the sign was never made, the passengers were safely delivered, and Father rode to change the boss's damaged tire.

The very next day our first answering machine was purchased.

I CAN START THE CAR

Our ten-year-old son demonstrated a keen aptitude and talent for motorized and household repairs. He continued to be an active contributor in assisting Dad with his chores. He was skilled in driving the country home tractor lawn mower and would spend hours mowing the grass. Under the apple trees were two rows of picnic tables. Part of his recreational activities involved backing the tractor and connected trailer around and between the tables.

He was highly proficient in all these many demanding challenges. Whenever the vehicle needed a repair or adjustment, he would diagnose the difficulty, open the tool box, select the proper equipment and fix the problem.

At home while dad was working with his band on a Saturday night, Mom decided to take our children and two nieces to dinner at a local restaurant. When the meal was finished, they returned to the car for the trip back home.

After several unsuccessful attempts, the automobile would not start. The only male passenger boldly stated that he could solve the problem. The teenage girls looked and laughed at the young boy. He popped the hood, opened the trunk, got the tool box and tinkered with the motor. Within a few short moments, he told Mom to crank the engine. Magic! The vehicle started and they safely returned to the house. Needless to say, the four girls were impressed with the confidence, expertise and abilities of the young mechanic.

WHY IS A TEN-YEAR-OLD DRIVING THE CAR?

Whenever possible, our family week ended at our farm located in the Massachusetts Berkshire Mountains. The car would be packed the night before, Dad would get a ride to Upper Saddle River on Friday morning and he would be picked up after the children were dismissed from class. He quickly changed into farm clothing and drove the three-hour trip to "Shangri- La" which was deep into the country woods. Before entering the dirt road, we would stop for dinner, use the civilized bathroom, and buy fresh milk and cold beer.

On Saturday, the gang would arrive for two days of partying. While the girls visited the tag sales, Dad and Rob remained behind to cut firewood, mow the lawn and tend the fires that produced hot water and heat for the cold, crisp, clear, dark and star filled evening, fall skies.

When time permitted, the pre-teen son would be given daylight driving lessons on the farm acreage. Late one afternoon, the ladies drove through the large entrance gate to observe a young, smiling driver behind the wheel of the family white Cadillac. "What is he doing in the seat steering solo in our new car?" The answer was, "To prepare for a potential emergency". In the event of an accident, someone would have to take Dad to the hospital. Since we were the only two remaining on the remote and desolate property, he must serve as the designated driver.

Fortunately, his pre- license driving skills were never required for main street driving.

YELLOW JACKETS

It was a perfect fall Saturday and we were fortunate to be invited by my secretary's family who had two sons attending West Point. The football game was played at Michie Stadium. We arrived early and assisted in arranging their party area. As the other guests appeared, they placed their various assortments of goodies on the lovely breakfast table. Realizing that it was a brisk morning, someone was wise enough to grace the setting with coffee augmented with tasty Kahlua. This was absolutely appropriate to take the chill from the crisp air!

Nancy slowly took a sip from the cup and immediately felt a sharp pain on her tongue. There was a yellow jacket, enjoying the refreshment and the last swim. Instantly, the tongue proceeded to swell to a point that it did not fit in her mouth. Everyone was concerned and suggested we quickly report to the medical center.

Upon entering the facility, two young cadets were on duty. They ushered us into an examining booth and pulled the sheer curtain. On the other side of the thin separation, her situation was being discussed. Throughout the conversation, it was clearly stated that last time a patient was seen with this problem, she died because breathing mechanisms were completely blocked by the swollen tongue. In the state of sheer panic, Nancy hung on to me for dear life.

At that time, the doctor appeared, took charge, gave a shot of Benadryl, sent her back to the stadium and said take two pills every other hour. After a while, things became normal. In the meantime, the medication made her sleep through the entire game. From then on and whenever drinking outside, she examines the cup and contents FIRST!

AUTUMN
From Ages: 41 to 60

THINGS TO CONSIDER:
Splitting the Restaurant Check

Restaurant dining is a delightful experience that progresses, over years, and with the passing of time. The social sequence begins in early childhood with small treats being bought by parents, relatives or adult close friends. An exchange of a few dollars provided fond meals and memories which continue to remain. The teenage practice carries on this ritual with individual "pay as you go" food purchases which may include simple treats such as: candy, hot dogs, pizza, soda or ice cream.

The social high school scene introduces the shared interaction of enjoying snacking in small group settings with acquaintances that may be gathered together after a dance or an athletic event. Because participants shared the same items in very similar quantities, the bill payment was easily divided evenly. Restaurant dining is a delightful experience that matures, over years, and with the passing of time.

Eventually, the dining succession progressed to dating relationships and the applied rule was that the male picked up the tab for the occasion. Double dating followed a similar procedure and the gentlemen split the bill. For the most part, money issues were resolved right at the table. In most situations, cash was the common means of paying the check.

Due to a much wider medley of selections, assorted dining atmospheres, price ranges, cocktail mixture tastes and budgetary alternatives, the grown-up restaurant practice sets the stage for a more complicated know-how. Within this backdrop, some conditions are conducive to beating the system and getting stuck when one individual decides to be extravagant knowing the bill will be uniformly divided.

Described next is a potential challenge presented for consideration and resolution: Before going out for a meal, a group decided that each party stays within the same price range by all selecting hamburgers and beer. Consistent requests were made until the last couple ordered Prime Rib. They knew how to beat the system!

Months later the same four-some reluctantly scheduled to go out for a second time and they agreed that the original arrangement be implemented. To ensure a most proper and predictable final outcome, The Prime Rib pair was positioned to place the first order with the waiter. Everyone comfortably complied with the prearranged understanding. However, the system beaters called the service person back before the kitchen was entered and asked to change their selection to Lobster Tail.

The problem was solved the next time out by all parties receiving separate individual checks. This arrangement was resolved and all individuals selected the same meal which was hamburger.

What suggestions might Miss Manners make?

COMPUTER AND ME

The Upper Saddle River School System took pride in being at the leading edge of current and new innovations that are related to the instructional process. Staff members were encouraged to participate in professional development programs by attending graduate school, national, state and local conventions or workshops. As principal of the building, I fully participated in many of these activities as a motivator, presenter or participant.

The introduction of the technology age brought a wave of new excitement to the educational community and several opportunities were available to appreciate and understand the impact of these highly powerful devices. While this township continued to promote forward thinking, they were influenced by a conservative budgetary philosophy and the cost per pupil ratios. They were receptive to introducing computer science to the student population but reluctant to appropriate funds for administrative purposes. Although my experience had been limited to a theoretical understanding, I accumulated an appreciation for the tremendous potential available for a managerial application.

Eventually and after examining the availability of products, a recommendation was submitted to acquire the first computer dedicated for office utilization at a cost of $5,000. The request was approved by the superintendent and business administrator. Once submitted to the board of education, a request for more information was required. An invitation was extended to attend a public meeting and provide the essential support they needed to understand the acquisition of this expensive equipment.

Basically, the question was, "What was the advantage of a computer when compared to a replacement $200 electric typewriter?" After an in-depth comprehensive presentation and a very detailed dialogue, the purchase was approved. Although there was reservation relative to this large expenditure, the trustees indicated their decision was based on the meticulous report, explanation of implementation options, strategies and my reputation.

Upon delivery, the secretary attended a two-week training session, a technician appeared at her desk for a few days and the school was electronically connected to a consultant providing guidance services. Within a month the device and operator were inundated with requests from other building offices to help complete their projects.

The costly typewriter replacement promptly developed a demand and demonstrated that the expenditure was well worth the dollars. That single computer, over time, multiplied dramatically as new technology became a vital component in the entire managerial operation of the school district.

DAD I CAN FIX THE DISHWASHER

Our thirteen-year-old boy was mechanically inclined and very skilled in efficiently completing household chores. Additionally, the young man also displayed a unique ability to fix or repair complicated things. The original dishwasher was in the home for sixteen years and ran very well. However, the interior area that contained the vigorously moving hot water began to show indications of failure. The signs were obvious that the appliance needed to be replaced.

Rob confidently announced that he could solve the problem and he was told to go for it. Upon entering the kitchen early Saturday morning, parts and pieces were spread all over the floor. It was suggested that he mount and label all the components on a large cardboard sheet for reference. He instinctively responded that everything was under control and he must be left alone to concentrate. If Dad continued to interfere, the "mess" would be left and he would leave the project. His strong recommendation was respected.

Later in the day, he stated the task was completed and successfully tested. The fine "professional" quality work enabled the service life of the machine to be successfully extended for several additional years.

HOW-TO PICK-UP CHICKS WITH A "*FRANMOBILE*"

We were fortunate to own a new white Cadillac with a green leather top. Because of the color combination, the four door, hardtop sedan, created the appearance of being a "mile long". Installed was a musical horn that played over forty tunes. When the children saw a friend, as we drove by, they chose a musical selection, pressed the button and shared the melody with their sidewalk buddies.

Within a short time, the classy car was identified as the *FRANMOBILE*. When it was time to transport teams to their games, youngsters created a line outside that wrapped around the entire vehicle. Each door was a potential entrance to the plushy appointed luxurious interior.

Our son was in middle school and it was obvious that a progressing interest was developing in young ladies. On a local journey in town on a lovely, lazy, late, autumn afternoon; we were alone and shared the front seat in the automobile. As we stopped for a traffic light, a car full of attractive high school cheerleaders returning from a football game pulled up beside us. I said to him, "It is time to learn how-to pick-up chicks".

As I played the musical horn song, *A Pretty Girl*, his face turned brilliant red; he then slid off the seat to hide under the dashboard and gave me a killer look. The traffic signal changed to green, the girls smiled, waved out of the windows as they drove off into the sunset. He did, however, not stay under the dashboard very long and he eventually did learn the lessons of how-to pick-up damsels.

VETERANS OF FOREIGN WARS

It was well known in Washington Township, New Jersey that I was a musician and performed with a popular band on weekends. A neighbor, who was a member of the VFW in town, asked if I might be interested in donating music for disabled veterans or special needs children.

I volunteered for my services and arranged to provide a band for their many programs. This commitment expanded to having me sponsor music for the organizations' charitable events during numerous occasions throughout the next several years.

Immediately, the frequent functions became favorite activities for military service people and challenged children. The entertainment was donated over a period of decades and the advertised dates became very popular with various audiences. The hall always drew excellent capacity crowds.

Our daughter was approaching her sixteenth birthday and asked if she could have a party and invite her relatives and high school friends. Since the VFW hall was a large attractive facility and, in our town, I said that I will make the necessary arrangements.

The request was made to the banquet manager, who checked the date for availability. The evening was open and boldly stated that the rental fee was three hundred dollars. He was reminded that I was the person who supplied the music for all the special occasions at no charge and we filled the house with well-behaved participants who thoroughly enjoyed every presentation.

Further it was explained that my family will set up, monitor the teenagers and clean-up after the party. Once again, he insisted that the fee had to be paid. I reminded him of my several contributions and gave him an opportunity to reconsider. The response was that the policy is fixed! A counter offer was proposed and he would be receptive to waiving the customary fee under the condition that I donate music for New Year's Eve. I concluded that he might have been a brilliant war hero in the past...but today he is a poor businessman.

I said, "Thank you very much and don't ever call me to provide free music for your charitable affairs. We then decided to put the rental fee towards removing a lolly column, finishing the basement and having the party at our home. The conversation did not end at this point and the VFW continued to telephone and request that I provide complimentary music for their future events.

A PROTECTIVE PARENT'S PERIL

New Jersey provides sixteen-year old's an opportunity to obtain a driver's learning permit. After a good solid year of practice and supervision with Mom and Dad, our daughter successfully completed the process in her junior year of high school. Since she exceeded all the expectations that were placed on her responsible shoulders, we were confident and comfortable that she would become a competent, solo and safe independent driver.

While parked in the high school student area during the first snow flurry of winter, an accumulation of white sleety powder swiftly stacked to several inches. Coincidently as dismissal time neared, Mom was returning from completing her errands and passed the school as she headed home. Instinctively, she pulled off the road and into the lot to clean the child's car windows and ensure that the novice seventeen-year-old motorist has a clear unobstructed view. With that gesture of kindness finished on this cold frosty day, Mom continued the journey home to await the protected, secure, arrival of our young lady.

Shortly, the house storm door sprang open and then slammed shut followed by shrilling, staccato, sounds. "When I came out of class, my windows were the only ones cleaned! How embarrassing and please don't ever do that again". While distressed for the moment, Mom taught her a valuable lesson that is implemented each time the snow falls. Clean all the windows!

WESTWOOD HIGH SCHOOL MARCHING BAND

On a late July afternoon, our daughter, Rene, had a visit from an excited classmate who ran into the house to enthusiastically announce the marching band was looking for a girl to carry the American flag during various functions for the coming year. The task involved half-time football shows, holiday parades, band festivals and evening concerts. While our young lady was reluctant to sign-up, Dad forced the issue and the two young girls completed the application process. Since there were no other pupils interested in carrying the stars and stripes, she got the job.

Under the leadership and influence of a very capable, talented music director, the marching band ranks included a combination of over one hundred instrumentalists and color guard members who were able to consistently provide excellent performances. Lined up shoulder to shoulder, the youngsters extended from one goal post to the other at the opposite end of the football playing field.

Their red and white, crisp, traditional, uniforms added to the spectacular presentations they perpetually created. As a transformed hesitant member of this prestigious group, she influenced her younger brother to become involved during his high school career. Active participation in this organization afforded children an opportunity to play in a European summer concert tour which was scheduled every second year.

After a long tenure of excellent service and in our son's sophomore term, both the choral teacher and the band director announced their retirements. Once their farewell letters were accepted, the school superintendent telephoned our home and asked if I might be interested in becoming the next president of the parents' music association. Realizing the demands of this appointment included working with a new music staff, assisting in the planning of the extracurricular schedule, formulating the next summer concert tour, and the feelings of our son, I said that my response would be provided within a few days.

Our young man encouraged me to assume the position, join him in the venture and accept the responsibilities associated with this most important office. The challenging assignment was taken and, fortunately, the supervisory committee consisted of many supportive parents and volunteers that included very competent people who worked vigorously and in close harmony. In preparation, the new director, who came from Vermont, spent a week at our home during the summer vacation and we planned the events for the coming September.

As a result of our seven-day strategy sessions, we mapped out the August band camp, created organizational guidelines and formulated preliminary plans for the next European Tour. During the interim, we accepted an invitation to have the band march at the halftime show in Giants Stadium.

Nancy and I were among the many proud spectators in the grandstands who were able to observe our 6`9`` son dressed in white drum major's attire and his flag twirling sister entertaining a full arena of energetic football fans. As an aside and on two separate occasions, both youngsters, while in high school, paraded on this Meadowlands field.

An additional bonus allowed us to become deeply involved in the European concert experience which numbered over one hundred junior and senior vocal plus instrumental students. With the assistance and cooperation of a core of child-oriented chaperones, we enjoyed a flawless three-week excursion on the continent, proudly displayed the talented students and showcased the excellent mature young adult representatives from Westwood High School. They also served as outstanding teenage ambassadors of "goodwill" from the United States of America.

FIRST MEMORABLE DRIVING LESSON ON THE GARDEN STATE PARKWAY

In the event of an emergency and because of the remote location of our summer farm country home, it was desirable for our ten-year-old son to learn how to drive the family car. He was an experienced lawn mower and attached utility trailer driver who had acres of lawn on which to practice.

Acquired skills included cutting the grass in straight lines and backing the vehicular combination between and around a dozen large picnic tables. With this background of proficiency and using the backyard as a practice parking lot, it was comfortable for him to advance to the automobile.

With this profile and years of a perfect safety record, the car was second nature when the time arrived for him to obtain a New Jersey learner's driving permit at age sixteen. In preparation for his test, we decided that he would chauffeur us on the Garden State Parkway for a trip to visit his college attending sister in Trenton. Before taking the wheel, he demanded the STUDENT DRIVER sign be removed from the rear window. Once this request was honored, the journey began.

An assortment of minor suggestions was provided by Dad sitting on the passenger side and Mom occupying the back right seat. The ride and dialogue proceeded nicely. Immediately, after passing through the Essex Toll Booth, however, he surprised us by pulling to the side of the road and getting out of the car. While asking Dad to continue the driving he said in a calm voice, "Enough, you drive!"

He did earn his license on the first attempt. Currently, he is a proud father with three children of which the youngest is a teenager near driving age. I am interested to observe if and when his history is repeated.

DAD, I CAN FIX THE CAR

Our son inherited from his grandfather the talent and skills which enabled him to fix most things. His extensive list of accomplishments included: large or small appliances, general household items, electrical projects, computer problems, plumbing, carpentry, construction, fine decorating, tile work, lawn or garden maintenance and automotive care.

The strategy, as a dad, was to identify the task, discuss the sequence of steps necessary to make the repair, select the proper materials or references, provide the tools, and ask questions. Once comfortable with the scope of the situation, he was left alone to do his thing. Inevitably, the task was professionally completed within a timely fashion.

As a thirteen-year-old, he confidently volunteered to restore the malfunctioning car trunk lid hydraulic closure mechanism. Broom sticks were used to support the deck while the door pistons were removed. Then, it was suggested that a blanket be placed to cover the locking devices while the cylinders were replaced. This procedure would provide the extra safety margin in the event the support poles slipped.

With the exception of the blanket as a triple precaution, the planned course of action was implemented. However, the sticks did slip and the trunk lid slammed shut! Due to the cold winter weather, the connecting garage door to the family room was closed. In the meantime, moments quickly passed while the other family members continued work on their weekend chores.

When, low and behold, his sister asked for the location of her younger brother. The fire proof door was immediately opened to hear a banging noise on the closed trunk deck. Our son was immediately rescued by opening the lock. Now, the suggested safety blanket was correctly used to cover the latch, replacement trunk door pistons were installed and the repair was satisfactorily completed.

SENIOR CITIZEN SEASHORE STOLEN SUPPER

On a weekend visit to my brother's beach house, we went to a local store front family restaurant for a fresh fish supper. At the time, our daughter was thirteen years old and had some interesting views on life. Sitting at the next table was a grandmother accompanied by her relatives and grandchildren.

During the course of the meal, the elderly woman showed signs of physical distress. Perspiration beaded on her forehead, skin tones were pale and summer slacks were rolled up in an attempt to be more comfortable. As that group finished dessert, she collapsed and slumped in the chair.

The ambulance arrived immediately and placed the patient on a gurney for transportation to the hospital. A relative asked for the check and the café owner said, "Take care of the lady and the bill is on me". The people in the establishment were then requested to assemble outdoors for a time while the staff regrouped. The adult members at our table were very upset and the feeling was we could not finish our food.

In an attempt to comfort our dinner party, words of wisdom were shared by our worldly teenager lady," Don't worry, that's an old senior citizen's trick so they can eat for free!"

SENIOR CITIZEN FORCED TO PLAY IN A TEENAGE ROCK AND ROLL BAND

The Washington Township residence, in which we lived for thirty-eight years, was a comfortable place for our children's friends to gather on weekends and during vacation periods. It was a welcome, safe, secure, environment which operated around a set of simple rules and behavioral guidelines. There was never a concern with alcohol, drugs, tobacco, inappropriate language or manners.

Nobody had to explain the principles; however, if a serious infraction of the unwritten code was ever broken, the offender would be removed from this home for a lifetime. Not one single youngster had to be dismissed.

Most Friday nights found teenagers in the family room watching a movie on a VCR that they chipped in to rent. While the package included an assortment of snacks, Nancy, who served as chaperone and treasurer, was the provider of soda and Dunkin Donuts. These parties occurred while I worked with weekend music engagements.

During the summer months, the young high school group assembled on the deck next to the pool. This nightly ritual involved setting up, swimming, snacking and housekeeping. Before departing for their homes at the end of each party, all furniture had to be put-away and stored in the cabana. It was a pleasure to observe these fine young people working together for the good of the group.

Because of our close bond with the children over the years, we were extended an invitation to a classmate's high school graduation party. The young man, who was the guest of honor, was our school marching band drum major, talented percussionist and leader of a local "hard rock" band. This combo provided the evening's entertainment. The aspiring musicians knew that I was a professional accordionist and extended me an opportunity to join them in their jam session.

They chided me throughout the evening and eventually made enough of a commotion that I went home to get my instruments. While setting up, slick smiles were casually observed from my young counterparts as they anticipated hearing squeaky sounds from an ancient squeeze box.

While their rock selections were unknown to this senior citizen guest, this was an easy gig. All the tunes, in their special library of "hard metal", followed the standard twelve bar blues pattern which incorporated less than five basic common chords in the root position. Even easier, their vocalist could only comfortably produce undistinguishable words in the key of "E".

As an invited back up fill- in guest, I quietly joined them in their next selection. To their amazement this sophisticated, electronic, synthesizer placed in my hands produced the sounds of a full-sized theatrical organ. I timidity demonstrated to their tender ears the multitude of variations that could be produced using chord inversions, substitutions and multitude of colorful embellishments that could be added to their basic structures.

When given an opportunity to take a solo, I was able to implement all the skills that were accumulated as a result of my night club entertaining experiences. The right hand played the piano side of forty-one keys and the left hand worked the bass notes which numbered 120 buttons.

These fingers played deep notes which were written below the staff and were powerful enough to drive a full band. In addition, several sound registers on both sides of the accordion produced all combinations of instrumental sounds that could be heard when listening to a complete orchestra. They were in awe of the surprises that came from this square, amplified, modern electric accordion that had the appearance of something other than a guitar.

Before the evening ended, the old corny accordion player was given an opportunity to join the group. *Interesting!*

CAMERA CONQUERS COLLEGE ENTRANCE CHALLENGE

From the time our children were born, the topic of college education was emphasized. Frequent discussions centered on the importance of doing well in school and participating in its related activities. As the years passed, we talked about graduating with a marketable skill which would then evolve into a career to support a comfortable and productive lifestyle.

These lessons were well learned as the youngsters progressed through the twelve grades. As high school commencement approached, college selection and potential courses of study were examined. Fortunately, the children selected a fine university and curriculum major. Both chose Trenton State College as their preferred option.

Since this institution earned and enjoyed a reputation for excellence at a rather reasonable tuition, competition for acceptance was intense. While both children were fine students with excellent performance records and superior recommendations, the stages were set for an aggressive and convincing campaign.

A favorite tool was put to work as we attended all the admissions presentations in the area. Each meeting was followed up with a thank you letter that was attached to a picture of the school representative. In most cases, the photograph also included the new potential student's picture who was easily identified. The procedure continued as the campaign for early admission and acceptance accelerated. Eventually and happily, the connection was made between applicant and snapshot. Because of multiple visits to the same repeated establishments, the prospective pupils were frequently recognized and introduced from the audience as people interested in attending their fine institution of higher learning.

Together, both goals were successfully attained and the young adults graduated with certificates and training to enter the teaching profession. Each has earned advanced degrees and are currently major contributors to their family, schools and communities.

HARD TIMES

While growing up, both children, whenever possible, were encouraged to acquire an appreciation for the value of money by working at small jobs. During one summer, our son started a neighborhood lawn cutting service. Due to being supplied by dad's basement tool collection, his operating expenses were minimal. Therefore, his fees were economical when compared to those of local professional landscapers. Within a short period and because he was a responsible young business person, his list of customers quickly expanded to generate a substantial monthly income.

Mid-point during the summer vacation, he was invited to spend two weeks at the shore with his cousins. The problem was presented to his family, and Dad offered to cut his lawns while he went to enjoy the beach. He departed for the seaside and his experienced free worker continued the schedule.

Late one afternoon, a close friend invited the parents to an evening barbeque. Father's immediate response was that he had a full agenda behind the mower. In order to attend the dinner, Mother volunteered to assist by operating the weed whacker. This combined team effort enabled the tasks to be completed in time to clean-up and attend the social gathering.

The next morning the phone rang and an acquaintance stated we were seen cutting a stranger's lawn. And… since Nancy was involved, had we fallen on hard times and taken on extra work to meet expenses?

PAID VACATION

While waiting for our friends to join us on a trip to a local restaurant their son, who was a recent high school graduate, ran out to our car and exclaimed in an excited voice, "I am going to Australia next summer!" When asked how this happened, he quickly said in a happy high-pitched tone, "My company has a paid vacation policy". He was immediately saddened and deeply distressed when the concept was carefully explained to him.

JACKSON JONES

From the time as a toddler, my Dad could tell stories and jokes using a variety of ethnic voices, mannerisms, dialects and body language. They were very authentic. The complete package, when implemented, augmented the all-embracing imitation presentation. Being at an impressive age, I was intrigued with this unique talent and practiced to develop this amusing skill.

Eventually, some of my dialogues were perfected to proficient levels of development. Jackson Jones, a fictitious character from the deep south, was one of these eccentric personalities who effectively used the telephone lines for personal entertainment. During the highlight of this rather unconventional individual's new character, he unleashed interesting conversations with some acquaintances.

The first episode involved my dear friend, Olga, who was kind enough and volunteered to babysit for three small children whose parents had an opportunity to enjoy a free paid vacation in Italy. The father of these youngsters owned and operated a successful dental lab that specialized in producing exceptional quality crowns and false teeth.

While in the home one early evening, she answered the telephone to a masculine voice who spoke with a distinctive southern drawl. The gentleman was difficult to understand, used a disguised voice with rapid velocity and expressed much anxiety and excited, high, emotion. It was clearly conveyed to the sitter that this was a very serious, emergency, situation and he desperately needed his new replacement dentures.

Throughout this rather frantic experience, the young, compassionate lady thoroughly searched the large house. Unsuccessful, the desperate investigator sadly reported the inability to locate the misplaced treasure. Now, the so-called agitated client requested that a secret special hiding place in an open-ended plastic imitation ceiling beam, that was located midway up the staircase to the second floor, be examined.

After about fifteen minutes of my hysterical game, the mystery farce was uncovered. An immediate sigh of relief was heard in the receiver followed by a lengthy exchange of hearty laughter.

A few years later and relaxing at her home, our wonderful friend received another phone call from a voice with a distinct deep, Dixie accent. Obviously, the Jackson Jones memorable episode was immediately recalled. After kindly listening to what was thought to be a repeat of a dramatic, previous, humorous, escapade, she said before hanging up, "I know that it is you, Bob Franchino."

Well, low and behold, the voice was from a genuine, professional talent agent for a popular game show. Fortunately, the representative redialed and was successful in convincing Olga that this was the real thing! He was employed by the television game show, *Winning Streak.* As a result of this authentic conversation, she was invited to be a contestant on a program hosted by Bill Cullen.

JACKSON JONES STRIKES AGAIN

A few weeks later the deep, Dixie, imaginary. voice used the wires to prank another victim. This prey, a proud father, was very honored that his oldest son was accepted to Georgetown University. He was very delighted to share this wonderful information with friends and family. This news provided another opportunity for the southern, mystery man to strike again.

The personality of our elated parent provided a golden opening for this prankster to enjoy some fun. In a telephone conversation, the jokester explained in detail that their sons were selected to be roommates at the college. The Dixie Dad explained that his boy was a resident in a very, low, poverty, environment and his excellent football talent was instrumental in making this full scholarship and superb benefits possible.

Throughout the bulk of what seemed to be a one-way dialogue, the child's indigent daddy bragged at length about the incentives used to entice the gridiron star to attend this prestigious institution. In addition to a generous scholarship, an extravagant expense account was provided. The deal was sealed when the celebrity jock was provided a bright, red showroom "Amtrak" Pontiac convertible automobile.

The other parent at the receiving end of the one-way conversation was a member of a two-member, hardworking family who were potentially challenged by the expenses associated with this educational experience. As the boasting continued, the quiet frustrated father at the listening end, experienced silence, emotional anxiety that accelerated with the growing list of enticements. Included was the fact that the southern superstar played "sack-a-phone" in high school.

The last segment of bodacious words occurred when the megastar's dad masterfully suggested that the employed folks from New Jersey finance the cost of room decorations, matching bed spreads, draperies and linens. At about that time in the sales pitch I, the impersonator, identified myself. Well!! The telephone exploded with dramatic relief and an abundance of belly laughter.

JACKSON JONES RETIREMENT

We moved to Four Seasons at Mapleton, which is an age restricted community. This location is six miles from our daughter's family home in Bordentown, New Jersey. Our spacious dwelling is in a well-maintained community that is in a beautifully landscaped setting.

The well-appointed clubhouse contains: management offices, meeting rooms, billiard area, cardrooms, library, fully equipped fitness facility, large size multi-function room, spacious indoor swimming pool, hot tub, locker rooms and sauna. The outdoor portion of this area accommodates a large fully appointed and furnished patio plus gazebo, spacious outdoor swimming pool, four bocce lanes and two tennis courtyards.

Because this is a retirement community, it is imperative that all facilities and individual homes be immaculately upheld. The retirement age of our residences mandates that maximum property values be maintained for resale purposes.

These combined factors account for the easy, efficient and rapid transfer of individual owners. In addition, facility maintenance fees are very reasonable and have been consistent over the years. These extraordinary components can be attributed to the excellent, speedy, sales turnover at Four Seasons. Many properties exchange ownership before they are listed.

The time arrived for a nearby neighbor on Ellington Drive to sell his home and relocate to a warmer, year-round, climate. The news of this decision became popular knowledge in this delightful suburban community. The area trickster, Jackson Jones, decided to telephone and express interest in the available estate.

The deep, southern accentuated voice was rather animated as it began to seek very detailed information. The responses were concise and lacked embellishments. The excited, highly motivated, prospective purchaser, Mr. Jones, was thrilled with the scant detail that was provided. His overwhelming joy was accelerated when he learned the street is named after the famous jazz musician and composer, Duke Ellington. At this point in the one-way dialogue, Jackson shared an abundant amount of knowledge about his idol. The extensive presentation was made to the seller in depth for a lengthy period of time. Although very patient, the listener became frustrated in his inability to end this challenging conversation.

Sensing these negative vibes, Jackson Jones clearly stated that this was a cash deal, no mortgage or inspection was required; and because he was ready to immediately move in and occupy, an offer to purchase was made well over the asking price,

Now the local con-artist realized that his friend was in a most impossible situation with an offer that could not be refused. The jokester switched voices and identified himself! The perplexed seller, who was obviously on the verge of some sort of a breakdown, instantly realized this was a hoax. Once grasping this was a prank, he was immediately relieved of tremendous pressure, frustration and anxiety!

Times have dramatically changed and with the implementation of caller identification, Jackson Jones has retired and his career abruptly ended.

I DO NOT WANT TO ATTEND COLLEGE

Attending college and the importance of education were major topics of conversation while the two children were growing up. The concept of "the more you learn, the more you earn and the longer you live" was ingrained in their developing minds.

One day while an upperclassman in high school, our boy casually announced that he was not thinking about college because he was going to be a truck driver. Rather than over react and give a thesis on the topic, the proclamation was permitted to pass without commentary. A few days later, a friend and owner of a moving company was contacted. His response after hearing the tale was, "Send him to me!"

He got the position and started a summer job. To his surprise, the first day's assignment was to move a family, living in a mansion, to a location several miles across the state. Being the new man on the crew, he still remembers having the trivial task of digging up a large swing set in a soaking rain storm. He did not come home until near midnight. Exhaustion was so extensive that the novice transportation specialist fell asleep on the family room floor.

Although he made rapid advancement through the company organization with several promotions, stories of that nature occurred frequently. By the end of that vacation, however, he was elevated to foreman of the warehouse operation and offered a full-time position. He learned that this was a work experience which would not be repeated, returned to school and successfully sequenced through the system.

He graduated from high school, earned a Bachelor of Science which was followed by a Masters of Arts. Today, he has a PhD, works in one of the nation's most prestigious high schools, and is an assistant principal and an adjunct college professor. While our son is long retired from the trucking industry, he is now focused on moving many young minds in a multitude of interesting, exciting and positive directions.

INSTALLING A SPRINKLER SYSTEM

The Franchino home enjoyed the prestige of a premium prize lawn. A procedure and schedule were implemented for seeding, fertilization, weed control, thatching and aeration. The property displayed a consistent high quality luxurious green carpet of healthy turf. A most important component in the list of tasks involved watering. Whenever necessary, hoses and sprinklers were dragged, moved and precisely located to satisfy the requirements of the demanding needs of the thick green blades.

Our son, while attending college, worked during the summer with a prominent landscaper who provided excellent services to his customers. In the role of helper, Rob absorbed all the necessary skills to be successful. After assisting in the installation of several home sprinkling systems, he was confident in having a mastery and proficiency of the essential procedures.

He offered to connect an underground, automatic, irrigation system as a Father's Day gift for me. My requirement was to purchase the materials and leave the home on the date of installation. Within the week, he produced an engineering plot plan, a design and a full parts list. The equipment was purchased and a construction date was scheduled.

During the next week, he announced the project would begin on Saturday and requested that he be left home alone. While gone, he and a friend dug the trenches by hand, laid out the plastic pipe, connected the new watering heads, wired the system with electrical timers, tested the job and refilled the ditches with the lifted sod. The mission was completed long before my return at the day's end. Within a week, the lawn was restored to its natural condition and the watering process became automatic. His accomplishment operated flawlessly well past the time we sold the house.

RENE'S COLLEGE LAVISH LINCOLN

While in her junior year, our daughter's car was no longer reliable to make the journey from college to home. Since Mom's trips were mostly local, it was decided that they would swap their vehicles. As a result, Rene drove a lovely, luxurious, rosewood, colored Lincoln Town Car. She soon became the uncomfortable campus celebrity and topic of conversation.

One day, she met a handsome young man who asked her for a date. In the process of making arrangements, he stated his only means of transportation was a heavy-duty construction truck that was desperately overdue for complete cleaning. They agreed that her automobile could be used for this special occasion.

Since an intense rainstorm set the stage at pick up time, Rene wisely decided to park in front of his house and summoned him by sounding the distinctive horn. After several unsuccessful attempts to attract his attention, she reluctantly walked up to his front porch and quickly rang the doorbell. He immediately greeted her with open arms.

In response to an explanation for his lack of attention to the blasting sounds coming from her fancy coupe`, he stated that he was confused and thought the beautiful limousine was there for one of his neighbors. Needless to say, this very stormy start of a social relationship began on a rather cloudy note!

SANIBEL SEASHELLS

While both youngsters were attending Trenton State College, we offered each of them an opportunity to invite a friend to join us on a family vacation. Mom and Dad would assume all the expenses connected with the trip. Waiting for them to adjust their schedules was difficult. As patient parents and waiting for their time selections to be identified, the summer passed and we remained home.

The next year the same proposal was presented. However, they were provided with a specific two-week period which was available for them and their guests. Our son immediately said that he was not interested and our daughter, eventually, arrived at the same conclusion.

We arranged to be away for a complete month to relax and enjoy the sunshine in beautiful Sanibel Island, Florida for a two-week period. On the way south to the destination, the first seven days in July were used to explore the Smoky Mountains. Prior to August 1st, the return trip home involved sightseeing along the Atlantic Ocean coastline.

After reaching our destination and settling in at the condo, our young lady, who was distressed over a broken romance, telephoned. In the conversation, we encouraged her to join us and agreed to purchase a round trip airline ticket. Hopefully, the warmth of a tropical beach would provide the young lady an opportunity to rest, recuperate, and reorganize.

At the airport arrival time, we masquerade as a pair of limousine drivers and displayed a name sign at the top of a tall, black, men's umbrella. The damsel in distress slowly and sadly, sauntered down the escalator wearing a white sailor hat that was yanked down over her ears. Under this Navy boater was a hairstyle that severely lacked its traditional top-quality grooming. She was attired in a well-worn Trenton State sweatshirt that was pulled over loose fitting pajama type cotton boxer shorts. In a display of dramatic disgust, a facial expression demonstrated the lack of appreciation for being picked up by a pretend, professional, car service. The drive to the resort was very quiet and without meaningful dialogue.

Her plan was to "veg out" in the heated pool, search for seashells along the famous Gulf of Mexico coast and stay in her room in the evening. We coaxed her to join us at a fine seafood restaurant and the reward for the indulgence was a good case of hives that did not agree with the red, raw, recent sunburned skin.

Valuable time was consumed with tasks associated with gathering, sorting, cleaning and bleaching tattered, vacated crustaceans' carcasses. I finally asked what she was doing. The curt, brisk, response was collecting these fragmented morsels to make a nautical lamp! These efforts consumed the bulk of available sand searching time. In due course, I asked if a sample of the finished product was available and could be observed.

We visited a store, Seashells of Sanibel, and was shown an example of the desired fixture which was on display. The sales person was carefully requested to wrap it up and gently present it to the emotionally tormented school girl. This delicate, fragile package was carefully taken home to New Jersey and has continued to occupy a permanent place in her guest bedroom.

NOTEWORTHY TIPS

The tipping custom is a well-established tradition that has long been enjoyed by club date musicians. The practice generally occurred at parties, in banquet facilities, cocktail lounges or restaurant areas. My experience with this ritual was introduced as a small child responding to requests from guests who were visiting our home. I was asked to show how tall I am getting, and then play the accordion.

I reluctantly responded to both directives by standing-up straight and walking to the front sunroom which was adjacent to the parlor and the location of my daily practice area. While playing a few tunes, the visitors would place a hush-hush quarter in my hand. Within moments after the exchange, the adults continued their conversation and I provided the short session of entertainment. I got the message, quietly put the instrument down, responded to gentle applause and left to place the coin in the bedroom, a small, silver bank.

My first professional performance, as a fifteen-year-old entertaining at a local neighborhood tavern, institutionalized the custom. Again, the pattern continued. The variation of transactions went from an image of a shiny metal coin to a printed portrait of George Washington on green paper. This represented quite a change!

Except for a five-dollar tip for playing the *Grand March from Iota* at my first New Year's orchestra engagement, the standard token of appreciation remained a dollar bill. While playing several high school dances, a specifically shy student would consistently request and tip the band for playing a Latin Rumba. Once again, the favor was acknowledged with the prevailing amount.

Wedding receptions conducted in church basements or firehouse halls presented a different picture. These activities generally were "beer and bun" affairs that were restrained to very conservative budgets. The band's goal was to provide participants with a great and memorable evening and to thereby encourage them to extend the party. In most cases, the host and hostess did not have the finances to compensate the musicians for overtime. Eventually, someone would step forward, pass a hat and collect money to continue the celebration. There was always enough in the fedora to lengthen the good time. On some occasions, the cap funding technique was circulated for a second trip.

As a parent with two young children, Nancy and I planned a surprise vacation to Disney Land. The fancy hotel in which we stayed for the week featured a fine restaurant. On the first night, we decided to have dinner on the premises. The evening's entertainment included a singing, strolling guitarist. *Raindrops Keep Falling on My Head* was our daughter's favorite tune and a gratuity was provided when the request was made. As the vocalist's words were heard by our young lady, she shyly slipped from her seat and slithered beneath the table.

There were two additional notable tipping events during the period in which I primarily performed as a strolling musician. The first occurred while entertaining at a mini-mansion wedding cocktail party reception. A gentleman, in an attempt to romanticize a sententious female, asked if I knew her favorite song, *Satin Doll.* After playing the selection, he palmed me with a twenty-dollar bill. During the evening's festivity, the sauntering accordionist continued to mingle among the elegant guests. The dauntless, dapper, dude who was on the prowl, and seemingly involved in a serious seduction of the desirable damsel, made this same request three additional separate times. He repeatedly rewarded me with a green representation of Andrew Jackson. Instantly, this became my all-time favorite melody.

The second event, worth noting, occurred when I was hired to play a Saint Patrick's Day grand opening at a popular and prominent Irish Pub in Bergen County. The proprietor put a program together which included: bagpipers, an Irish band, an ensemble of step dancers, a house full of well liquored, loud, lively, lousy, amateur off-key vocalists and me.

During all the raucous, rowdy, hullabaloo of dancing, heavy drinking, singing and boisterous merriment in this high-spirited setting; my major role was to wander around the establishment, compete with the fun-loving crowd and play requests. With the exception of a few tunes from the Emerald

Island that were known to me, most songs in my repertoire shared the same basic melody line.

In preparation for the gala, however, my library was searched and several additional tunes were photocopied and reduced in size to fit in a small cardboard container. This contraption was mounted on the top of the squeeze box. I was ready to use this miniature music portfolio and respond to the anticipated assortment of ethnic or cultural requests. Interestingly, I knew from memory all the songs that were required. Basically, it was the same variety that was common to the general public. However, the patrons thought this was a vessel to gather gratuities. This money-making, portable, cash register had to be emptied several times during the evening. Regrettably, this was the only time this unique cash box was used!

A DEFINITION OF TIPS

While walking into a local Florida restaurant that was affiliated with a national chain of eating establishments that we enjoyed patronizing during our travels, two stools were almost available at the bar. Greetings were exchanged and the cocktail order was taken. Before the beverages were delivered, the party sitting next to us finished their meal and paid their dinner check. Dishes, glasses and eating tools remained at their place well after they left the area.

Approximately fifteen untidy minutes passed, and the unappetizing clutter was unchanged. The barmaid was nicely and appropriately requested to clear the mess and restore the station to create a pleasant dining atmosphere. The curt response as her arms were firmly folded was, "I am doing the best that I can".

Within the next forty-five minutes, our meals were delivered, the lady had time to casually converse at length with several customers and continue to ignore our distasteful condition. In the meantime, the manager passed through the area and also chose to overlook the situation.

During the interim, another unsuccessful request was made. In the course of a conversation with a couple sitting at the very opposite corner of the counter, a person asked the meaning of the term, tips. My response was "to *insure* prompt service and tips are earned –not given".

The dialogue continued and we communicated our daughter's profitable experience in the restaurant business and shared that her excellent income was a reflection of the fine services she provided. Immediately, the message was processed and an instant metamorphosis transpired. What had taken well over an hour to implement was swiftly resolved in seconds with a shining smile and a sweet voice stating that the next round of drinks was being prepared.

While the liquid refreshments were excellent and the meals were very good, we were needlessly exposed to an unacceptable and uncomfortable experience due to a very negative attitude of the server and an incompetent manager. When the bill was presented and totaled for payment, a note was boldly written on the gratuity line, "I am doing the best that I can". The tip amount was $0.00. Hopefully, this person learned an important lesson. Actions speak louder than words and tips are earned!

In the food industry, you have only one chance to lose a customer.

HER-O

Excitement mounted with less than one-minute remaining in the last basketball game of the season. The winner of this pivotal contest would be invited to advance into the NCAA national championship tournament play. The Trenton State Men's basketball team was leading by two points when Jersey City State took possession of the ball in the back court. A trap play was effectively executed by an aggressive defense. The JCSC guard, realizing the situation, instantly signaled for a time out.

The referee's whistle sounded and the action came to a screeching stop. As the almost "out of control" crowd calmed down to await the important call during this sudden reprieve, our little lady and daughter, wearing the striped shirt of the official scorekeeper, boldly marched on to the court and gave the unmistakable signal for a technical foul that was charged against Jersey City.

The host team's spectators in the bleachers went ballistic. In the meantime, the game officials met at the scoring table to review game statistics. Yes, the violation was correct and TSC was awarded two foul shots that were magnificently made with a swishing, swirling net string sound. They then were given the ball to continue play.

Obviously, it was held until the final time expired and the competition ended. While the defeated dejected home team silently departed to their locker room, exuberant excitement and rowdy raucous behavior engulfed the arena as the victorious visiting squad and their out-of-town fans celebrated.

Ultimately, the Trenton State Basketball Team, of which our son was a member, was invited to participate in the national tournament in Wittenberg, Ohio. It was a thrilling and memorable experience to watch them play in the final game of the playoffs.

Twenty years later, the entire group of national men's basketball champions was placed in the college Hall of Fame. Our "**her-o**" daughter and entire family attended the induction ceremony and banquet to once again support the team. Rene`, who was the score keeper, was never mentioned by name during the formal procedure. She remained at the side line to witness the showering of accolades and gifts for these talented men. As is the case in countless instances, numerous heroes pass through life without ever receiving the recognition that was earned but never rewarded.

THE ST. LOUIS MAGIC STORY

While attending professional sessions at the National Association of Elementary School Principals Convention in St. Louis, Missouri; Nancy was free to explore the city and locate points of interest that we could enjoy at night. Lena Horne, one of my favorite jazz vocalists, was in town and scheduled to appear in a concert that evening. That afternoon, my lovely spouse volunteered to locate the theater and purchase two tickets for the evening performance.

In line at the box office was a young couple who were obviously excited about getting one free admission to the show. The pair was asked, "What's the story?" The response was whispered, "Say magic". This password made patrons eligible for a free complimentary entrance for one person. The transaction was properly completed and she returned to the conference hospitality area with the good news

We stayed in a hotel that provided a courtesy van to the theater which was on the same avenue at a distance of two miles. Interestingly, the same young folks, who shared the special word, were also in the lobby before the presentation. After I was briefly introduced to the couple, we separated and moved to the seats and experienced a fantastic performance.

The curtain closed at the end of the final selection and we headed to the street. Since our timetable that day did not allow for dinner, we were very hungry. A policeman, directing traffic, was asked for a restaurant recommendation and he confidently pointed to the corner and a New York City style steakhouse. In the same café appeared our new friends who were now in trouble with a flat tire.

They agreed to use my AAA card to telephone for assistance. While waiting for help to arrive, I bought them a drink. Once again, we parted as our table became available. After a delightful meal we then proceeded to the street and attempted to hail a taxicab for a return ride to the hotel. Now, the earlier friendly crowded neighborhood was desolate and the environment began to show obvious warning signs of an imminent threat. The search for transportation was futile and we returned to the bistro. We were now informed that a bus stop was two blocks away.

While returning to the darkness, minutes crept by, night sounds became scary and signals of mysterious activities in a deprived dangerous criminal area began to emerge. I asked to hold Nancy's umbrella and grasped it in two firm hands with a protective offensive weapon position. We placed our backs against the brick building wall to watchfully wait.

A police car then pulled up, rolled down the window and asked why we were in that part of town at this late hour. The officer stated that under normal conditions he would provide us with a ride. However, there were two handcuffed characters in the back seat. He then radioed for another squad car to come to this location and pick us up for a secure ride to our hotel.

Realizing that this current dangerous dilemma was accelerating; emotional anxiety peaked when two bright headlights pulled to the curb, the driver opened the door and said, "Get in!" Ready for action and prepared for confrontation, I recognized the same two new acquaintances that we had crossed paths with for the fourth time during that very long trying day. They invited us into their automobile and drove us safely to our hotel destination. Much magic occurred on that memorable date and does it matter that these were young, caring, kind black folks?

I HAVE A WARRANT FOR YOUR ARREST

Both our children were excellent automobile drivers. They each had their own cars and enjoyed an unblemished safety record. Since the college they attended permitted them to have vehicles on campus, we comfortably accepted this arrangement. While our son consumed extra hours playing varsity basketball and had no hours for employment, his older sister obtained a part time job to produce extra spending money. Both, however, had the responsibility to do well in school. The students began classes early in the day and returned to their apartments well after dark.

One day a local police officer came to our home, rang the doorbell and delicately announced that he had a warrant for my arrest for a series of parking violations from Lawrence Township, New Jersey. Those dramatic words had immediate shock value on Nancy.

The explanation was that the young serious athlete lived in a complex with limited parking facilities which were compounded with his late arrival to the lot after games. As a result of these circumstances, he parked in restricted areas. He neglected to pay his fines, which elevated the seriousness of the problem.

Since Dad was the registered owner of the vehicle that he used, the responsibility to pay the ticket costs became this parent's obligation. An immediate telephone call was placed to Trenton State College with a careful explanation of the ramifications related to his carefree attitude on this important matter. In essence, if Father is sent to jail, everything that the family enjoys comes to a screeching halt. Fortunately, this tale has a happy ending and the matter was quickly resolved.

THE LAST STOLEN SANDWICH

The farm in Tolland Mass. was the place where the family gathered for weekends. The annual schedule began in May and extended to Thanksgiving. It was common that all sleeping quarters were used to accommodate our many weekend guests. On several occasions, more than twenty people filled the house for the two-day period.

Visitors provided an abundant supply of groceries and drinks to support the festive, party atmosphere. Some meals were served buffet style on the picnic tables under the shady apple trees. The outdoor stone fire pit and grill were used to heat the servings which had to be warmed. Once ready, we sat together as a group to enjoy a sumptuous, dining, delightful day.

I took joy in waiting for a tender teenager to carefully prepare their plate and select a spot to sit. Generally, the young, hungry, unsuspecting, victim would get everything set, lay down their meal of choice and walk to the iced coolers for a refreshing cold soda. The seasoned villain waited for the optimum moment to pirate on the unguarded food. Slyly, the heaped dish was stolen by the famous family felon who then sauntered to a secluded spot to salivate over the stolen supper.

This game was played over several years and the host was identified as the food villain. Knowing my reputation, the children began their own particular protection procedures. During the cuisine gathering process, they hid their delicious, decorated, dishes in secluded, secret, places. Once finished they proudly sauntered to the eating place to benefit from the fruits of their toils. Once settled, they shot a slick smile and wholesale wink in the hunter's direction. They were even more amused when my plate remained empty.

The last successful theft occurred as my lovely niece, Kara Dawn, vigilantly filled her platter of specially selected salads and sweets. These gastronomical, gourmet, choices were topped off with an appetizing Dagwood style scrumptious looking tuna fish salad sandwich. As she went to select a frosty drink, the harvested, tonsorial, treasure was left unattended. I speedily swiped the complete serving and sauntered south.

While I thought this was amusing and part of the traditional game, she felt quite differently. The innocent child was devastated as she eloquently expressed anger and frustration. It was clear that the young girl loved tuna, the meal was properly prepared and she was totally devastated and disappointed that this was the last portion of her special fish on the banquet table. Her point of view was augmented when the return of the unspoiled stolen portion was refused!

While several youngsters were targeted over the years, this "humorous" ritual produced a lasting impression on the adults and the game came to a permanent and screeching halt. Her justifiable, realistic, reasonable, rage eventually subsided and the smoke emitted from a set of red ears gradually segued into a subtle, sad, smile. This favored lovely lady is currently the mother of her own daughter. When we meet at family gatherings, both of us recall this challenging episode and chuckle.

Lucky me!!

UNDER SURVEILLANCE

The Upper Saddle River School District earned and enjoyed an exceptional reputation for providing an excellent educational and a fully diversified program. Because of this distinction and a close proximity to New York City, and the large commercial complex next-door Montvale, NJ; the borough attracted corporate executives from the entire international business community.

The municipality's pupil population profile included mothers and fathers who placed a high priority on school and learning. The effect of this profound influence was obvious and had a positive impact on student performance. In many cases, children attended our public school during the regular schedule and then they enrolled to participate in a variety of supplementary outside private instructional establishments on weekends.

Prestigious homes located on well landscaped plots were large and multi-level. Youngsters were well attired in the latest high fashioned clothing and were driven to the educational park complex in late model luxury automobiles. Highly motivated learners arrived prior to the bell to participate in an assortment of extra help and pre-class academically oriented activities.

Similar programs were available during the lunch recess period and included: free time, recreational options, athletic games, club selections, cultural presentations and instrumental music or special choral rehearsals. These many supplementary programs were made available through the combined coordinated efforts of dedicated teachers and talented parent volunteers.

A startling, strange, situation occurred early one spring morning. While at the main entrance door to greet the arrivals, a unique, uncharacteristic, dead-beat car was observed to be parked in the first spot in the visitors' lot. Generally, these spaces accommodated current models of extravagant well-polished sparkling vehicles. In this mix was a single, tired, tarnished and gently dented sedan.

Realizing that this was obviously out of character with traditional standard means of transportation, I walked from the building to the distinctively, different, defective set of wheels. Once spotted, the man in the driver's seat quickly pulled up a newspaper to hide his face.

I briskly rapped on the side window and motioned to have the non-electric handle rotated. He lowered the glass and dropped the journal. His response to the inquiry that followed was that he was with the county sheriff's office and on surveillance in a criminal investigation.

It was suggested that he look around the area and observe that his undercover coupé stuck out like a "rusted bucket of well-worn bolts" and his well-known head hiding technique had been extensively exploited by the detective entertainment film industry. As I was easily able to single him out…so was the person he was assigned to observe.

His official wrinkled credentials were requested and police headquarters contacted. Actually, he was the real thing! Before preparing to leave the rather affluent municipality, it was suggested that he take more care in creating a disguise which blended in and to concentrate on using a cover which is commensurate with the clientele being scrutinized

THE GREATEST GIFT A SON CAN GIVE HIS FATHER

He asked me to be the Best Man at his wedding!

BLASTER BOYS

Current technology can be applied to yesterday's tradition when employed to dig an old-fashioned hole. The luxury of trash pick-up is unavailable at the Tolland farm. Therefore, the problem is resolved by burning garbage and hauling recyclables to the town center.

Gramp implemented his own custom by having newcomers to Shangri-La dig a worthless hole to bury rubbish that could have easily been set on fire and reduced to ashes. He notified the grandchildren of this assignment weeks in advance of their visit to the Berkshire Mountains.

On this weekend, our three men who were now old enough to be indoctrinated became the subjects of this well-established ritual. After settling in following their long drive to the country, the site was located, dimensions provided and tools supplied. Detailed directions were given to Charlie, Franch and Web.

The ground selected was rock solid and required mighty muscle, substantial sweat and enormous energy to complete the arduous job. Once instructions were completed, the senior supervisor chuckled as he walked through the rear gate opening and returned to the picnic table under the shade of an old apple tree to sip a cold beer.

In about fifteen minutes, there was an explosion that shook the entire area. The confident, relaxed foreman shot-up from his cozy seat and scrambled to the excavation spot. As his feet scrambled forward, expletives that were never heard from this fine gentleman's vocal cords rocketed forth to fill the air with rather colorful sounds.

The location was instantly transformed into a large smoky crater of dispersed dirt and smashed stones. Two of the young workers placed their shovels so that the handles touched the ground. This positioning enabled them to hide their laughing faces behind the spade's pointed blade which was at their shoulder level. Rob, our son, stepped forward to diffuse the verbal tirade.

The parties approached this conversation from two dramatically different directions. While Gramp realized the potential danger of detonating two quarter sticks of dynamite in this escapade's remote, rural, location and the serious threat of a devastating injury; the blasters accepted the hazing challenge and concentrated on an instant solution to a labor-intensive project.

Wisdom which accumulated with age conflicted with youth's quest for a quick easy labor reduced solution. As a result of this brief heated discussion the message of safety was explicitly emphasized. The excitement of the moment was beautifully resolved when the wise elderly man ended the conversation by calmly stating to the boys, "Nice job!"

A PARENT'S WISH

My wish is that our daughter and son become parents that are equivalent to their Mom and Dad. Over the years, we have spent a great amount of time visiting them in their homes. It has been impressive to observe two devoted and dedicated family settings that are positive and wholesome. Their youngsters are surrounded with love, compassion and caring. Together, our adult children and their spouses satisfied this goal and have exceeded this expectation for our grandchildren.

FINAL SHOPPING FLING

The beautiful first lady of our house continues to enjoy an enthusiastic excitement for varied department stores and extensive mall shopping in Bergen County. After completing daily chores, her very distinctive automobile could be found in one of the several large regional retail centers. She remains talented in scoping sales throughout the area in world record times. Expertise is in the vast domains of product location, competitive pricing and merchandise quality. Bargains are and continue to be her forte.

Prior to our relocating to Four Seasons, newspapers contained many dramatic headline stories about the after dark hazards and dangers associated with women cruising the outlets, shopping centers and mega boutiques by themselves. So, I implemented a marriage procedural change and we traveled together to these establishments.

Knowing that her husband despised this pastime with passion, she eventually became seriously suspicious and apprehensive. Located between the kitchen and family room in our sugar maple split home are two stairs which were used to place our heads comfortably at the same level. This special area was properly labeled a kissing step. Recalling that her all-inclusive annual physical examination was recently completed, she placed us carefully on this selective landing; wrapped her arms warmly around my neck and whispered in a weepy, weary, wobbly, sigh; "Am I terminal?"

MRI

Well past his eightieth birthday, my father was asked to go for an MRI. After the procedure, he asked the technician if there were stones in his head. Pebbles do not form in that part of the body! Dad's immediate response was, "I have been married for well over sixty years and my wife frequently tells me that I have rocks in my head".

ELIGIBLE WIDOWER

Soon after my Mother passed away, the single senior ladies in Dad's neighborhood began to descend on him. In fact, even at Mom's wake, they stated to Nancy that we would not have to worry about Mike because the females will take good care of him.

They continually rang the doorbell with a variety of casseroles and wanted to visit. He never let them in! Nancy suggested this would be an opportunity to cultivate a few friendships. He just was NOT interested.

The door was always unlocked and we walked in one afternoon to visit him. As the kitchen was entered, he was observed crawling across the floor from the sun porch into the living room. I said, "Dad what are you searching to find"?

His surprised remark was, "Nothing, I am just getting the mail that was dropped from the door postal slot. If the widow across the street sees me through my window, she will be over here in a minute and I will never get rid of her"!

With the exception of his shared driveway mates, no neighborhood lady ever entered Dad's home!

THE LAST PAINTING CONTRACTORS JOB

Our son, Rob, and his fiancé, Lisa, were fortunate to be able to build a new home prior to their wedding day. Our first project, after the structure was framed and closed in, was to install the preliminary burglar alarm wiring. Charlie brought a portable electrical generator to the site to power the tools. Within a day, this project was completely finished.

Nancy and I volunteered to be the painting contractors. The biggest job was to fill in what seemed to be thousands of nail holes created by the trim finish carpenters. This task encompassed several very cold, bitter days. Our fingers were raw, frozen, and exhausted. Once completed, we attacked the painting of two coats on the multi paned windows, decorative doors and all the trim molding.

Shortly after the harsh winter season ended, we were ready to paint all the recently sheet rocked surfaces. Rob and I were assisted by his friend, Bob Lock, and Uncle Bob's paint sprayer. While our son operated the electrical device, his partners followed to back roll the white, wet color. In six hours, this team applied fifty-five gallons of paint and produced a highly professional job.

After the honeymoon, the happy couple moved in to organize their brand-new place. Within a short time, we were invited by them for a Sunday afternoon dinner. During the relaxed conversation I was asked to fix a simple ceiling nail pop. Surprisingly, this was not the real problem. The weight of an inferior second floor joist split along its length and protruded through the sheet rock.

By the time this was discovered, it was 5:00pm and the stores were near closing time. We hurried to Home Depot to purchase a new 2``x10`` beam. While the open hole ran the entire width of the ceiling, we successfully removed the damaged section of the original board and bolted the second timber to it. This was identified as a sister structural repair. Within a few days, the ceiling was spackled, painted and returned to its original condition.

SHE WILL NEVER REMEMBER AND GRAMP WILL NEVER FORGET
(CPR Story)

From the time our granddaughter, Lauren, was a few months old until she moved to Minnesota several years later, we had the pleasure of babysitting for her two days per week. Since both parents had full time jobs, we volunteered to take care of the little bundle of joy each Thursday and Friday. The newborn was picked up on Wednesday evening and driven eighty miles to our residence in Bergen County. She returned home, to join her family, late Friday afternoon. This was a standard weekly schedule.

One evening before retiring to bed, Gram, in her nightgown, went to check the infant who was sleeping in the crib. The baby was making barking sounds and throwing up thick rubbery like materials. Grandma immediately shouted for Gramp who was working in the office on the first floor. The distinct sound of her stressed voice, unmistakably, was a warning signal that an urgent situation was occurring.

Entering the nursery, his first aide squad training of several years kicked into high gear! Evaluating the situation, it was determined that there was no breathing, a heartbeat, bluish skin tones and rolled back eyes. "911" was instantly telephoned.

The little tender infant child was gently positioned for respiratory resuscitation and the procedure began. Within a few short timely puffs, independent breathing was restored which was followed by an expulsion of a hard, white, solid, food substance that traveled out of the tiny mouth and across the room.

The beloved girl was very warm and appeared to have a rather high body temperature. The township ambulance was telephoned, and it seemed to instantly arrive on the scene. Fortunately, this very competent and professional crew took charge and prepared the tot for hospital transport. Upon arrival, the emergency room staff treated the little one and quickly resolved the health concern.

After completing their long, anxious journey to the medical center, the parents entered the recovery room to comfort, cuddle, and care for their newborn who by now had completely recuperated from this traumatic experience. Once the hospital paperwork was completed, five exhausted individuals returned to our house. The precious princess, however, was the only one able to finish the evening with a well-earned restful sleep.

In summary, the child will never remember this incredible incident; the grandparents will never forget.

THE HAIR STYLIST

During a very recent visit from my twelve-year-old granddaughter, she shared a deep dark secret that was kept from the time the child was four years old. In a conversation about the "Olden Days", the youngster asked if I remembered when we played Beauty Shop. My recollection immediately flashed back to those wonderful days when I had a substantial head of black hair.

Thru that period while I positioned myself at her feet and on the floor, this lovely toddler would sit on the sofa to brush my thick locks. At the same time, she would use a spray to moisten my head to create and style my new exciting coiffeur. During one delightful experience she was asked if water was being used from her magic squirt container. An immediate resounding yes was the response! This pleasant relaxing experience frequently continued over the years.

Before this recent trip down memory lane ended and she had to return to her home in Minnesota, my dear young lady made her confession. She announced in a rather timid voice, "Gramp, I want you to know there was Windex in the bottle that was used on your head". My surprised but affectionate delayed reply to her was, "Oh, now that clearly explains why and how my hair color has changed from coal black to snow white".

THE GREATEST GIFT A DAUGHTER CAN GIVE HER FATHER

Please stay with me until I am taken into the baby delivery room!

PARENT'S INCOME TAX SHOEBOX

Income tax, Medicare and family record keeping were responsibilities that I assumed early in life. The first assignment, while a college student, was to take care of my grandmother's medical and fiscal affairs. Accurate records were maintained to ensure that government entitlements were in order and eligible to be received.

Later the task expanded to include my parents' money matters. Each tax season, an overstuffed shoebox was presented to me that contained every paper morsel that was collected over the year. The information was disorganized, mostly unnecessary and essentially inappropriate. The overstuffed container was presented to me immediately following Mom's sumptuous Italian home cooked dinner.

After finishing the lengthy sorting and separating process, an arduous filing procedure began. Voids in their documentation keeping activities were resolved. Before the evening ended, their state and federal income tax reports were completed. Over the next few days, they reviewed the data for comfort and accuracy. The following week's dinner assignment involved Dad copying the corrected and revised returns.

Finally finished, the forms were mailed. The purpose of my entire assignment was to make sure they always received a refund. Once posted, they patiently waited for the arrival of their treasury checks. The annual challenge was always successful, and I continued to serve as their only accountant for several years.

The financial guidance supervision journey continued when Nancy's parents reached the time when their data keeping issues became cumbersome. For one winter season while in Florida, they were our next-door apartment neighbors. Within a short time, it was obvious that maintaining their asset portfolio presented a major challenge.

They were relieved to have their daughter, Nancy, volunteer to manage their business transactions. While statements were not in a traditional financial shoebox, their investments were scattered among a variety of mutual funds and several banking institutions. During the next few years, their profile was reviewed, updated and consolidated.

When the time arrived for them to move to Ann's Choice in Pennsylvania, their monetary matters were in excellent condition. They easily qualified to meet the necessary requirements for relocation to the Erickson property in Warminster, PA. This complex was an excellent, supportive and nurturing facility for them.

They were now in a place that was free from home maintenance concerns. In addition, there was easy access to professional medical resources, entertainment explorations and availability to meet many new friends. Most importantly, they were in a wholesome environment that enabled them to continue enjoying a lifestyle to which they were both accustomed. In essence, their living expenses were greatly reduced; quality of life was enriched, recreational or social activities enhanced, proximity to their both daughters and family life dramatically improved.

These series of experiences, over time, can be used as a preview of my future coming attractions.

ONLY TWO MORE WEEKS

During my teen years, Dad frequently expressed, "Only two more weeks". At the time, these words were considered a joke and amusing. It took me well into adulthood to realize the profound wisdom and impact of this very powerful phrase. I realized the significance of these important few words.

Listed below is my interpretation and application of his message:

Cherish family, friends, and heritage

Take care of loved ones

Love God and country

Practice the Golden Rule

Define your purpose in life

Enjoy the present

Plan for the future

Take advantage of all educational opportunities

Habits are cumulative

Respect honesty and integrity

Have money in the bank

A dollar can be spent only once and use it wisely

Maintain accurate and current records

Minimize unfinished business

Avoid unnecessary debt

Define your desired legacy

FALLING OFF THE ROOF

Our family was fortunate to live in a comfortable three-story home in Bergen County, New Jersey for thirty-eight years. The residence grew with us over time as it went through several renovations and major additions. Fortunately, I had the skills to do most of the work and keep maintenance and routine repairs current.

The abode was always in excellent condition from the chimney top to the footings in the basement. While living there, it was common to find me on the top of the building cleaning rain gutters, replacing missing shingles or tarring separated vent pipe flashings. In addition, I installed a new roof before moving.

As the years passed, the mother of our precious two children stated with sincere determination; "If you fall off the thirty-foot-high roof, please pray that you die because I did not choose to be a nurse for the rest of my life".

So low and behold, we eventually moved to an up-to-date address at Four Seasons in Columbus, New Jersey where reconstruction and refurbishing requirements would be at a minimum. The lovely lady of this house has been freed from this potential caretaker burden and is now able to shop or concentrate her energy as a social creature that flits from one party flower to another.

SNOW SHOVELING

While living in a lovely residential suburban community, upkeep of a home was the sole responsibility of each individual owner. Duties were year-round and included general maintenance, decorating, construction, lawn care and the full variety of all the other chores.

During the last winter in Washington Township, the white fluffy, frosty stuff began to fall from the dreary, dim, cold, gray sky. The predicted accumulation was for several inches and the removal was clearly defined as a very harsh, brisk, laborious assignment!

After properly dressing for the task at hand and before walking outside and into the frozen evening darkness, I asked my faithful spouse to periodically check on me. The confident response from Nancy was, "There is no need to examine the work because you always do an excellent job"! The concern, however, was not to evaluate the finished product but to ensure that the snow shoveler was not under a car suffering from a heart attack.

WINTER
From Ages: 61 to ....???

WHERE DOES THE TIME GO?

While deeply involved in thought, my three-year-old granddaughter asked a profound question, "What happens to today?" A simple answer to the complicated subject was that it became yesterday. Over time, however, I have pondered the thoughts relating to this interesting matter and concluded that yesterday is gone forever, and what remains are today and tomorrow.

Dwelling on past events tends to be counterproductive and a rather inefficient expenditure of energy. Making the best of this present day and preparing for the future is where an enormous effort should be expended. Every day is a gift, and those precious moments should be spent wisely.

A full lifetime consists of an accumulation of many episodes, measured in seconds, which occur in bits and pieces. While these small segments collect into minutes, hours, days, years, decades, and generations; they are an assortment of combined valuable encounters that reflect the past and determine a person's future. Hopefully, worthwhile daily deeds result in positive rewards that impact individuals, their families, and friends.

On the other hand, harmful habits merge to produce less than desirable consequences. With the passing of time, well established and distinctively defined patterns can be used to predict and determine a quality of life that can be expected and experienced.

As an active participant in the AARP age group and described as being "over the hill" I hear conversations from peers that day's fly by with the speed of a downhill skier. This is a wonderful sign for folks who are continuing the race through life and taking full advantage of the many marvels that are available in this beautiful and exciting world!

Remember: Yesterday is history. Today is the present and the reason why it is called a gift.

Tomorrow is a mystery.

THE GREATEST GIFT FROM GRAMP

During the infant and toddler times of our first granddaughter's early years, many cheerful hours were devoted to singing the alphabet song and listening to nursery rhymes. Later large picture books were used to establish connections between illustrations and descriptive words or phrases

This was followed by a causal study of consonant and vowel sounds and how they were combined to form blends. As she grew, the repertoire expanded to include classic children's literature with an introduction to easily recognizable words.

When ready, we developed lists of word families and the relationships to their collections of letters. Over the course of her preschool years, a certain magic occurred, and she learned to figure out the code and begin very basic reading.

Several years later, I received a Father's Day card which contained a thank you note. It was neatly written in a child's hand and stated, "Gramp, you gave me the greatest gift ever. You taught me how to read".

While I was given much credit for this celebrated accomplishment, it is well known that several other factors and numerous dedicated people contributed to this important achievement. The spotlight should be opened, spread, and shared with the many special individuals who were not mentioned in the little girl's profound letter. Parents, relatives, neighbors, and fantastic teachers are all invited to enjoy the accolades associated with this very special compliment.

RETIREMENT

Nancy and I continue to enjoy all the wonderful benefits associated with retirement. We have an abundance of time with nothing to do. However, there are seldom enough hours to accomplish all that is planned for each day and the overload must be scheduled for the exciting future. Recently, a need has developed to cut back on our numerous high energy activities.

Hours are now consumed with a new and frustrating adventure. Currently, we find it necessary to dedicate many more waking moments for the purpose of locating items that have been filed for safekeeping or inadvertently misplaced. It is now a poor sign to walk into the garage and forget what I seek to find. The next unfortunate step is to again walk the same path and realize that I am lost!

Actually, both of us feel so good that we are beginning to worry. Life is fantastic!

MOVE TO FOUR SEASONS

We moved into our three-story Washington Township home as newlyweds and planned to remain there until "death do us part". Because of the close proximity to family, friends and employment, this concept was firmly established in our long-range future plan. Through the following years, the home was well maintained, modified, renovated, and expanded to include: nine rooms, three lavatories, swimming pool, cabana, and two large decks. After thirty-eight years of raising a family and accepting the lonely "empty nest", we finally completely redecorated and began enjoying the comforts of retirement.

During the next few years, our dear friends continued their search for a retirement home. While our map was fixed, we enjoyed sharing conversations about their final move. Eventually, their time arrived, and they found a perfect location in Columbus, NJ. In the meantime, we were committed to babysit our young granddaughter who lived in Bordentown.

While returning the child to her parents after the eighty-five-mile drive, we were invited and made a date to visit the models in our friend's chosen new destination. Near the end of the turnpike trip, the little girl fell asleep, and it was decided that her nap was important enough to not be interrupted. Therefore, I remained with sleeping beauty. Nancy visited various styles of new homes. Upon her return, she stated that the designs were attractive, and an age restricted community was an interesting concept.

Since our trips to Bordentown were a weekly event, we frequently accompanied our friends to the sales office to help them during their selection process of upgrades. These visits consistently coincided with the slumber session of the precious princess and Gramp elected to remain in the car with the child.

Late one evening as we returned to Bergen County, I noticed that Nancy was very quiet and I wanted to learn about her deep thinking. The response was that I would not believe what was on her mind! With a little bit of coaxing she said, "I would like to move". As a joke, I responded, "Start cleaning the accumulation of almost four decades of attic stuff".

The very next Saturday she was found in the storage loft, teary eyed, and filling a collection of large black garbage bags. She was serious!

The rest is ancient history, the move occurred, and we lived happily ever after.

LIFETIME OF LESSONS YEAR `ROUND TAN

During the great depression, my mother's oldest brother had to leave school to find work and contribute to the household income. After several years as a career bus driver, this strikingly handsome young man found employment as a family chauffeur. Over the years, the daughter of the wealthy businessman fell madly in love with my fortunate uncle and they eventually married to live happily ever after.

As a young growing child, I had a few memorable opportunities to visit their mansion located at the New Jersey shore. In addition to all the traditional rooms, their lavish residence had a study, library, music room and a fully solid raised cherry paneled spacious dining room. They were serviced by a live-in-maid and full-time gardener. The few trips taken to their residence required wearing a suit and tie.

On occasion when the "distant relative" stayed with my grandmother who lived in Northern Jersey, he would also stopover at my home. He was generous and frequently brought along special gifts. His full head of stylish white hair was set upon an easily recognizable summer and winter golden bronzed face. Attire was augmented by fine tailored clothing that created an elegant appearance.

In addition to his collection of beautiful suits, shirts, slacks and sweaters, his country club apparel included a brilliant solid red sport jacket that completed the picture. He presented a fashionable and distinguished image of a well-groomed successful individual.

As a teenager, the wonderful thought of a year around healthy-looking complexion was impressive. This gentleman's quality representation, as a role model, did establish several subtle standards for me to enjoy a wardrobe which is now comparable to his and it, too, includes a stylish scarlet coat. Needless to say, my hair is now a color of chimney smoke and wintering in Florida has supplied the source for the desired yearlong tan. Now, retired to Four Seasons introduced me to the "Too Old to Be Cold" philosophy.

Life is good!

THE MISSING PROFESSIONAL SILVER COFFEE URN

We moved into the Four Seasons on January 16, 2001. Once settled, we shared a mutual goal to establish a new circle of friends. Within the next year, our home was identified as a major community entertainment center for neighbors and acquaintances. Evenings provided many opportunities to mix, mingle and socialize. Ultimately, folks gathered at 35 Ellington Drive after scheduled activities.

Nancy was quickly identified as a magnificent hostess with a gracious home which had a full liquor cabinet and several table tops that included a complete variety of interesting, bursting, candy dishes. These were always available to visitors. While she provided coffee, an assortment of snacks and desserts; my role was to be co-host plus bartender.

Before the second year in our new home, we accumulated a magnificent mixture of new acquaintances. At that time, it was decided to have a Christmas party for the new combination of neighbors and guests. When completed, the list included over seventy people. Although our home could comfortably accommodate all these folks, it was determined that two separate brunches be presented on a weekend. In order to enjoy this affair and free us to participate in the event, it was arranged to hire a waitress.

The week prior to the gathering, our "Mr. Coffee" pot broke and was put in the trash barrel. Although we had a thirty-cup maker for a regular brew, it was necessary to have a second machine for decaf. Happily, a neighbor, Ursula came forty with a beautiful, professional, silver brewer that produced seventy cups. Between both machines, more was produced than required. As a matter of routine, the broken container was placed in its box next to the garbage can in the garage by Nancy.

Renee, the waitress, (not our daughter) was a tremendous asset that allowed us the comfort of completely enjoying our open house. Her talent and abundant skills enabled us to totally participate in the morning functions. She magically remembered each person's choice of beverage and maintained everyone with a fresh glass or cup.

During her time in our entertainment areas, she kept the home pin neat. When finished, there was nothing left for us to do! A magnificent job was completed in a timely manner and very well done.

On rubbish day, I asked if the coffee maker should be thrown out with the other debris. Without checking with me, Nancy said, "Yes". This assignment was completed and mistakenly Ursula's borrowed pot now in the refuse was placed curbside for collection.

Soon after the rubbish was gathered by the truck, empty cans were returned to their normal storage place. Later in the day, the lady of the house went to the garage to return the special, fancy, silver urn. It was nowhere to be found. She came into the house and excitedly asked, "Where is Ursula's urn?"

My reply was, "I don't know and show me where it is." She took me to the spot where the big white and blue box was located. It was gone! Now, the very distressed wife asked, "Where did you move it?" Obviously, our interpretation of the previous brief conversation was dramatically different! "I threw it out".

Needless to say, my conscious spouse was very upset. She immediately went to the telephone to call Ursula and explained that there was something important to say. It was necessary to tell her in person. The friend's response was, "Just tell me over the phone".

Nancy replied, "It has to be done in person" and she then drove to Ursula's and gave the bad news. This beautiful person was relieved and subsequently upset that she took the distressed messenger by the shoulders and shook her vigorously to cause her head to rotate. While at the same time proceeded to tell Nancy that she thought the conversation would be about cancer or divorce. In this comforting exchange it was stated that a new one was located, and it was about to be picked up at the store.

Ultimately a few years later, Billy and his wife moved to the Villages in Florida. This urn and its legend were "gifted" and resides in our attic ready to be shared by anyone who needs to borrow a seventy-cup machine that is attached to a profound story.

ASTHMA

As a child, I knew very few people who suffered from breathing disorders, asthma. I enjoyed excellent health, actively participated in athletic events, and played competitive basketball in high school and college. I was selected to represent my district in a summer tour playing in a variety of tournaments throughout the United States. I was also fortunate to make the starting team as a freshman in college. Except for struggling for air while playing in the mile-high city, Denver, breathing endurance and stamina were never a problem.

Towards the end of my studies at Paterson State College, I developed a persistent cough. The throat tickle and attempts to get some reliefs were always more embarrassing than uncomfortable. I was always strong enough to sustain the rasping sounds which now migrated from the mouth to the central chest area.

Eventually, I visited a doctor friend that I grew up with and he prescribed an antihistamine. This medication brought the problem under control. However, the side effects made me sleepy and required napping when not involved in classes, working in the shoe store, operating a music studio or playing weekend band jobs. While on campus, employment activities frequently exceeded eighty hours per week. Considering these factors, I could accept the need to rest during down times.

The hacking coughing problem became more intense as years passed. My persona was identified with being dressed in a suit or tuxedo seven days per week, actively involved in family activities with the children, maintaining a home, caring for a swimming pool and severe coughing. While my lungs never experienced the impact of cigarettes, my life was always consumed with the deep sounds of a heavy smoker. Teachers in my building claimed that my sounds provided them with a warning signal of me being in their vicinity. A problem never occurred while teaching, demonstrating lessons or presentations before large groups.

One day while sitting in my principal's office, it was realized that I was running out of physical strength to endure the stressful sounds that were being emitted from my lungs. I telephoned home, explained the desperate situation, and said that I needed to see a pulmonary specialist immediately. Nancy was always tuned into the situation, had done some previous research and knew of a well-respected doctor who was located about forty miles from our home.

Without delay, an appointment was arranged. After extensive interviewing, testing and a thorough examination, a diagnosis was provided. The physician confidently stated the difficulty was determined and his prescription protocol would enable me to enjoy 80% relief. He was accurate! We departed from the medical facility with a bag containing pills, inhalers, and detailed instructions. Within a few hours the comfort level continued to improve, and the welcome growing sense of satisfaction remained.

This improved level was enjoyed for many years and the doctor was visited twice annually for consultations and minor tweaking of the medication protocol. My last appointment to the medical center was profound. The doctor who "saved my life" was not there. Because of the several miles traveled, it was suggested that I be seen by one of the associates. As was the situation in the past, the prescription was slightly modified. While the minor coughing condition was stabilized, there were side effects that were intolerable. I experienced: body trembling, excessive perspiration, memory loss, cognitive difficulties, out of body sensations, sudden weight loss of thirty pounds and an inability to work at school. Competency levels deteriorated from very normal to much less than adequate. What a disaster!

Out of desperation, an appointment was scheduled with our local family physician. He listened to my current prescription protocol and recommended that aggressive medications be stopped. Within a few days, the body chemistry issues were resolved and I was able function confidently, comfortably and to return to school.

Once located in our new location at Four Seasons, I sought recommendations for an area pulmonary specialist. Under his guidance, I enjoyed a conventional lifestyle by adhering to a moderate medication program. In addition, I visited a hypnotist for a few sessions that were related to relaxation training. While serving on the Mansfield Township Zoning Board and involved in a variance hearing, I exhibited a few coughing symptoms that were related to asthma. After the meeting, a neighbor approached me and inquired about my respiratory difficulties. After discussing my history, he presented a very convincing detailed case in support of taking a daily tablet of bee pollen. Magically, it worked, and all the medications have been eliminated! Finally, after many years, the breathing difficulties have been resolved.

MOTHER HUBBARD MISSING WEDDING DRESS MISSES THE RECEPTION

From the first moment of meeting my future spouse, while in the Paterson State College Library, I was impressed by the appearance that played before my eyes. She sat graciously at the table to prepare for the next class. My friend and I asked the pair of girls if we could share and use the empty chairs and do some homework.

Ultimately, this relationship evolved into an appropriate conversation. I slyly lifted her textbook cover and shrewdly recorded the telephone number. This positive experience was the beginning of a wonderful lifetime of adventure, happiness, excitement, fulfillment, deep love and an incredible successful marriage.

Always, and from that first moment we met; she was the "attractive lady" who was well groomed, exceptionally attired and really put together. Most of all, her clothing was handmade and carefully tailored by her mother. In most instances, she was the best dressed person at all the functions we attended. Consistently, I was very proud to have her at my side and on my arm. This wonderful pattern has continued to the present moment. It is noteworthy to state with utmost confidence that her beautiful gown at our son's wedding was a sensation! The only time this standard changed was for our daughter's nuptial day a year later.

The search began and the mother of the bride found "a must have outfit" which included a matching jacket and a very full gown that was tastefully beaded. In my opinion it did not match her history for selecting sensational, appropriate, stylish apparel. Because the shop owner strongly insisted that a larger size be ordered and reluctantly placed, an ill-fated disaster began to unravel over time. The crux of the problem was the garment was way too big and impossible to remedy!

During the arduous, time consuming, fitting process that included many devastating disappointments, the "Mother Hubbard" dress continued to deteriorate. It got worse with each successive visit. Ultimately, a master men's tailor was engaged to address the sad calamity. The downhill pattern continued!

The week before the big day, Nancy," the mother of the bride" finally realized this was an impossible circumstance that was well beyond mending. A second hunt began, and her exasperation was resolved when an alternate ball gown was located on the rack in a prominent boutique shop. My perplexed wife placed a deposit on the elegant garment, telephoned me at work and asked that I join her at the salon for an opinion. While there, the outfit was modeled for me. She radiated and looked stunning. "Now what?" she asked. I suggested that she sit on my lap and suggested that the Mother Hubbard "costume" be worn in church and the newly purchased "Cinderella" dress, which was fantastic, stunning, stylish and extremely suitable to be presented at the reception.

While Rene was the bride and the focal part of the party, Nancy's very magnificent gown presentation certainly complimented the wedding group as we received guests and poised for wonderful photographs. The dress episode was eloquently summarized when this now outstanding attired lady stepped from the hotel elevator for a grand entrance into the wedding reception ballroom. Rob, our son excitedly and accurately expressed, "Now that is my mother!"

ST. PATRICK'S DAY

As the calendar approached March 17th, our primary grade youngster stated with wisdom beyond her years, "St. Patrick's Day is one the friendliest holidays of the entire year". She gave several reasons to support her statement.

Everyone in school including: pupils, teachers, visitors and the principal seem to be Irish and the event is celebrated as a national feast. Green is the color of the day, and it is seen throughout the building. Clothing attire, wall decorations, balloons, four leaf clovers, shamrocks and shillelaghs are all over the place and everyone seems cheerful. It's also safe to say HAPPY SAINT PATRICK'S DAY with no fear of being uncomfortable with children and grown-ups from other national, ethnic or religious backgrounds. We sang and danced to Irish music and shared a really good time. I also saw people wearing bright KISS ME I'M IRISH signs.

As she left the conversation, I took some time to internalize her observations and reflected on the shared thoughts. In conclusion, likewise, I will be delighted to also be Irish on that special occasion, eat corned beef and cabbage while drinking green liquids.

Maybe this is the preverbal "pot of gold" that is at the end of the global rainbow that can surround us in this troubled world!

SURPRISING SENIOR WEDDING

While waiting to be seated in a fine Florida restaurant, a stunning young beautiful bride stepped from the stretch limousine and was escorted by a handsome young man wearing a tuxedo. Shortly an elderly gentleman who appeared to be the great grandfather hobbled on a wobbly cane into the lobby. It appeared that he had one foot on the proverbial banana peel and the other on the direct path to the golden gates.

A member of our small dinner party, in the spirit of joy and happiness, extended congratulations to the aged white-haired chap. He said with a cheerful, sincere, smiling face, "Your granddaughter, all dressed in white, is a beautiful bride". The elderly man's curt and less than kind retort was, "I **am** the groom!"

SARAH THE HORSE

My three-year-old granddaughter, Alyssa. trained me to be her indoor prancing pony. Using a variety of household treasures, the little child outfitted me with a bridle, reins and a saddle. Like a precision machine, I was guided around, over and through a variety of obstacles in the house. Once routes were mastered, she would steer me in reverse though the same path.

The complicated course changed frequently, and the white-haired stallion could never memorize the ever-changing route. The exercise continued until the story period which was followed by nap time. Then, the old steed would retire and rest on the couch.

This activity progressed in a variety of forms. As a pre-teenager, her parents graduated her to a real horse owner and contest rider. Persistent habits, dedication and rigorous training have rewarded her with being the proud winner of many show ribbons.

While enjoying playing dress-up and applying "make-up", she would much rather spend time in the barn cleaning stalls, grooming the horse and training the 1,800-pound steed. At this point in her young and developing life, she set a goal to attend Rider College and become a member of the equestrian team.

NINE- ELEVEN THROUGH THE EYES OF A THREE-YEAR-OLD

Shortly after moving to Four Seasons at Mapleton on January 16, 2001, the ten-minute drive to babysit in Bordentown became a safer trip and more comfortable pleasurable weekly routine. While Gram was involved with exploratory road trips centered on shopping and becoming acquainted with the new geographic area, Gramp became the designated person in charge of childcare.

After breakfast chores and while the infant, Chad, was prepared for a morning nap, his three-year-old sister, Alyssa, set up her retired grandfather for an early workout to play "Sarah the Horse". While a soft scarf was placed in his mouth to be used as a bridle, a towel was positioned on his back to replicate a saddle. A gentle tug on the silk rein signaled the direction in which the white-haired senior stallion trotted. Each time the rider approached a fluffy chair, the steed reared up to throw the junior jockey gently off his back.

The mount would fall in a face up position with four hoofs pointing toward the ceiling. He would then produce pony sounds which signaled the need for "ENERGY". The little lass quickly jumped from the sofa to smother him with a bounty of beautiful kisses. Once fully refueled, the pair took to the trail for another challenging, wild adventurous, journey around the house.

On Tuesday morning, September 11, 2011, the telephone rang and the little girl's Dad told us to turn on the television. There, and before our eyes, we saw the continued developing saga of the complete sequence, setting, and a shocking series of historical events! The sickening descriptions and variety of scary scenes sequenced over and over.

Eventually, my sad and very young impressionable granddaughter asked me to turn off the TV screen. Expressions on the tender tot's face were combined with streams of tears rolling from her set of upset eyes. This permanently embossed a mental memory in my mind that tore at my heartstrings. These dramatic sights will never be forgotten. By no means will I even understand or ever know the impact of these poignant images and the lasting impressions that she must have internalized.

I AM NOT GOING TO MARRY GRAMP

From the day my granddaughter was born, she would curl up on my lap while I sang an ABC song and told her stories. One of her favorite tales was about us getting married when I grew up, living in a large palace and riding horses. Grandmother's tasks will be to take care of the castle, cook and clean the horses. This yarn was spun so frequently that she thought it was going to eventually occur when Gramp was old enough.

Well… shortly after her tenth birthday and sharing this romantic fable once again, she placed tiny hands on her hips, shyly looked at me and glibly smiled; "Gramp, I can't marry you". I asked, "Why?" Her response will be embossed in my memory forever, "You have too many wrinkles!"

CRYING DOESN'T WORK

We have five beautiful grandchildren. Two of them live in Bordentown and three live in Apple Valley, Minnesota. Because of the location, we spend many more occasions with the New Jersey children. Over time, they have made remarkable adjustments to our simple rules and behavioral standards. They know that we give directions once and they comfortably comply. When an adult response is "No", it is consistent and remains unchallenged.

Recently, the long-distance Minnesota youngsters had an opportunity to visit their east coast relatives. During the vacation, the four parents planned to go out for the evening and left the babysitting duties to the very capable grandparents.

Within a short period of time, the out-of-town toddler Michael, made a request that could not be granted. He processed the information and then began shedding tears. With that, the little local cousin, Chad, walked over to him and clearly stated, "Michael, Crying doesn't work!"

HANDYMAN IN MINNESOTA

Our vacation schedule included a visit to Apple Valley, Minnesota during the first few weeks of August to celebrate the first granddaughter's birthday. We enjoyed taking her to the zoo, swimming pool, amusement park and the Mall of America. Between these excursions, grandma took over household chores, food shopping, cooking and attending to the children.

While she took care of these responsibilities, Gramp worked on the fine lawn, trimmed the shrubs, washed the windows, painted the garage doors, and refinished the front porch banister and furniture. When not with the youngsters, he actively worked on these projects and did a professional job.

One evening, as we gathered for dinner, the telephone rang. Our daughter-in-law answered the call. Within a few moments she laughed as the conversation continued. In essence, the chat was very complimentary to the handy man that was described as working nonstop from early morning to late afternoon.

As the accolades continued, a contact number for the workman was requested. The neighbor asked permission to hire the gentleman after he completed the projects at their home. Lisa, our son's wife, explained that I was her husband's father, and this was part of his vacation and is not interested in taking on any more assignments before returning to New Jersey.

POP

We moved to Four Seasons on January 16, 2001. Within two weeks a scheduled vacation was taken in the Dominican Republic. Upon our return, the house, garage, and storage attic were organized. Eventually, days became warmer, and the weather took on spring-like characteristics

It was now the season to work on the grass. Although landscape maintenance was included in the monthly fees, I wanted to duplicate the "picture perfect" lawn that surrounded our Bergen County home. A local commercial nursery was visited and several bags of lime, pre-emergence crabgrass chemicals and fertilizer were purchased.

A conscientious counter clerk spotted my full head of white hair and helpfully said, "Pop, would you like me to carry the supplies and load the car trunk?" I was taken-aback by this genuine offer and gesture of kindness. However, pride, self-image and masculine identity were tarnished and challenged. My instinctive response was less than gracious! The need to demonstrate my youthful strength, vigor and independence had to be illustrated and I quickly packed the auto.

While in Pompano Beach, Florida, a second test was encountered relative to my age. Our winter condo was directly across from a large Publix food store and located on a very busy street. Several senior citizens walked their loaded shopping carts across the six lanes to our apartment complex. Unfortunately, they left their empty wagons in the residential parking lot.

Because this created an unsightly situation, I would frequently collect the empty carts and return them to the shopping center. Early one morning, while waiting for a break in the traffic, a police car with flashing lights stopped in the middle of the roadway. The officer exited his vehicle and halted traffic speeding in both directions.

Realizing this was an authentic, dramatic, and serious, security, signal to help me; I quickly proceeded across the avenue and enthusiastically thanked the man in blue who clearly was concerned for both my health and safety.

Lesson learned; graciously accept assistance when it is sincerely offered.

MUTUAL RESPECT

We have three teenage granddaughters who are proud honor roll students in school. Over one thousand miles separate them from spending more time together. The oldest of the trio lives in Minnesota, is a proficient dancer, a very positive role model and is held in high esteem by the younger sister and New Jersey cousin.

During a visit to Bordentown, Lauren and Alyssa decided to visit the barn to groom, exercise and ride "Tundra", an 1800-pound steed. It was interesting to observe that the young horse lady's talents were immediately recognized and respected by the Midwestern relatives.

While there is a three-year age difference between the two older children, the farm field experience developed a wonderful opportunity to create a chance to admire and develop a mutual respect between both youngsters. This occasion, through the eyes of Gramp, was a milestone event and both learned to appreciate the differences, abilities, skills, and gifts of each other.

UNTIMELY HEADACHE

While swimming at the condo pool in Pompano Beach Florida during a fine February afternoon, a cluster of senior citizens and snow birds reminisced about the "good olden days". In that conversation a lovely attractive widow of many years expressed to the group, as her sparkling smile glistened in the warmed glare of delightful sunshine, "My only wish is that I didn't have so many headaches when my husband was still alive!"

CLOTHING CAPERS THROUGH THE YEARS

Clothing makes the person! My tale begins with homemade outfits that were hand sewn by my mother and constructed from recycled hundred-pound chicken feed bag liners. This inexpensive textile was made from a tightly woven cotton material that separated the poultry food from the raw burlap outer covering. Because hens and roosters were raised by several neighbors during World War II, this salvaged fabric source was readily available, and it came in a variety of practical patterns which were used to construct sun suits for toddlers.

The boy's design had an open "fly" seam in the appropriate spot which signified the distinction from a girl's chic style. During these difficult economic times, hand-me-downs were an important resource in creating my wardrobe. There was an established line of succession as the garments passed to different homes.

Normally, youngsters had three sets of clothing. Brand new articles were worn to church on Sunday, next was school attire, and last was play wear. This sequence was repeated when the fashions passed to the next family. Lucky, I was always the tallest child in my age group and was, therefore, early in the sequence.

Except for socks, shoes, hats and handkerchiefs, Mom had difficulty finding other items when shopping for me. Usually, things in my size or the selections were very few in number and less than desirable in appearance. On one memorable desperate occasion, two shirts exactly the same were purchased so that they could be washed and worn on alternate days. In response to a classmate's question about always wearing the identical striped red, blue, black and white polo shirt, she suggested the classmate be told that they are two of the same kind and, if required, they can be worn together on the same day. Knickers and a matching double-breasted jacket were worn for my first communion celebration, and they eventually went through weekly church dress succession. However, it was passed on before it hit the play wardrobe pile. My aunt would commonly buy new outfits for Christmas and Easter, and they would generally be passed on after they graduated from Sunday duty.

The warmest winter wear in my closet was a cousin's retired Navy pea coat which had his name stenciled on the outer breast pocket. Although the names were different, nobody ever made a comment about its original ownership.

I remember that only "poor kids" wore sneakers and jeans to school. You had to carry the black PF Keds on your shoulders on gym days and protect them from being thrown over the telegraph wires by some wise guy. Because of my size, I was lucky and never had the problem of defending in-flight sneakers.

For grammar school graduation, I wore my first new store-bought suit complimented with a herringbone and tweed full length topcoat. These remained essential articles in high school and the dark blue suit was worn on my first band job as a fifteen-year-old accordion soloist in a local beer joint.

A sports outfit was later purchased to match the dress apparel of a musical combo that I worked with on weekends. As the group became more popular, tuxedos, in many colors and styles, were added to the collection. An interesting accessory to complete the picture was the utilization of formal white pleated stiff paper shirt fronts and removable separate collars that were rather comfortable after moistening with performance perspiration.

During college, I operated a music studio and managed a chain of cancellation shoe stores. Suits and ties were a part of the required attire. It was always difficult to find a selection in my size until I met my future father-in-law who was in the men's tailoring business. He had stores filled with shirting and men's stylist woolen fabric samples. Finally, my dressing dilemma was resolved, and I could now accumulate a wardrobe collection of custom-made suits, sport coats, slacks and monogrammed shirts.

My favorite is still a blue and white striped short, sleeve shirt with my initials stitched on the tattered button-down collar. Nancy has written on the pocket, "OLD SHIRT", to remind me that it must not be worn in public. However, it has been seen on several occasions as I traveled to various shopping centers in and around the Four Seasons.

ROB'S DOCTORATE

When the news from Minnesota reached New Jersey that our son was to be awarded his doctoral degree, the east coast relatives determined they would be in Apple Valley to witness the proud event. As it turned out, this required more determination than they had any reason to foresee.

On October 14, 2005, all eight of us, which included grandparents (ages 88 and 87) aunt, uncle, daughter and her husband met at Philadelphia Airport. It had been raining for seven days and people were sitting, lounging, and sleeping in every available space. A multitude of flights were terminated as the storm worsened.

The US Airways flight was scheduled to leave at 6:00 pm. Before getting on the plane at 8:00 pm, they moved us to six different gates. After sitting on board for a half hour, the tired travelers became very upset when told the most significant flight of our life had been canceled,

Our ticketing and jetway agents, who had been helping us during the disaster, recognized the importance of this occasion and quickly began the process of relocating another flight. These several complicated multi-tasks were masterfully managed at the very highest professional level and these extremely competent folks must be complimented for their actions.

They located an aircraft that was departing in ten minutes with three available seats. We raced through the corridor to arrive at the next gate. A customer rep immediately boarded the airliner and passionately described our situation and announced to the passengers that five more seats were needed by a family who are attending a graduation the next morning. A magical atmospheric quality passed through the travelers' compartment as one person at a time graciously offered their place.

A gentleman next to Mom quickly stood up, and then another pair of men followed him. Now only two more vacancies were needed. The spokesperson appealed again and one more male left. As each passenger donated their place, another family member boarded and heard cheering and clapping. Everyone was rooting for us. Now. only one more spot was needed for our son-in-law. Again, the agent made another heartfelt speech. A lady sitting across from our daughter clasped her hand and said she would exit.

Finally, all of us were on the flight and able to enjoy the tremendous cheering that took place. In order to exchange reservations, the entire process of luggage handling and reissuing of tickets had to occur. We patiently sat still for another hour and a half. Through the entire ordeal, not a negative comment or complaint from anyone on board that flight was stated. Throughout this entire adventure, the many unnamed heroes remain a mystery.

With all the switching of people and parcels, only two suitcases did not show up in Minneapolis. In his infinite wisdom, the new graduate said, "You could all be in Philly with the baggage here or in town helping me celebrate with the clothes you have on". This was an excellent point of view.

Compassion and very sincere concern for a family in distress was dramatically demonstrated as total strangers worked together to bring this story to a happy conclusion. To all who were involved in this adventure, and especially to US Airways personnel, a very sincere expression of thanks and gratitude is expressed. The graduation day arrived with something that was a stranger to the sky…sunshine.

RENE'S MASTER'S DEGREE

A very significant educational goal was attained when Rene announced her graduation with a Master's Degree from Grand Canyon University in Glendale, Arizona during May, 2006. Her brother, Rob, earned a Doctoral Degree the prior year and we were all there to witness that special event. Now, it was her turn to celebrate this distinctive achievement. Our proud daughter then told us she would not be able to attend the ceremony because it was too far to travel.

It was explained that these distinguished formalities are designed for parents to celebrate the successes of their children. We told her that all the travel arrangements would be provided so that the three of us could attend the occasion. She was thrilled! A few weeks passed and she called to say that Charlie would like to purchase a ticket and also attend. We stated that the matter will be taken care of by us, and we will fly together.

Days later, they decided Alyssa and Chad would like to join the group and try to squeeze in a trip to the Grand Canyon. Again, the airline was contacted and the group to Glendale Arena was extended to six.

Because we arrived a few days early, Grandmother managed all the final arrangements for hotels, automobiles, restaurants and the full day tour of the Grand Canyon. They flew in on Thursday night and spent the evening relaxing and having dinner around the swimming pool. On Friday morning we got up bright and early to enjoy a guided tour by travel van through the magnificent Grand Canyon. Our grandchildren were the only youngsters on the vehicle. Their attention was intense, behavior excellent, excitement spectacular and enthusiasm catching. While at a restaurant for lunch, many fellow passengers purchased gifts to reward our fantastic youngsters for their cooperative spirit.

Saturday was graduation day. The Glendale Arena is a huge indoor stadium with a gigantic jumbo TV and each graduate could be viewed life-size as they participated in the heart-warming commencement. It was an exciting day and we were extremely pleased with Rene and her wonderful supportive family. Mom and Dad were honored and thrilled to share these very precious moments. We then celebrated at the Red Lobster to enjoy unlimited delicious king crab legs and the cold bucket of a bottomless supply of frosty beer

Sunday was our last party day to recuperate around the pool. At sunset, the Lintz group finished packing for the drive to the airport. This was an incredible whirlwind delightful experience of four incredible days that remains deep in our souls and those of the Lintz family.

CHAD'S FIRST DAY OF SCHOOL

On the first day of school, our grandson, Chad went to his new teacher and stated that his grandmother and her mother are very good friends. The educator asked her name and he quickly responded, "Grandma!"

THE OLD MAN WHO SWIMS WITH A HAT AND GLOVES

The children grew up in a home that had an in-the-ground swimming pool. It was installed when Rene was approaching her fourth birthday and Rob was well into his first year. The pool was an extension of our recreational area and was the center of our entertainment activities from Memorial Day to the first day of school in September. Family, friends, and playmates shared many wonderful experiences during the warm, sun, filled months.

While my total pool time over the thirty-year period was less than two dozen dips, Dad's role was to keep the facility in pristine condition, preserve perfect clear water chemistry, serve as captain of the maintenance team and celebrate that we never lose a day of swimming.

However, the most memorable swim occurred on a cold, windy, wintery February afternoon when the severe conditions caused the solid aqua blue vinyl cover to slide off the deck and into the icy water. I jumped from the redwood walkway into the arctic liquid to rescue the cover and returned it to its proper place for winter protection.

Swimming became a prominent routine when we moved to Four Seasons which had a beautiful indoor pool. The activity continued in Pompano Beach, Florida. Within a short period, I was easily comfortable swimming a mile per day. But, due to my light sensitive, tender skin condition, diving gloves and a long brim hat had to be worn for sun protection.

While at the Virginian for ten years, grandchildren of the condo owners would ask why the old man with white hair dressed that way. His answer was that his mother frequently said, "Always wear a hat and gloves for the winter". Their quizzical facial expressions clearly indicated they were confused as they walked away. Over the years the returning youngsters would ask residents, "Does the old man who wears a hat and gloves still swim here?"

The special water attire was shed when we relocated to Sun City, Florida for January, February, March, April, and May.

The water exercise program once again returned to an indoor pool.

BOWLING BITS AND BANQUETS

Our long family history includes a fair list of proficient bowlers which included my dad, uncles, aunts, and cousins. Conversations, while growing up, involved a wide variety of tales associated with sport. As a youngster, several trips were to the alleys for the purpose of watching relatives throw the large ball at those elusive white pins, enjoy the social component, thrive on the competition and anticipation of winning prize money at the season's end.

I recall going with my father to a bowling sports store and observing the long-involved process of selecting and engineering a new ball. After several hours of knocking pins down, a special custom design was finally selected, and an appointment was made to test and pick up this special creation the following week.

As a musician, May was a magical month, and much cash was earned from entertaining at these banquets. The band would be on stage for a short time while the guests arrived and picked up their drinks. Rivals then would report to their respective team tables and await the serving of their victory dinners.

Shortly thereafter, the music stopped for distribution of trophies and sports awards. It seemed that every participant was provided with a rather lengthy discourse on their valuable achievements which was followed by a presentation of their plaque and a cherished money envelope. The festivities finished with just enough time for the music to end the evening with a good night's song.

A Four Seasons tournament saga continues with my participation in the Tuesday morning league. In preparation for the opening day, and to look good, proper attire and equipment had to be purchased. Mid-season and in the process of exchanging gifts at holiday time, our son-in-law said he had my father's ball in the attic. He retrieved the treasure and positioned it in my palm. Gripping the memento created the feeling of shaking hands with Dad who was honored with scoring a perfect game of 300 points.

At the final feast and with a second season average of 109, I was awarded the "most improved bowler". A few years later and with an average of 120, my team won first place for the initial starting half of the season. When considering the competition has many players with averages close to 200, I continue to have difficulty understanding how a person with less than a mediocre performance can win a championship.

BETTER ACCORDION PLAYER LAST YEAR

Once a year, the garage is given a thorough cleaning which includes moving all the items on the floor to enable complete sweeping and vacuuming to take place. During the process, my accordion and amplifier are temporarily relocated to spruce up the crowded storage area under the attic staircase. Generally, this task completes the job.

Before returning the musical equipment to its proper place, an urge occurs to test the instrument and determine if it is still in working condition. Eventually, the paraphernalia is set-up, and the fingers are applied to the keyboard. The challenge begins. After about a long hour of struggling and dealing with enormous frustration, tunes become remotely recognizable.

Because this is usually a summer project, the double garage doors are open to allow the dust and "music" to scatter into the fresh air. My good neighbor, who was working in her garden, appeared in the driveway with a spectacular smile on her glowing face. I stopped playing to say hello and then, she slowly responded with a laughing voice and exclaimed, "You sounded much better last year!"

While repeating this session again the following year, this lovely lady appeared and presented the budding celebrity with a beautiful bouquet of her home-grown garden flowers. She created a pleasant encouraging experience and a lasting memory!

DO I SMELL?

While wintering in Pompano Beach, Florida and enjoying Nancy's eighty-year- old parents as our next-door neighbors, we observed, they were experiencing increased difficulty in confidently functioning independently. During this short season we began to realize that basic upkeep, repair, maintenance, and financial matters became more challenging and beyond their ability to manage.

In increments, Nancy and I assumed the tasks of administering their household affairs. Ultimately, investments were recorded, charted, consolidated, and put in order. The checkbook was turned over to us and she and I began to direct these important living matters.

As part of this observation process, the family realized that their independent living in a lovely large, beautiful home in Elmwood Park, New Jersey was beyond their capabilities. The time had arrived for them to downsize and relocate to an apartment with assisted living components.

In their future, these excellent financial resources could be utilized if and when it became necessary to implement and relocate. Another positive factor was that they would then be a short driving distance to the daughters, cherished grandchildren and great grandchildren. The research process began and an interesting setting, Ann's Choice, was found. This facility incorporated the features and lifestyle needs that met the requirements of Mom and Dad.

Eventually, the Russell Court home was prepared for sale and this process consumed several long weeks. This task involved sorting and separating a huge collection which was accumulated over a period of sixty years. In August of 2006, the chore began. While this occurred during the hottest days of summer, their thermostat was constantly set at 85 degrees.

In his confusion and since Dad returned "valued" trash to the garage during night fall, the workday began in early morning by placing discarded materials at the curb for the refuse truck to remove. The selection process continued until late afternoon. Because of the tremendous heat generated by the basement blast furnace, we ended our day with an abundance of emotional tears and sweat, soaked clothing.

On the way to our hotel, we stopped at a local tavern for a few quick long cold beers to replace the salt lost to heavy perspiration. The combination of relaxation, frosty pilsners and air-conditioning helped cool us down before reporting to the motel. There we showered, changed clothing, and dressed for dinner with friends living in Bergen County.

After enjoying a delightful soapy soaking, I stepped out of the bathroom in complete, fresh, crispy, clean attire. As Nancy prepared to duplicate the bathing routine, I said to her, "Why do I still smell?"

The answer was that, while in a newly laundered, sparkling, outfit, the offensive odor was coming from the wet clothing that was hanging in the open closet that was opposite the lavatory. Once I moved to the furthest side of the bedroom, the benefits of the refreshing, shower and sterilization were fully enjoyed.

THANKSGIVING AT THE FARM

For several years, our family enjoyed an old-fashioned Thanksgiving Holiday weekend at our quaint farmhouse that is neatly nestled in the southwest corner of Massachusetts and near the crest of the Berkshire Mountains. It is situated on a one hundred-forty-acre, wooded parcel on a desolate, twisting, dirt road located several miles from the nearest town. A 10,000-acre state forest is directly across the street.

This pretty paradise is properly called Shangri-La, for it is truly in the heart of God's good country. In the past, it was common that days would go by before a stranger - who was probably an explorer or lost - would appear on the roadway.

The charming structure was constructed by a dairyman and his neighbors over a hundred years ago. Beams and floorboards were cut from local lumber and hand finished by primitive craftsmen. Walking on the quaint irregularly leveled linoleum surface, which covered the uneven wide boards, changed according to season or relative humidity and became a constant challenge for a person to maintain proper balance or stability. Absent are running water, central heat, electricity and indoor plumbing. In essence, the home's one modern convenience was a telephone party line and the only modern connection to the outside world. It was installed for emergency purposes.

As the stunning foliage began to take on an autumn magnificence, the New Jersey folks' excitement radiated and exploded with the daily thoughts of returning to their country hideaway. During the next few weeks, supplies were slowly gathered to prepare for the anticipated coming festivities and celebrations. Items were purchased to include the extra-sized bird and ice chests to be loaded with staples.

A few days before the expedition, the grandparents departed to make the long-established retreat ready for the weekend migration. Eventually, the date arrived to make final arrangements for the anticipated gigantic reunion. The car was packed on Tuesday evening and loaded to the brim with essential stuff. Since school was dismissed near noon on Wednesday, the goal was to leave early to beat traffic. The car was gassed, and Dad was picked up immediately after work near the last exit of the Garden State Parkway.

With luck, the taxing trip to the mountain haven was successfully navigated and the highways were cooperative by being uncongested. As darkness approached near the end of the three-hour journey, we stopped for dinner, gasoline, fresh milk and cold beer. Shortly, the rustic, rural, road was reached, and the car horn sounded to announce our imminent arrival.

Customarily, about half-way up the trail, a pause was made on the old rickety wooden bridge and the headlights were briefly turned off. The young children were amazed at the instant total darkness that resulted and they immediately pleaded to turn the lights back on. Driving up, the old house windows radiated with a yellow cast produced by several glowing antique kerosene lamps. Waiting at the patio door with extended outstretched arms, the grandparents anxiously stood to welcome us and exchange affectionate greetings of hugs and kisses.

As we settled in, a shot and cold beer was handed to the driver. Leisurely, the suitcase on wheels was unloaded, beds prepared, and the children tucked in for a well-deserved nighttime rest. Mom and Dad chatted, shared a few more drinks with our parents and, together, looked forward to the arrival of the other relatives.

During this period, fresh water was drawn from the Jack and Jill type well. Firewood was stacked near the wood burning stove which supplied heat for the cold night. Kettles were placed on top of the outdated heaters to produce boiling water for cooking and washing. After all the additional people arrived and cars were unloaded, the long day ended with a plate of German wurst and steak tartare on rye bread.

Before Mr. Sun peered over the horizon to announce the arrival of Thanksgiving, this farmhouse came alive as the cooking crew went into pre-dawn action. An important first step, using a flashlight, was to take cautious strides over the slippery, frozen, frost coated hard ground to the outdoor well to draw clear, fresh, wintry water once more. A return to the house and the comfortable coziness caused by the crackling log fires, created a sense of contentment and peace. The next task was to separate ice cubes from the cold turkey cavity.

This was then followed by carefully washing and salting the bird. Stuffing was then prepared using and mixing the pre-cooked provisions that came from home. Kitchen chores and their special, shared, sounds slowly stirred up the children who were now wide awake and ready to traditionally "pat the turkey" prior to its placement into the oven.

Before their feet hit the frigid floor, "Kids were given an important safety message, "Walk, don't run and be careful about knocking over the fragile lighted lamps." The table was now cleaned for Gram's presentation of a full farmstead gourmet breakfast.

After the morning feed, the ladies continued to prepare for the afternoon feast and the men worked outdoors. Pine boughs were placed around the rear and sides of the outhouse to minimize very uncomfortable chilling updrafts. Between checking the water supply and keeping the fires going in two wood burning stoves; new timber was cut, split and stacked to prepare for next season.

While the amateur lumberjacks prepared future fuel, the weekend landscapers cut the grass, raked fallen leaves and collected kindling. A scouting party, led by Gramp followed by a trail of children and their moms, then searched the wooded section to tag Christmas trees which would be taken home for the holiday season.

At 11:00 am, Gramp would sound his special signal to stop the outdoor work. He always displayed a happy face and a sparkling smile that provided a ray of sunshine on this comfortable, cold, crispy morning. His loaded arms carried brandy, beer and thick whiskey glasses. While the farmhands assembled, we would sit, sipping, sharing stories, and sincerely enjoying each other's companionship.

Children surrounded the "senior citizens" and were intent on absorbing the long-established tales that were tied to the family historical tree. The women continued to scamper and prepare for an expected house filled to capacity with guests who were there to share the extraordinary meal that was about to be served at 1:00 o'clock.

Finally, the bountiful feast began and continued... and continued... and continued! With stomachs satiated through several passing hours, the table was cleared and decks of playing cards came out. While some elected to join in games, others took out their singing voices and assorted original musical instruments. The contraptions included: spoons, washboard, pots, pans, trumpet, ukuleles, combination pole plus rawhide string fastened to a board that was mounted on a wash tub, harmonica, drum sticks and accordion. The rafters rocked into the wee late hours with boisterous singing and vigorous playing.

From their bedroom perches, the children continued to absorb a culture of family images that would be permanently embossed in their tender young memories. During the action, someone always emerged to take care of the fires, water supply and refreshments.

After breakfast early Friday morning, the girls eagerly drove to town for bargain shopping and lunch. While the fathers, on the other hand, remained at the farm to finish chores, take care of the children, tend the fires, enjoy their shot and beer break, and make a noon meal of Nancy's nursery school homemade vegetable soup.

Our teenage son would enter the woods and pick wild grape vines and mountain laurel. He then spent the next few days constructing winter wreaths which he took home and sold to floral shops. Enough money was earned to fund his holiday gift expenses.

Later in the afternoon the women returned to present a fashion show and display their shopping treasures. They certainly budgeted enough time to prepare a dinner of leftovers which were as good as or better than the prior day's feast. The evening's amusement included more friends, cards, and a return engagement of the musical Mass. Mountain Men.

Saturday marked the last full day of a wonderful weekend. Dawn broke with Gramp marching through the bedrooms waving a flag, playing an eight-track tape recorder along with having fun blasting an accompaniment through a bugle made from a long blue plastic funnel. He proudly produced abrasive sounds. The children groaned by the earsplitting use of this inventive alarm clock. Their dramatic moaning motivated him to continue his solo parade.

However, they all woke up, washed and dressed to enjoy a breakfast which included fried eggs, hot dog pennies, toast, coffee and fresh orange juice. The youngsters and grandfather then went into the forest to cut and drag the evergreens that were to be made ready for their journey to New Jersey.

Basically, this day was used to rest, relax, and get ready for more afternoon guests who all remained for a typical New England super of boiled hot dogs, sauerkraut, salad, and baked beans. The program for evening entertainment remained the same of cards and raucous melodious harmony. By this time, the wood burning infernos were crackling at full capacity and the sweltering temperature was enough to bring out the bikini bathing suits.

Sadly, Sunday morning arrived, and we prepared for our eventual return to civilization. The anticipation of running the city treated water, an indoor bathroom, hot shower, centrally controlled heat, a washing machine and clothes dryer were a mild incentive. These thoughts might have brightened the day; however, I doubt it!

The morning meal was awfully solemn for we knew our Shangri-La would be closed for winter. It would be covered with a blanket of bottomless, beautiful, pure, silky, soft, smooth, snow that would help our country "estate" rest, revive and recover to get ready for our marvelous spring return to this splendid sanctuary.

The few families four wheeled supply vehicles parked, pointed south, and packed with the trees tightly secured to the car roofs. While hunters lashed deer on their automobiles during this season, we transported trees to fill our living rooms at Christmas time. As an aside, the small Scotch spruce sapling in its natural setting becomes a super, sequoia when stationed in a family living room!

A quick residential inspection occurred to make sure all the gear was properly stowed. The family lined up for their goodbye embraces and we entered the car, waved, and drove through the white painted gate that led us to the highway home. The grandparents were the last to depart and they carefully rearranged everything in the event a fashion magazine decided to visit the place to photograph and publish a feature article on the homestead.

My safe drive back from the wood burning smoke scented scene to a sophisticated society was always quiet and lonely because the passengers were fast asleep. They appeared to be enjoying the tender thoughts that must be dancing through their beautiful dreams. It was many years since we took time to be together, as a complete family, at this sensational spot. In the meantime, Gramp and Gram have passed to their well-earned resting places in the eternal puffy high white clouds above this green, natural farm paradise. It is interesting to reminisce that at their memorial services, every word spoken during their testimonials were a reflection of all the many fond and lasting wonderful memories they helped create for us.

MESSAGES

The intuitive message board is illuminated at the instant conception is achieved. Once the chromosomes align to combine, organize, or share genetic data, DNA information is in place and the gift of life is magically established. A brand-new clean stage is set in motion for nature and the nutritional components to coordinate energy to foster forward progress.

An appropriate combination of these elements in a wholesome environment should encourage the embryo to properly develop and fully mature. This phenomenon occurs, regardless of size, each time an organism is created. The numerical combinations for individual species to procreate are beyond comprehension.

It's a simple matter of the parental pair being in the same place at the precise moment. During the gestation sequence, decision choices are beyond the influence or control of the unborn. Essentially, one does not have a role in choosing their parents in the ordinary world.

Once born, the progeny is exposed to an ever-expanded source of physical and sensual stimulation that is derived from a variety of resources. Initial contact broadens from the immediate environment and expands in a multitude of outward directions. The supply scope of influence extends from the concrete to the abstract. Complexity of the thought procedure is directly related to a developmental sequence of the young and the hierarchy of the organism in the chain of life.

As it relates to human beings, the process is influenced by everyday surroundings, spontaneous occurrences, life experiences, educational opportunities and nourishment. Some believe in a variety of influence sources which include and are not limited to religious beliefs, divine interventions, mystical principles, solar alignments, luck, angels, demons, dreams, and an inordinate assortment of more mysterious communiqués.

In most cases, these factors combine to produce a unique individual profile. It tends to be a stimulus response for locating in the right place at the right time or the converse of being in the wrong place at the wrong time. These incentives can be perceived consciously or subconsciously through a thought activity or an instinctive reaction to an event.

A response ranges from an immediate reaction to a long-delayed reply. The combination of these experiences, throughout a lifetime, maps out the path the individual chooses to travel as a result of the choices selected. As one journeys life's conduit, several opportunities are experienced for important messages to be delivered.

The transmission can be categorized in two columns which range from constructive information to undesirable data. The individual is presented with many alternatives and combinations to the decision making, sorting activities and a multitude of several selections over time. Once the stimulus is internalized and synthesized, the impact of these experiences are consequences. The results of these decisions are cumulative and encompass a scope which extends from extremely positive to excessively negative.

IN TIME, THE CHILD BECOMES THE TEACHER

From the first crack of dawn's early light at the start of history to the fading glimmer of stars that mark the birth of a new day, civilization has continued to improve, advance and move forward. Older groups have been surpassed by the energetic youth of the next generation. As an outcome of this phenomenon over centuries, advancement has resulted by accepting their gifts of fresh new ideas and inventions.

Persistent, persuasive, progress has occurred which evolved from the normal acceptance and implementation of discoveries and innovations supplied by the young. Eventually and through eons of time, students have become society's new teachers, leaders, scientists, and philosophers. They have perpetually contributed promising visions or perceptions to enhance the world and make it a better place for all of those who have followed.

The wireless communication explosion, which began at the beginning of the twentieth century, is a classic example used to illustrate this point. Early in the last millennium, people were intrigued by listening for sounds created from a crude, crystal radio. Hours were devoted to scraping a shiny, clear, colored stone for that specific, special, spot. Once located, with assistance from a battery and attached wire to a simple electrical circuit, unamplified scratchy signals were heard through a large headphone. Success resulted from chance rather than skill.

Today, our sophisticated children are connected to complicated devices which instantly calculate, produce telephone rings, play assorted music, provide clear speech, include geographic positioning systems, construct written text, and contain a variety of literary masterpieces. Amazingly, these mechanisms can be handheld and operated with just thumbs!

Parents also marvel at the skill level of their own adolescent youngsters who may even be more technologically talented than them. It is increasingly interesting to observe these mothers and fathers asking our grandchildren for help when they open the cutting-edge expensive package housing the latest, magical, miniature, and up-to-date gadget. Year after year, minutes pass, milestones slip away, and their new developments eternally encourage society to travel faster and in more exciting directions!

TWO BIRTHDAYS PER YEAR

During the year-end hectic holiday season of 2008, I experienced mild difficulty with breathing, perspiration, jaw pain and fatigue. These symptoms were brought to the attention of the family doctor who immediately scheduled a complete physical examination that involved a cardiogram. The results were excellent, and the respiratory problem was attributed to my chronic asthma which was probably brought on by the changing temperature associated with the coming winter.

The dentist dismissed jaw discomfort with a possible muscular strain. However, throughout the height of the active social season, it was necessary to find an excuse to return home early and go to bed. Assured that health was not a concern, I was confident that a change of address and the next three months in Florida would help the ailments improve. On the way south, we experienced an effortless trip. A first stop was to visit friends in the Villages for a few days. Next, the journey continued to our destination in Pompano Beach, Florida where we quickly settled into the apartment. Physical condition issues seemed to improve in the sunny and warmer climate.

Our friend and downstairs neighbor had just returned from an extensive hospital stay and wanted to have his condo painted. I volunteered to do the job. With less than ten square feet remaining to complete the second coat, I experienced a mild pain in the center of the chest and immediately connected the medical dots of all the previous warnings.

As I sprawled out on the wet, spotted, drop cloth, Nancy entered the room and was told to call the ambulance. She thought this was a joke and responded in an ethnic accent, "So, should I call the doctor?" and in her fancy glittering outfit, proceeded to finish the archway. Finally, the message was processed when she heard that this was a heart attack! Before the stressful telephone conversation ended, the paramedics were at the door. They assessed the situation; said I was a big person and asked if I could get up from the floor and move on to the gurney. I complied and was quickly wheeled into the emergency vehicle.

During the necessary medical stabilization period which consumed a few minutes, Nancy concluded that her husband had expired. She pounded on the door, told her the situation was under control and gave instructions to meet at Holy Cross Hospital in Fort Lauderdale. Lauderdale, Florida. Fortunately, this episode occurred across the street from the first aid squad and down the road from the regional cardiac center. Upon arrival, immediate surgery was scheduled, and a prominent highly skilled physician was chosen to perform the procedure. Before entering the operating room, Nancy anxiously appeared in the corridor with all the unread signed documents.

Then, placed a kiss on the cheek, wished me good luck and wept on the way to the visitors' station to begin the strenuous waiting process. Within a few hours, three stents were inserted in the heart and the sleepy patient was moved to the recovery area. Upon waking, Nancy was at the bedside side, holding my hand and explaining that she did not have time to read the lengthy forms. Eventually, I was transported to a room, settled in and visited by the doctor. He confidently and professionally explained that the procedure was successful, a rapid medical intervention was quickly provided in time and there was no permanent damage. His major concern was that the groin region in which the incision was made had to remain immobile. The reason was the opening would be used in two days to insert four additional stents.

In less than a week, I was back to the Virginian to begin the recuperation period. Within a three-month period, I had an excellent nuclear stress test report, returned to swimming a mile a day and was able to drive home to Four Seasons.

The cardiologist, Dr. Purrow, dismissed me with this sentence, "Consider January 12, 2009, your new birthday." Therefore, this explains my two birthdays per year.

GRAMP, HELP ME WITH MY ITALIAN PROJECT

Our second-grade grandson knew about my Italian heritage and ability to play the accordion. He asked for assistance on his social studies project. I was informed the assignment was a research project on Italy and my role was to provide background Italian music while he made the class presentation.

Since punctuality continues to be a very important component of my profile, I arrived in plenty of time to get ready and make an appearance. After explaining the reason for my request to visit his classroom, the school secretary stated she did not have this on her agenda. However, there was a program scheduled for an international music festival that was to begin shortly and each class was selected to sing a national song which was representative of a foreign country.

Since the assembly program took place in December, I volunteered to welcome the student body as they entered the room by playing holiday songs. His group was the first to arrive and the second surprise occurred when my grandson entered the auditorium wearing a Mexican costume.

Considering my performance was in progress, I asked him to help lead a sing along. He was an instant hit, and the teaching staff encouraged this new school celebrity to remain on stage for forty-five minutes. JOY TO THE WORLD!

NEW YEAR REFLECTIONS, AN AMERICAN DREAM

Recently time was set aside to review, reflect, and count my blessings. This flashback began at the turn of the 20th century when both sets of grandparents decided to migrate from their native land and relocate to the United States of America They must have been motivated by the potential for an improved way of life, hope for employment and the abundant educational opportunities available for their future children.

In addition, they were certainly encouraged by former countrymen who preceded them in this very courageous adventure. It must have been comforting to have this new network of acquaintances on hand to generously offer them guidance and support at their new address located in Paterson, New Jersey.

Shortly after completing their crossing, necessary steps were taken to study English and become American citizens. They were pleased and proud to attain these wonderful goals. During the following years, the four grandparents found jobs, raised children to firmly impress, inspire and influence them in regards to the importance of school, study and the rewards associated with hard work.

My parents absorbed these principles and ultimately passed them to their next generation. Throughout childhood, education and learning were significant components that were emphasized and well respected. As a toddler, I vividly remembered Mother reading to me every day.

Through these formative years, Dad taught valuable skills which continue to serve me. Fortunately, the local school, at the center of the neighborhood, had excellent facilities and a staff that demonstrated a strong commitment to assisting pupils in their variety of journeys towards a successful future.

While the specifics differed in each household, the pattern seemed to be firmly established across American society. This, certainly, was the model that fashioned our generation while growing up. Families, friends, and fellow citizens, across this great nation have collectively shared or experienced similar ideals, aims, challenges, ambitions and celebrations.

This resulted in a wonderful nation coming together. Our Four Seasons has adopted these fine characteristics and has taken them to a higher level to include care, concern and compassion.

As we enter a new century, I am grateful for the bold steps my forefathers took to provide my place on this planet and the magnificent opportunities made available for me to enjoy "the good life" **GOD BLESS AMERICA!!!**

BROKE WITH A POCKET FULL OF CREDIT CARDS AND CASH

We have been fortunate to enjoy the luxury of travel and have visited all the United States and several countries around the world. Our experience, over the years, has been that the mighty American dollar and credit cards were gladly accepted throughout the globe.

Recently, on a trip to Sicily, Italy; this was not the case. Many establishments did not accept American Express or Visa and the almighty bucks were rejected. Attempts to exchange currency in hotels or banks were refused and it was a dicker for dollars atmosphere.

Because we were comfortable and successful in the past with a cash/credit card environment, a major problem developed and grew due to never using an ATM card. Fortunately, we met a concerned young couple who was well experienced in modern electronic banking. I was escorted to a nearby ATM and tutored in the efficient usage of this contemporary convenience. Within seconds, the problem was solved.

DO A GOOD JOB GRAMP

As a fourth grader, our grandson invited me to help him with another report on Italy. The assignment was to locate a person with an Italian background who could talk about his assigned country. Because of a very full lifetime involved with immigrants from that Mediterranean nation, I had mastered, over the years, an ability to speak Italian with a broken English accent.

In preparation, the pupils were carefully informed the dialogue would be presented in Italian. A red, white and green "I Love Italy" cap was introduced, and it was explained that while placed on my head, they would easily understand my words.

Before we joined efforts to make the brief discussion understandable, Chad robustly said, "Gramp, you better do a good job!"

HAIRCUTS

From the earliest years, I can remember the attention that was devoted to my haircut and the emphasis which stressed the importance of proper grooming. My first childhood professional portrait had me photographed with an over the ear Buster Brown hairstyle. During the toddler years, a trip to the barbershop was scheduled in two-week intervals and Mom, who escorted her little man, seemed to be the only female in the place of business.

Eventually, in this safe neighborhood setting, I was permitted to walk alone to Joe's Barber Shop and patiently sit a long time while waiting for my turn. The owner carefully picked up the small customer and placed me gently on the booster bench that was supported by the thick, leather arms of the grown-up white porcelain, revolving chair.

Early tools included a manually operated neck clipper that was used to trim fair hair. This portion of the procedure was rather painful for the ancient device seemed to specialize in yanking fine fuzz from their firm follicles. The standard routine ended with a neck rub of scented, strong, stinging Witch Hazel and a brisk brush down with fancy, fragrant talcum powder.

The cost for this service was fifty cents and the ritual ended when the large silver coin was exchanged for a waxed paper, well, wrapped large lollipop. The final act was completed when the ornate metal cash register drawer opened to receive the coin and the loud bell rang as the secure door closed to end the transaction. During this World War II period, the practice of prior arrangements and tipping were never a thought in this factory, working class area.

Over the years, patrons were conditioned to respond appropriately when the man dressed in a well starched white jacket protecting a shirt and tie gently provided a clue by lightly touching the customer's head. Instantly, the necessary maneuver was executed and the cutting continued. Throughout the entire ordeal, there was a continuous chatter of meaningless conversation that centered on local gossip and regional politics.

My very thick abundant head of black hair included a distinctive widow's peak which extended to cover both temples.

Mom would plaster these stubborn locks with a quick drying, green, gluey substance, *Wave Set*. The product had a distinctive unpleasant odor. Once dried, the hair produced a cracking sound when the comb made last minute adjustments. This process took place in the morning before leaving for school and after the home lunch recess period.

Turning thirteen years old, the family moved to a new home that was constructed by Dad, friends, relatives, and me. The new address was on the right side of Paterson and in a suburban, middle, class setting. Resulting from this upper mobility progression, the barbershop's identity changed from an owner/operator to a proprietor/stylist with a proportional increase in selection offerings at higher prices. The twice a month schedule remained constant and rituals in the changed location were similar with different characters placed in comparable conversations.

The owner, however foreign born, spoke without a heavy Italian accent. Since the cutting procedure was well established for everyone, there wasn't a need to ask what was to be done or required. As a teenager and young adult, this males' only refuge was cherished and well appreciated. My silent resentment was stimulated, when a female had the audacity and nerve to invade this seemingly masculine sheltered sanctuary to be styled by the guy's skilled sharp scissor.

My horizons widened while working in Newark, NJ. Next to the shoe store in which I managed part-time was an upscale men's hair salon. On the team was a manicurist, shoeshine person, washer and a private back studio for wigs and hair piece fashioning. This establishment was patronized by successful upper management executives and numerous celebrities. That situation was too rich for my emerging tastes and modest income.

Once married and living in Bergen County, a change in the procedure was introduced. The master barber/stylist was a graduate of a special school, earned a license and worked in a place with eight chairs. In addition to a selection of several staff salon specialists, an appointment was strongly suggested.

Wood paneled walls were decorated with pictures of handsome models posed to show sophisticated, tonsorial techniques. At this point in my experience, a new trend emerged which deviated from the past, standard, predicted, excellent, consistent, long-term service. For about a year of using the same "expert", the time spent with each cut shortened and the quality or standard of satisfaction slowly deteriorated. The lifetime loyalty factor as a "regular" had changed, and it became necessary to periodically search around for a new professional stylist.

From a man's perspective, this became a "Hairdo Hell"! Within a few visits at the new establishment and explaining what was requested, my standard response to how I wanted my hair cut was, "In silence". The motor mouth at the other side of the shears did not have to burn or bend my overburdened ears with meaningless gossip and well-rehearsed repetitive rhetoric.

After visiting several shops in the area with the same eventual disappointment, Nancy suggested that I visit her beauty shop and have a girl cut my hair. The introductory remarks were exchanged, and my request was resolved when she was told that I welcome her judgment and do what is necessary. She went to work and implemented a different approach by using very small scissors. Early on, she proclaimed that my hair was cut by a man. The next remark was that he was an Italian. Both comments were casually acknowledged with a slight nod. For, this was the profile of most barbers in Northern New Jersey. Next, she stated with confidence that his shop was in Emerson and his name was Luigi. I was amazed at her accurate assessment of this situation.

While a vow was made to utilize the gentle, soft touch of a female for the future, the regressive pattern continued, over these long years of caring for my precious strands that have changed from dark black coal to a shade of smoky, snow; I have continued my search for the "olden days" of uniform consistency.

Obviously, my bride shared the same encounters with beauticians, and I followed her for the next adventure to Hans Maxim who had a full complement of competent, cute, cutters wearing small, slim mini-skirts. While the location's, interior decorations and gender continuously changed, the introductory interrogation seemed to be institutionalized with the same time-worn questions!

The attractive beautician asked, "What is your name?"

"Madeline"!

"Is that a lady's name"?

"No, it's mine".

"What do you do for a living"?

"Gynecologist".

The dumbfounded girl then asked, "How do you want it to be cut?"

"In silence and you're the boss"!

Finely, she got the message, discontinued the dialogue, and did an excellent job. Madeline became her steady customer until we moved to Four Seasons.

While Nancy and I used the identical unisex salon, we were never in the establishment at the same time. However, one day my wife brought photographs that I took at a family wedding. As the pictures circulated, the operators commented on the variety of hairdos that were captured in the prints. Ultimately, my secret identity was revealed when the girls saw an enlarged color picture of me, Nancy exclaimed, "Madeline, Madeline! MADELINE".

"That is my husband." Immediately, there was a choral response from the girls, "Madeline, the gynecologist, is your husband?" "Yes, and don't let him examine you because he is an elementary school principal"! While they continued to call me Doctor, my cover was exposed.

The pattern of excellent initial starts and declining finished products continued over the next twenty years of searching in the Columbus region. To date, I have changed hair cutting firms many times and the search will probably continue well into the future.

FLORIDA FLAT TIRE

After spending a wonderful week in Florida with Gerry and Mike, we decided to enjoy a leisurely lunch on the way to Tampa Airport. As the car exited, a loss of air in the rear tire was noticed. It was decided that the remaining inflation level was sufficient to safely complete the fifteen-minute trip to the terminal. The meal experience was good, relaxed, and delightful. Upon our later return to the vehicle, the tire was flat. Attempts to contact AAA were frustrating and unsuccessful. The passing of valuable time, now, had the potential of becoming a serious concern.

At about the same time, the restaurant staff was changing shifts and the servers appeared in the parking lot. It seemed a good idea to ask one of these tuxedoed attired young ladies if help could be provided with our transportation dilemma. An assumption was that a well-groomed person would drive an appropriate automobile…Not the case and the wrong character volunteered to help us.

We were escorted to an overused cargo van that was well past its prime, in serious need of sterilization and a thorough bath in a very good car wash. The vehicle was loaded with well-worn tools and an interior covered with several layers of used oil. As we placed the luggage in the unkempt, wheeled, mobile garage, the pretty driver popped the hood to check the water level… Not a good sign!

Upon entering the thick dirty black greasy limo with reservation, an assurance was provided that the potential overheating concern was under control if the vehicle maintained a speed of 70 mph. Because of heavy commuter volume, stop and go traffic was experienced and progress could be measured in footsteps. On the way the driver stated with confidence, this was a very familiar trip. She was self-assured in knowing the procedure and we would be taken to the seventh level and dropped off at the elevator. Driving past the elevated departing flight approach turn, she stated that her passengers are always taken to the top level of the parking terminal.

We safely arrived with plenty of time to take the elevator down to the proper area. When asked how much money was needed to make this favor profitable, she said one dollar was enough to cover the cost of gasoline. Two twenties were placed in her hand. The response was that one bill was more than enough. My response was that her kindness was greatly appreciated and please, take the second bill and treat yourself to a nice lunch.

HAIR STYLE GELS PERMANENT FRIENDSHIP

For many years our family enjoyed a Sunday morning breakfast at a local restaurant. Since band job commitments were seldom in the morning, this event was woven into a schedule to enable us the opportunity to appreciate each other's company during this comfortable time slot.

After Rene and Rob left for college and eventually married, Nancy and I continued this custom and gradually expanded our breakfast circle to include friends living in New Jersey and others wintering in Florida.

While sharing a before noon meal and sitting at a window table in Sun City with Bob and Linda Weber, my eyes focused on an attractive couple about to enter the eatery. The damsel was well groomed and sported an attractive, stylish, chick coiffure. Since Nancy was in a Florida "hair do hell", the observation was mentioned to my table mates. The sisters immediately agreed and this attractive damsel became the center of conversation.

Within a few moments, the spotlighted pair were seated next to us. A stage was set for the three girls to begin a detailed discussion on hair salons and various styling techniques. Inside a couple of moments, a magical moment transpired as the three beauty queens bonded. Telephone numbers were exchanged, Weber's stay extended and a new social circle was created.

In a few days, my bride contacted Sharon and a fresh, wonderful, lasting, relationship evolved. Interestingly, this phenomenon was enhanced by the fact that both husbands experienced a very similar rapport. I also acquired a new buddy that had a very parallel background of interests and experiences. While the wives immediately connected, the husbands enjoyed a very similar association. Because of our common backgrounds, lengthy detailed conversations were immensely enjoyed on a variety of assorted topics. Our diverse dialogue, while separated by miles of distance, continued via telephone, email and texting. There was never a lack of words.

Arnie is and was such a wonderful and dear friend that is always at my side and in my heart. His memorial medal was given to me by his lovely wife, Sharon. It is worn by me around the clock. We are only separated by swimming activities and showers. In time we will be reunited in the sunshine above the heavenly clouds and OUR days together will come again!

ACCORDION; A SECOND VISIT

    I have enjoyed several interesting experiences on my tour through life. Each sustained activity was valued and appreciated to its fullest. When the time arrived to move on to the fresh challenge, a comfortable transition was made for the next adventure. My interest and energy seemed to travel forward to accept the latest undertaking. When compared to a book, one chapter closed, a page was turned, and the next installment was initiated.

    Recently, an opportunity was presented to return back in history for a visit to a happy place in my former days. While sitting at the bar in the King's Point clubhouse and enjoying a nightcap to complete a delightful Sunday afternoon with friends, I sipped on a drink while watching a championship NFL game. Nancy became involved in a conversation with twin sisters who sat on the stools next to her. As the discussion progressed, the three ladies discovered that they had several things in common. Eventually, the banter included an exchange of experiences related to the accordion.

At this point in the new relationship, I was brought into the interesting chit chat. Within moments, one of the women offered me an opportunity to borrow her dated seldom used accordion during our Sun City, Florida winter vacation. We finished our cocktails and followed the pair to their home. The instrument was brought out and strapped to my shoulders. Instinctively, my fingers ran up and down the keyboard. The hostess then skillfully began playing her totally European button instrument.

Because of her German heritage, she played tunes which were native to her country. While I did not know the melodies, I was able to anticipate and play the assortment of common chord changes and comfortably accompany her with background harmonies and supportive ethnic rhythms. The collection of Rhine River selections included: ballads, waltzes, and polkas. During the following hour, the two accordionists were joined by a guitarist, and we enjoyably played together. I experienced fantastic pleasure and a tremendous sense of satisfaction. While my skills had severely tarnished since my last professional performance in 1988, the trip down memory lane was very emotional and brought tears to my eyes.

I was invited to attend the community Accordion Club and participate in entertaining with a fifteen-minute solo performance before the talented group. This has provided the motivation to practice and prepare. It has amazed me that the recollection of songs, chord structures, and patterns began to return with the passing of each study session.

That current melodious voyage has been both enjoyable and frustrating as the struggle for perfection continues. It is common for me to get "lost" in the middle of a musical selection or hit the wrong notes. Fortunately, I am getting better at improvising and compensating to cover for the multitude of mistakes encountered. The bottom line is that it has been fun, and progress has improved to the level that I then rented a vintage professional instrument to play while completing the Florida winter vacation.

A few years later, I purchased a new state of the art Roland FR-8x electronic computer driven accordion. I now play every day to hone dormant skills.

UNTIMELY WALK ON WATER

The family gathered to celebrate our granddaughter's thirteenth birthday at a party given in her Bordentown home. The arrangement was for Alyssa's aunt and uncle to drive her great grandmother to New Jersey. Later, Nancy and I planned to transport her return to Ann's Choice in Pennsylvania. A good time was enjoyed by all as we celebrated this important event. Early evening approached while the sky clouded over, and it began to rain with increased intensity.

When the time drew near to ride "GG" home, weather conditions deteriorated to a potentially dangerous situation. Visibility was awful and the car hydroplaned frequently on the New Jersey Turnpike as we carefully headed for her complex. Eventually, we reached our destination, escorted Mom to the apartment, and turned back to complete the journey to Four Seasons.

Because of some street drainage problems on a local winding desolate country road, we selected to take an alternate route. Suddenly, the chosen lonely road flooded, and the car stalled. While electrical components functioned, the engine would not restart. We were stuck! The police were telephoned for help. They quickly appeared, gave instructions to remain in the automobile and wait for a tow truck to arrive.

In the meantime, bright safety flares were posted to alert oncoming drivers of the impending condition. Eventually, we were encircled with emergency vehicles and an assortment of flashing red warning lights that defined the growing pond.

Sighted in the rear-view mirror emerged headlights from an oncoming car. All attempts to wave off the impending catastrophe were ignored. They failed to heed the signals and entered the growing mini lake. As their wheels crossed the pool threshold, the high beams became submerged and went out. The displaced water from this careless mistake created a large swell which quickly traveled towards the stranded two-ton Lincoln in which we were uncomfortably isolated. This sequence set our auto afloat and caused it to begin changing position. *Very Scary*!

We immediately decided to collect our belongings and abandon ship. Items on the passenger side were already damp as the rising dark liquid entered the floating vehicle. Our pants were rolled up, materials gathered, and the tight doors muscled open. We kept our shoes on, entered knee deep water and walked a distance to solid land. As the police greeted us at the end of the cold unplanned wade in the unexpected brook, the tow truck turned up to pull the white vehicle from the unwelcome stream.

He then drove us to a nearby hotel where the evening was devoted to recovering, resting and removing moisture from the very damp shoes with the use of a hotel room hair dryer. While wet and chilled, we did not have to deal with fallen high-tension power wires which would have very seriously complicated this precarious situation.

A few days after the encounter, Nancy visited the body shop to retrieve other items. Parked in the storage lot with an assortment of salvaged parts and wrecked autos was our spotless, distinctive Town Car. By comparison, it looked like it was a "showroom" new. The remote door locks responded to the code and unlocked. Next, the electric windows opened smoothly when activated. These seemed to be good signs. However, the collision shop owner dampened the mood by confidently stating this prize white automobile will probably be totaled by the insurance adjuster. Sadly, he was correct.

The emotional trauma experienced from this episode was unbelievably stressful and it took several weeks for us to accept and adjust to this life-threatening encounter with nature. Fortunately, we survived this ordeal and developed a new respect for driving in storm conditions.

TIMELINE

Since the past, present and future are structured one phase at a time, it is important to continuously stay on the correct course as one ages. Traditional history is segmented in clusters of eras. For example: this universe was created approximately 13.8 billion years ago, and 4.6 eons mark our globe's origin. The first humans walked the planet, Earth, roughly 200,000 years ago; civilization sprouted within the past six millennia and the Renaissance period began inside of the five previous centuries.

Interestingly and in this context, the current anticipated American life expectancy is estimated at approximately eight decades. Considering this constantly evolving clock cycle, a person is calculated to experience an existence and direct frame of reference that embraces less than one individual century.

From the instant after birth, an individual aging process starts and begins advancing forward in phases. A people, population, progression can be compared to an incredibly elongated parade through generations of time. The marching procession is organized in a succession of diminishing maturational lines that include categories of all individuals sharing the same sequence along the path of life. As each hour elapses, mortals expire, fall out of rank, and cause their rows to reduce in number.

Watched by intervals of seconds and minutes, the first or most mature members perish, and their diminished count is ultimately replenished by infants penetrating the entry level in this order. During the entire example, senior combinations of the leading columns are replaced by new babies that enter the cycle to eventually accept the worldwide challenges of growth, innovation, and advancement.

Therefore, and in the process of reflection, a profound question remains to be pondered. A person in their "golden age" should take several sensitive moments to collect tender thoughts and identify the purpose of one's own existence and then pass pertinent information to the next generation. For few leave a legacy that extends much beyond their own lifetime.

KNOW WHAT TIME IT IS

The clock of life continues to tick. It is set in motion with the doctor's gentle tap on the baby's buttocks to stimulate the first significant breath. It then persistently marches forward to mark off each successive respiratory cycle until the last bit of precious air is drawn into the lungs. Valuable experiences are gained with each passing moment. The celebrations of an increased number of birthdays provide a multitude of gigantic opportunities to encounter extra experiences.

The processing list of events is a phenomenon which extends over decades and creates a direct proportion between lessons learned and days spent on Earth. Over time and through a mounting anthology of assorted incidents that are constructed, classified, and maintained; life experiences should promote the excitement of an advancing maturational progression.

In essence, the longer one travels on the living path, the larger a quantity of assorted information is accumulated. In comparing or considering that knowledge gathering is cumulative, a child's album of data is far less in volume when judged against the amount accrued by an elderly person.

While a newborn has a tiny, assembled background of encounters which are short and limited, an older being has established a parallel platform which is, hopefully, long and extensive. Obviously, there seems to be a ratio between age, maturity, and possessions of the collected concepts. The generational weighing machine can be compared to a fulcrum centered on a long edification, equilibrium scale.

The creeping passing of time moves this balance point progressively forward along life's lever and travels from zero at birth's starting point to its end terminus at death. Each passing moment advances the pivot tip along a hierarchy of enlightenment which moves ahead as more information is harvested.

Experience is a valuable commodity and a treasured gift which should be cherished and invested wisely. Moreover, it is much too important to be wasted and too vital to be lost. During the vast passing procession of seconds, the chronometer's tender hands slowly advance in only one direction and cannot be retrieved. Retired moments are lost forever. It is essential that one always knows what time it is on the individual's aging time piece!

EPILOGUE AND PERSPECTIVE

LIFETIME OF LESSONS LEARNED

<u>EDUCATION</u>

A youngster's job is to do well in school

A parent's responsibility is to provide advice; a child's role is to listen, evaluate, sort out and apply what is pertinent

Listen to lessons of others, sort information and select points that are relevant to the situation

In order for civilization and society to advance, the student must exceed the teacher

A culture advances only when the achievements of one generation are surpassed by the next

An excellent way to learn a topic is to teach the subject

Appreciate all that has resulted from only ten digits in mathematics, twenty-six letters of the alphabet and thirteen musical notes

Attitude determines academic achievement

Children are gifted and it is the role of adults and teachers to draw these talents out from each youngster

Children are our most valuable resource

Education is one of the few things a child is given that cannot be taken away

Exceed expectations

Excellence in education

Experience is a tremendous teacher

In addition to schooling, a job is a remarkable source for learning

Literacy comes in many forms

Learning combines to establish valuable experiences and a background of information upon which to draw

Make pupils' intellectual participants rather than spectators

Nations that out-educate us today will out-perform us tomorrow

Read formal and informal learning material thirty minutes per day or a minimum of 10,000 hours before the youngster enters school

Read to succeed

The more a person learns, the more an individual earns and the longer is one's life

Recognize there are numerous styles in which a person learns

Auditory, Visual and Kinesthetic are the major domains

Respect the many settings in which learning, and education takes place

Spend time with your children. They will certainly learn from negative involvement; so, invest in and enjoy positive activities.

Happiness is the key to success

The passing of age should result in an accumulation of wisdom and knowledge

There are no shortcuts to learning

There is no such thing as a free lunch

Those who tell the story perpetuate the culture

Use eyes to see, ears to hear, mouth to question and hands to touch as major channels for learning. Words can be used to paint a verbal picture and tell a story

HEALTH

Be true to your teeth or they will be false to you

If you do not have time to be sick, make time to be well

Ignore irrelevant behavior

Recognize the importance of regular physical, cardio, respiratory, vision and dental examinations

Keep a history of accurate medical records

Listen to your body as it relates to health concerns

Moderation

Stay fit

Walk 10,000 steps per day

What is eaten today walks and talks tomorrow

Work hard…Play hard…Sleep hard

FINANCE

A dollar can be spent only once…so invest it wisely

A great investment is to pay down debt

Understand the value of an Amortization Chart in loan reduction

Appreciate the impact of compound interest

Be organized and maintain accurate investment records

Give your children enough money to get by; but not an amount for them to do nothing

Have a Living Will, Power of Attorney and Last Will and Testament

How many hours of labor are required to purchase a product and is it worth the expenditure of time or effort?

Know a banker, financial advisor, accountant, and attorney

Live for today but invest in family, future and prepare for retirement

Live within your means

The older one becomes, the more expensive are your mistakes

The purchase of an automobile is a necessary product. Keep it repaired and safe to last a long time

Maintain an excellent credit score or better

PHILOSOPHY

A person's word is their bond

Admit when a mistake is made, assume responsibility, apologize, and make the necessary corrections

All situations (problems) occur in a context.

Understand the complete perspective in resolving a dilemma

In a discussion or conflict, understand the other person's situation, perspective, and position

Appreciate and support the arts

Appreciate friends and respect advice of others

Be kind to animals

Be safe rather than sorry

Buy American

Celebrate holidays and family functions

Cherish life's simple pleasures

Count blessings and be thankful

Decisions are made by the heart and by the head and many times, they are in conflict. Select the proper method or biological organ.

Understand the importance of opinion differences

Dress for success

Every day is a gift and, therefore, use it wisely

Favors are accepted with gratitude and graciously returned

Focus on the future

Follow the "Golden Rule"

Freedom is not free

Help family, friends, neighbors, handicapped and the elderly

Implement a firm handshake while looking the person in their eyes

In a conversation, minimize using the word, "I".

It costs nothing to be nice

Keep communication alive with family and friends

Keep old friends while making new ones

Keep resume` current

Know one's specific strengths and weaknesses in business and personal situations

Success enjoys many partners while failure stands alone

Know what time it is in life and remember the clock continues to tick forward

Know your facts

Life is short, pray hard.

Love God and country

No God, no peace. Know God, Know peace

Only one chance to make a first impression

Maintain an emergency savings account to cover future essential expenses for a period of six months in advance

Pass through life with dignity and integrity intact

Pay attention to the messages sent to you by the heavenly father

Practice what is preached

Reputation is built from the accumulation of past deeds, behavior and performance

Respect elders and the contributions they have made over time

Spend time sensibly

The best things in life are not things

Thoughts – several are private, and others are public. Therefore, some are silent while others can be shared

If a task is important to meet a person's high standard, then that responsibility should be assumed by that individual (YOU)

Time is too valuable to waste

Today is the oldest you've ever been, yet the youngest you'll ever be...so enjoy the day.

Use a pencil and paper when confronted with a difficult decision. List pros and cons and the solution will emerge

Vote, it is the responsibility for liberty and freedom

We stand tallest when we stoop to help others

What is my purpose in life?

What will your epitaph read?

When at work don't stand idle

When in company, remember that what is presented on the table is not as important as the person who is sitting in the chair

When wishing for something, remember you might be disappointed if the desire is granted

Yesterday is gone, only today and many tomorrows remain

While the truth is never forgotten, a lie is seldom remembered

Worry is pulling tomorrow's clouds over today's sunshine

The role of parents changes from active participants to silent spectators as grandparents

LEADERSHIP

A leader is wise in being surrounded by smart, very competent individuals who are then, supported to make contributions that originate from their various talents

An important responsibility of a leader is to find a capable and appropriate replacement when the time comes

Know your spectators before communication with the audience

Ask rather than tell

At times, silence is deafening

Be aware of your place, status, and value in the organization

Be firm, fair, and consistent

Be kind to people on the way up, because they may be needed on the way down

Be prepared

Be punctual

Don't make your lack of planning or preparation my problem

In a belligerent conversation, state the dialogue over until it can be conducted in a civil manner

In business, involve those at the bottom of the organizational chart in the decision-making process. Their perception may be productive

In the corporate sector, many conversations are less than two minutes. Be careful at what is said by you and heard by others.

It is much easier to give a presentation before a large group than be engaged in a small face-to-face conversation. Very few, if any, challenges arise from the large audience

Keep current and up to date

Kind words make excellent echoes

Know the difference between public files and private notes

Know the location of resources, records, and tools

Know the power structure, identify the leader, and learn how to manage dynamics to your advantage

"No comment", is an excellent response when the media asks for a quote

Recognize and reward talent

Recreation and relaxation are meaningful and essential components of a competent and productive employee

Request help when necessary

Set reasonable expectations and timelines

Setbacks pave the way for comebacks

Ten-minute power meetings are effective

Implement a two minute, stand up meetings when possible

Thank you are potent words

There is no such thing as an off the record statement

When asked a question, respond with, "What are your thoughts and suggestions?"

When temper is lost so is the argument

If you're not part of the solution, then you must be part of the problem

HUMOR

A bright smile will always light up a dull room

A grandparent should keep quiet with opinions, because there is nothing to gain but everything to lose

Boredom is an excuse and not an activity

Complaining is like a rocking chair. It gives you something to do, but you don't get anywhere.

Engage mind before running mouth

Excuses are like armpits, everyone has them and they both smell

Be able to laugh at yourself

Forbidden fruit creates many jams

Generosity is the only thing you can be good at without practice

Happiness and laughter are catching

If you want breakfast in bed, sleep in the kitchen

It is difficult to hoot with the owls at night and soar with the eagles in the morning

Keep a smile on your face and a shine on your shoes

Keep eyes and ears open and mouth shut

Keep quiet so nobody knows how dumb you are

Life is a measure to be filled, not a cup to be drained

Make hay while the sun shines

Never eat in a restaurant with a skinny chef

No matter how high a crow flies; a window can be broken with a hammer

Retirement goal is to enjoy a year around tan

I am too old to be cold

The best way to have the last word is to apologize

A tongue weighs practically nothing, but few can hold it

There is no such thing as boredom for an intelligent person

Well, done is better well said

As a senior citizen, never pass up a bathroom.

POINTS TO PONDER
Making the Right Choices

Grandparents who migrated from Italy

Inheritance of positive genetic pool

Steeped in solid family tradition

Proper parents

Liberation from the dreaded disease, Polio.

Priority on education

Listen to advice and apply what is appropriate

Work ethic

Never stand idle

Money can be made. Just work for it!

Share and accumulate advice and apply what is fitting

Investment advice, stock market and banking lessons

Appreciated experiences as a studio music instructor

Insurance man who provided college direction, major impact on my life

On campus college professor strong recommendations

Delighted to graduate with a college degree in three years

Accepted USR teaching job in a small developing school so that I could grow with it

Accepted USREA treasurer as first year teacher

Accepted USREA president as second year teacher

Purchased correct home before marriage

Excellent marriage partnership

Strong personal family life

Modern automatic devices are excellent as long as they work properly

Master's degree earned at nights and summers in one year to qualify for principalship

Obtained principal ship at age 26 and youngest in New Jersey at the time

Retirement at age sixty

Move to Four Seasons at Mapleton, New Jersey

Winter months retirement in Florida

Habits are cumulative

Be safe and practice good health

What is my legacy?

NOT A GOOD SIGN

As residents living in an age restricted community, we collectively have encountered several signs or indicators to serve us as reminders that we continue to enjoy the" golden" years of our lives. Listed below are some thoughts that have been accumulated over time:

While on an exhausting, lengthy travel log type vacation, in which you are in a different hotel each night, there is a need to visit the bathroom during the late evening. You are not in the lavatory but in the clothing closet.

Laughing at your both sets of parents when they had difficulty remembering the names of you youngsters.

When excited, you now experience the same problem of attempting to recall the names of your grandchildren.

After setting out the daily pills, you cannot recall If they were taken.

Finding the inside of your car is wallpapered with reminder post it notes.

Dressing in very poor lighting and realizing when out; your selection of clothing is mismatched.

Forgetting that your reading glasses were left in yesterday's pocket.

In a social situation, having difficulty recalling the name of a person you should easily remember.

Writing a check and cannot recall if it was put in the mailbox location.

Cannot consistently recall your social security number.

Preparing to smoke a cigarette and putting the wrong end in your mouth.

Leaving home and not remembering if the doors are locked.

Grateful for a medical receptionist's telephone call reminding you of a future appointment that you have completely forgotten.

Remembering if you put sugar in the coffee or teacup.

Polishing shoes with the wrong color.

Selecting a pair of shoes to wear and putting on the wrong color or style socks.

Using a cell phone to call home because you forgot the shopping list.

Leaving the bowling alley and realizing you still have one bowling shoe on your foot.

Remembering the name of the team who won last year's World Series.

Consistency in remembering your pin number.

Confidentially, stating the number of years in which you are married.

Accurately declaring your age as of the last birthday.

Having difficulty operating your new technology devices.

Setting the dials for the new car is impossible.

Needing large numbers on your wristwatch.

Wearing a calendar watch to remind you of the current day and date.

Having nothing to do and taking all day to do it.

When preparing for a vacation, taking more time to pack pills than selecting appropriate clothing.

When your bowling average is much lower than your body temperature.

Going to work and your boss is half your age.

Placing on eyeglasses immediately improves your hearing.

Cannot remember what you had for supper last evening.

Fixation on bathroom locations when away from home.

Washing windows and not remembering if you did the other side first.

Only picking restaurants because they have an early bird menu.

Remember when your children had summer teeth (Some are in while some are out).

Remember your mother's darning socks.

Only poor kids wore sneakers and jeans to school.

Went to the airport all dressed up.

Went to religious service all dressed up.

Went to business all dressed up.

Visited a funeral parlor in a suit and tie.

Dressed up for the holidays.

Could go all day without using the bathroom and now you use the lavatory all day.

While listening to a conversation, a thought enters your mind; but when there is an appropriate break in the dialogue, the important idea cannot be recalled.

When you go into another room in the house on an important mission and upon arrival at the destination, you cannot remember the purpose of being there.

When your golf score is higher than your IQ and your intelligence level is well beyond average.

Making a very important telephone call and when the party answers, you cannot remember the purpose.

Bringing a decorative bib to a restaurant.

After finding a good parking spot in the shopping center lot you cannot locate the vehicle when finished in the stores

Remembering the ages of your children.

Remembering all the names, numbers, and ages of your grandchildren.

Recalling the taste of cod liver oil and castor oil.

When you are in a European or Asian country and the street entertainer is playing *Guantanamera*.

Learning that things taken for granted in the past now have meaning and purpose:

Arms on chairs

Handrails on staircases

Magnifying glasses

Walking stick or cane

Auditory beeps as reminders

Assist grips on automobile doors

Audio assists while in the theater or at the movies

Needing ramps in addition to stairs at the front door of public buildings

Eyeglasses to correct a once perfect vision

Hearing assist devices that do not function properly

GPS devices to help find your way

When you ask," What do we watch on TV and state the usual Sunday evening schedule"? A smile is generated when the response is today is Saturday.

Requesting a doggie bag and not owning a pet.

Requesting a doggie bag to bring home a left-over meal and forgetting to take it from a restaurant.

When retired, your task is handbag holding while the strolling wife is shopping.

Of the many things lost over the years, I miss my memory most of all.

When locating a misplaced item is the most time-consuming activity for the day.

QUIPS AND QUOTES

Appreciate the impact of compound interest and the accumulation of dividends over time

Attitude determines academic altitude

Children are our most valuable resource

Earn more than you spend

Education is one of the few things you give a child that can't be taken away

Every day is a gift to be used wisely

Excellence in education

Focus on your future

Freedom is not free

Happiness and laughter are catching

Honesty is the best policy

Invest in the future

Know your number facts

Love God and country

Minimize debt and avoid unpaid credit card balances

Excellent habits are healthy

Poor health habits are cumulative over a lifetime

Read to succeed

Retirement goal is to have a year around tan

Spend time with your children; they will certainly get it for bad things. So, invest it in the good and enjoy the delightful experienced throughout life

Stay fit and die fast

The more you learn, the more you earn and the longer you live

There is no such thing as boredom for an intelligent person

Those who tell the story perpetuate the culture

Time is too valuable to waste

Too old to be cold

Treat others as you would like them to treat you

When at work, never stand idle

Work hard, to play hard, to sleep hard

Yesterday is gone.

You only have today and many tomorrows

WHAT DO I APPRECIATE?

<u>MEANING...FREEDOM IS NOT FREE</u>

Being born and a citizen of USA

Love of God and Country

Veterans who have protected my liberties and freedom

Appreciation of Fire, Police, First Aid Services and Educators

Grandparents who migrated from Italy

Rich Italian heritage

Love, respect, dedication, support, guidance, and care provided by parents

Development of a positive moral and values system

Willingness to learn and work hard

All gifts available through life

Actively participate and enjoy family life

Life survival skills

Good eyes, ears, health, intellect and strength

<u>EXCELLENT EMPLOYMENT OPPORTUNITIES</u>

Orchard Hills Country Club

Accordion performance opportunities

Cancellations Limited Shoe Company

Music Manor Music Studio

Upper Saddle River Board of Education, New Jersey

Paterson State University, adjunct professor

Ability to earn a living and retire comfortably at an early age

Importance of educational contributions of teachers, professors, instructors and administrators

The unnamed Metropolitan Insurance agent who had a major influence on my wonderful, productive future as a college graduate

SCHOOLS ATTENDED

Paterson Public School System

Paterson State Teachers College

Montclair State College

Rutgers University

Harvard University

Lincoln Center Summer Institute

Desire to function independently and speak freely

Choosing the right path and following God's messages

Become the finest person possible

Paterson, New Jersey interactions

Circle of acquaintances in Washington, Township, NJ

Tolland, Mass. family and friendship associations

Four Seasons social experiences

Florida Friends relationships

Volunteer work with first aid squad, blood bank, handicapped citizens, senior citizens and town recreation

To serve community and country: educator, college professor and volunteer

US airlines staff whose names I do not know, that assisted in changing flights for Rob's doctoral graduation

Take pleasure and share the benefits of relatives, friends and acquaintances

GOALS AND IDEALS

Leave a legacy for which I am proud

Be a positive role` model

Make contributions to create a better world

Pass on to future generations knowledge, compassion, patients, and undertraining

WHERE ARE THEY NOW?
(Acknowledgements)

Pioneers and immigrants that settled our nation

Preakness farm friends

Peers who walked or rode the bus together on the way to school

Teammates from various athletic activities

Teammates on the city industrial basketball league who consistently scored over 100 points in a thirty-two-minute running clock game and remained undefeated.

People we have met on various vacations

Teachers, professors, and administrators who were influential factors throughout my entire developing sequence and educational process

Harold E. La Paugh, School #10, Principal

Public school friends

Religious leaders

Orchard Hills Country Club caddy buddies

Shoe store associates

Parties who hired me to play music during my thirty- five-year career

Paterson State College friends

Restaurants, banquet halls, clubs and homes that enabled me to perform for them

Salespeople and vendors who made home deliveries

Music Manor staff

Crown Four Band

The Sharps Band

Top Kicks Band

Bob Chino Combo

Musicians that shared the bandstand with me
Student teaching memories
Upper Saddle River School experiences and colleagues
National Association of Elementary Principals
New Jersey Association of Elementary School Principals
Ramapo Valley Administrators Association
Secretaries who have assessed me over time
Shangri-La friends and memories
Farm family reunions
The Mass. Mountain Men Band
Shady deals and experiences that challenged integrity
Washington Township friends and memories
Square dancing friends
Girl Scout leaders and troop members
Knights of Columbus activities
Bergen County Blood Bank
Tools that were borrowed and not returned
Westwood High School friends and memories
Westwood High School European Band Tour
Recreational team sports
Sink, sink, sink
Westwood High School Band activities
Westwood High School Basketball
Westwood High School Baseball
Designated shooter
444 Beech Street basement and swimming pool parties
Rene's high school and college circle of friends
Rob's high school and college circle of friends

Trenton State College Homecoming Weekends

Trenton State College Basketball activities

Washington Township Volunteer Ambulance Corps

Final Four National Basketball Championship Tournament

Rob's Final Four teammates

William Paterson College adjunct professor experiences

Paterson, New Jersey acquaintances

Washington Township, New Jersey associates

Four Seasons friends and memories

Pompano Beach, Florida contacts

The Virginian friends and memories

Sun City Center, Florida links

Kings Point, Florida groups

Tour guides on trip and vacation adventures

Travel friends

Bordentown Elks Club Activities

Rob's Doctoral Degree Graduation

US Airlines staff whose names I do not know, that assisted in changing flights for Rob's doctoral graduation

Rene's Master's Degree and Arizona vacation

Number of accordions I have played over the years

Volunteers who continue to make this world a better place

Military police, fire and first aid members who served to protect our liberty and safety

Workers in essential occupations

While many individuals have come before our time and some are with us now, we continue to have opportunities to learn from each of them.

CHRONOLOGICAL CROSSROADS
(Acknowledgements)

Grandparents from Italy

Mike and Rose Franchino, parents

Franchino Family

Iannacone Family

Nancy Lee Sattler Franchino, Wife

Lintz, Rene` Lintz, daughter

Charlie Lintz, son-in-law

Alyssa Lintz, granddaughter

Chad Lintz, grandson

Rob Franchino, son

Lisa Franchino, daughter-in-law

Lauren Franchino, granddaughter

Michael Franchino, grandson

Rachel Franchino, granddaughter

Vince Tressa Giordano and family uncle and aunt

Dominic, Rose Franchino and family, uncle and aunt

Tony, Elizabeth Franchino and family, uncle and aunt

Angelo, Mildred Franchino and family, uncle and aunt

Phil Franchino, Delores and family, uncle and aunt

Louie and Mary Giannone and family, uncle, and aunt

Marilyn Shutts and family, cousin

Dan, Patti Austin and family, cousin

Donald Shutts and family

John, Carmella Doyle and family, uncle and aunt

Jackie Doyle, Joy and families, cousin

Allan Doyle, cousin

Janet Crosby and family

Jerry and Margret Iannacone. uncle and wife

Art, Elvira Iannacone and family uncle and aunt

Pat Iannacone, Edna and family uncle and aunt

Franchino, Michael, brother and Maureen, wife, best man, and wedding party member

Patti and Steve Gambardella niece and family

Cheryl and Jeff Mucha, niece, and family

Sam and Lena Anello, "grandparent roll", wine maker,

Earl and Lee Sattler, in-laws

Dick, Connie Sattler family uncle and aunt

Jeff, Darlene Sattler and family, cousin

Drummer family

Bob and Linda Weber, in-laws, and wedding party members

Rob, Allison Weber, nephew, and family wedding party member

Jody Weber and family, niece

George Sattler, uncle, interior decorator, wedding party member

Rudy Hendric, family friend

Carl, Helen Heinicke and family uncle and aunt

Eric and Maryann Heinicke, wedding party member

Roberta, Terry Murphy and family in wedding party member

Ernest, Clara Chagnon and family

Bob, Nellie Proulx and family

Hank Romano, high school basketball coach

Mickey Spinelli, high school basketball coach

Charles Offenhouse, high school guidance counselor

Morris Waldstein, high school physics and electronics teacher

Ed Katz, financial mentor

Herb Raskin, business mentor

Metropolitan Life insurance man, career guidance

Prospect Park banker

Ellen Kiraly, public school friend lifetime friend

Ellen Rosen, public school friend lifetime friend

Ceil Edelman, PTA mother

John Saccoman, high school buddy and accordion mentor

Santo Giglio, high school friend

Tony Nicolini, high school friend

Bernie Friedman. High school friend

Carnie Bragg, high school friend

Steve Harrier, accordion teacher

Hank, Barbara Kalesa and family, wedding party member

Doug Ellsworth college buddy

Ed Petkus college buddy-WPC adjunct professor

Tom and Jody Snelgrove, mentor, wedding party members

Dr. Marietta Gruenert College biology professor

Emil A. Cavallini Upper Saddle River Superintendent of Schools

Jim, Pat Meisterich and family, lifelong friend, mentor, colleague, and member of wedding party

Tom Benson, Upper Saddle River Superintendent of Schools

Morris Corn Principal of Robert D. Reynolds School

John Prelich School Psychologist Upper Saddle River Schools

Upper Saddle River, New Jersey parents and community members

Upper Saddle River, New Jersey Board of Education Members

Upper Saddle River faculty and Staff

Upper Saddle River New Jersey Pupils

<u>FRIENDS and FAMILIES</u>

Roy, Esther Lombardo

Joe DeStasi, uncle

Terry, Reggie DeStasi and family

Lou and Lou Brizzi and family

Vince, Pat D'Agati and family

Tony, Barbara Nebbia and family

Rich, Anna Boggio and family

Bob, Olga Lisofski

Nick Morrizo, sax player

Clem Uliani, steel guitar player

Steve, Joan Heinzemann and family

Angelo, Camille Rinaldi and family

Joe "Be-hind-us", Janice Hernandez and family

Pete Visich and family

Phil, Kay Baecker and family

Jerry, Betty Krams and family

Bill, Judy Weisbuch and family

Mario, Ginny Catuogno and family

Al, Isabel Zeszotarski and family

Billy, Ursula Wells and family

Billy Wells mentor in the mechanics of publishing *FOUR SEASON REFLECTIONS, MEMORIES and FLASHBACKS*

Russ Commino, sax player

Tony Putz, trumpet player

Pete Mazza and friends

Kay Shelby

Dick and Joan Coughlin, assistant principal Edith A. Bogert School

Washington Township friends and acquaintances

Four Seasons friends and acquaintances

Pompano Beach friends and acquaintances

Sun City Center friends and acquaintances

Ariana Guido and family

Anthony Maimone and family

Arnie and Sharon Silverglade and family, shooting, cell phone and computer mentors

Frank and Madeline Cimmino, accordion buddy

<u>DOCTORS</u>

Dr. Santo   Chiropractor

Dr. Purrow Cardiologist

Dr. Sena Cardiologist

Dr, Ricketti Pulmonologist

Dr. Mavasheva, Family Doctor

Dr. Ralff, Dentist

CLUB DATES

Accordion Club Locations

Alexander Hamilton Hotel

American Legion

Apple Ridge Country Club
Art and Mary's Tavern***first band job
Arthur Murray Dance Studio
Bella Cucina Restaurant
Benedictine Academy
Bethwood Restaurant
Bow and Arrow Restaurant
Brownstone House
Cameo
Camp Arapaho
Carlucci's Waterfront
Casino D' Charles Restaurant
Clifton Manor
Club 17
Club 50
Cotillion
Cottage Inn
Dover Club
Elks Clubs
Elmwood Park Italian Club
Excelsior Restaurant
Fireside Inn
Florentine Gardens
Four Season's Clubhouse
Friar Tuck Restaurant
George's Restaurant
Hawaiian Palms
Imperial Manor

Independent Social Club

Joe Pipps

La Vie en Rose

Macaluso's

Manero's Restaurant

Manor Restaurant

Mayfair Inn

Michele's Restaurant

Morning Side

Mountain Park

Natoli's Restaurant

Nestor's Restaurant

North Pole

Norwood Country Club

Old Tappan Manor

Petrillo's Restaurant

Pink Elephant

Red Lion Inn

Ridgewood Country Club

Riverside Vets

Rivervale Country Club

Robin Hood Inn

Rockleigh Country Club

Rounders Restaurant

Shortway's Tavern

Silver Spurs

Suburban Restaurant

Swiss Chalet

Swiss Tavern

Thayer Hotel at West Point

The Barge Restaurant

The Opera

Tides Restaurant

Tony and Eddy's

Totowa Elks Club

Veterans of Foreign Wars

Villa Bagliari

Villa Nova

Warner's Grove

Wayne Country Club

Wayne Manor

Westmount Country Club

Westwood House

White Gables Supper Club

Windows on the World

Woodcliff Lakes Manor

NOTE

As I have traveled this fascinating adventure through a wonderful lifetime, there have been numerous individuals and groups that have influenced me to explore a multitude of adventures. Their impact, inspiration, encouragement, and guidance has continued to be the stimulation for me to take full advantage of the assortment of gifts that are associated with a rich and rewarding existence. In essence and unfortunately many of their names and deeds are not included in these reflections, memories, and flashbacks. To them, I express a most sincere apology.

A very special expression of appreciation and gratitude is extended to Billy Wells for his abundant amount of encouragement, guidance, patience, knowledge, and support.

RELUCTANT READERS

As I approach writing my last story, the realization has set in that few are interested in my trip down nostalgia lane. Close family members have reluctantly read some of these reflections and most emailed stories have remained unopened and eventually sent to the recycling bin to automatically be eliminated.

The joy of recording these experiences has resulted in resurrecting memories of the many encounters that have been accumulated and cherished throughout my lifetime. This venue has recreated accurate and detailed mental pictures of each event. Emotions have ranged from silent smiles to tender tears.

My most favorite and loyal reader remains to be the love of my life, Nancy; her reactions, comments and suggestions have helped refine and polish many of these reflections, memories and flashbacks. In any event, my journey will resume and, hopefully, my collection of tales will continue to grow with the passage of each precious moment.

Together, we have Lived a Royal Life!!

Made in the USA
Las Vegas, NV
10 July 2023

74442701R00223